American Terroir

American Terroir

SAVORING THE FLAVORS OF
OUR WOODS, WATERS, AND FIELDS

Rowan Jacobsen

BLOOMSBURY

NEW YORK BERLIN LONDON

Published by Bloomsbury USA, New York

All papers used by Bloomsbury USA are natural, recyclable products made
from wood grown in well-managed forests. The manufacturing processes
conform to the environmental regulations of the country of origin.

LIBRARY OF CONGRESS CATALOGING-IN-PUBLICATION DATA

Jacobsen, Rowan.
   American terroir : savoring the flavors of our woods, waters, and fields /
Rowan Jacobsen.—1st U.S. ed.
       p.   cm.
   ISBN 978-1-59691-648-7
   1. Gastronomy.   2. Food crops—Ecology.   3. Cookery.   I. Title.
   TX631.J335 2919
   641.01'3—dc22
   2010006125

First U.S. edition 2010

1   3   5   7   9   10   8   6   4   2

Designed by Sara Stemen
Typeset by Westchester Book Group
Printed in the United States of America by Worldcolor Fairfield

Contents

American Terroir

Introduction

M Y NEIGHBOR PAUL has a field that grows great carrots. That's a good thing, because Paul makes his living off that field, but it's also a bit of a surprise. At first glance, you wouldn't expect it to grow great anything. It looks too high, too cold, and too poor. The soil is little more than ground-up schist. After a rain it looks like old pavement. You have to live there for years and learn to read the land, as Paul has, to start to recognize what works there.

Paul's place is called High Ledge Farm, with good reason. It's the kind of glacially scoured, hardscrabble New England hill farm that was settled only after all the choice river floodplain was taken. But it has wonderful character. The site has good exposure and drainage, so it dries out quickly and prevents the carrots from bursting open along a seam, which happens when carrots get too much water and try to grow too fast. "Vegetables are just crunchy water," Paul likes to say. "Sometimes they can't keep up."

The best thing about the carrots is the taste. They're amazingly sweet and flavorful, a little more carroty than most. They have a distinct bright flavor, and Paul thinks he knows why: "This soil is really mineralized. When we tested it, we were off the charts for magnesium. I've always felt that higher mineral content made things taste better."

Paul might be on to something. Magnesium ions are what give certain mineral waters their refreshingly tart taste, which is a pretty good way of describing these upland carrots. Then again, they are less uniform in appearance than river-valley carrots grown in deep, rich soil, which don't have to punch their way through and around rocks. Some people would argue that those lowland carrots are superior. For our purposes, what matters is that they are different. Same carrot seed, same year, two different farms, two different carrots.

That's all you need to understand to begin to explore the idea of *terroir*, a French term, usually associated with wine, that can be translated as "the taste of place." (Don't worry about sounding like Inspector Clouseau when you pronounce it; just say "tare-wahr.") Like *terrain* and *territory*, it stems from the Latin word *terra*, earth. It's a new concept in the world of gastronomy, yet it's not a new idea. If you grew up or spent time in the country, your family may have loved to get sweet corn from a particular farm stand. There may have been lots of farm stands in the area, but Farmer Brown's corn always tasted better. There was something about Farmer Brown's land—the soil, the water, the microclimate. He had the best spot, and he had the best corn.

That's terroir. And it's that simple. No one would argue that site conditions don't affect how things grow, that certain areas consistently produce better-quality food than others, yet somehow when the words to capture this take on a Gallic flare, the notion becomes a bit slippery and daunting. That's too bad, because seeing food through the lens of terroir makes it more colorful, more meaningful, and even, I would argue, more delicious. My goal in this book is to demystify the concept, to wrest it from the sticky clutches of wine writers, and to present some shining examples of great foods that are what they are because of where they come from. Rather than any sort of encyclopedic coverage, I've chosen a handful of foods to explore in depth. By understanding their essence, we can begin to understand our attraction to them, and maybe even learn a little about our place in the world.

The title of this book is anathema to a certain conservative European school of gastronomes, who believe that the Land of the

Golden Arches is incapable of producing foods or drinks that em-
body a particular "somewhereness," but I believe that North America, with its dazzle of terrains, climates, and cultures, holds terroir
to rival Europe's. We have a long way to go to tease out the best
expressions of the terroir of many places, and an even longer way to
go to cultivate a society that appreciates the attempt, but the past
few years have seen such a blossoming of enthusiasm and creativity
that I feel confident in asserting that American terroir's time has
come.

The subjects in this book span the continent, from salmon in
Alaska and apples in Washington's Yakima Valley to chocolate in
Mexico, coffee in Panama, cheese in Vermont, and wild mushrooms in Quebec. They ignore political boundaries but pay close
attention to geological ones.* Terroir almost invariably finds its
roots in bedrock, in the workings of tectonic plates and glaciers,
along with the realities of climate and geography. For this reason,
my favorite work on terroir is not from the bottomless vat of wine
writing. Rather, it is John McPhee's magnum opus *Annals of
the Former World*. In that work, McPhee traverses the continent,
showing how the patterns of life of its inhabitants, human and
otherwise, were set long ago by the deep movements of the earth.
McPhee has a forerunner in Paul Vidal de la Blache, whose 1903
Tableau de la géographie de la France argues that "the rapport between the soil and the people is imprinted with an ancient character
that continues through today." As Amy Trubek points out in her
wonderful book *The Taste of Place*, Vidal de la Blache shows how
everything from the food and drink to the architectural styles of
different regions of France has been influenced by climate and ter-

---

* In the name of sanity, I limit my range to North America, and use "American"
  to refer to the whole continent, not just the United States. Admittedly, I creep
  down to Central America a wee bit, but officially that isthmus gets lumped
  with North America anyway.

rain. In doing so, he adds depth and definition to the character of each region.

But terroir encompasses more than just geology. The great wine writer Hugh Johnson says it best with a beautiful definition in his foreword to James Wilson's 1998 book *Terroir*: "Terroir, of course, means much more than what goes on beneath the surface. Properly understood, it means the whole ecology of a vineyard: every aspect of its surroundings from bedrock to late frosts and autumn mists, not excluding the way a vineyard is tended, nor even the soul of the *vigneron*."* It's a partnership between person, plant, and environment to bring something unique into the world. The soil and climate set the conditions; the plants, animals, and fungi respond to them; and then people determine how to bring out the goodness of these foods and drinks.

My salmon chapter, for example, explains how the spectacular richness of king salmon comes from the years it has spent stocking its body with the raw materials necessary to complete one of the most extraordinary journeys in the animal kingdom. We catch those salmon just as they begin that journey—we co-opt that vitality. Understanding this, you can't help but feel respect, even reverence, for the salmon on your plate.

You also can't help but admire the Yupik Eskimo, who have worked with these fish for thousands of years. It was they who learned the life cycles of the salmon, as well as the necessary preservation techniques, in order to survive in a precarious subarctic environment. The story of the greatness of Yukon salmon is inseparable from the story of the Yupik, and that's the dynamic you'll find again and again in this book. Ultimately, it's about the human response to the deals that nature has offered. It's about the soul of the vigneron and the cheesemaker and the fisherman.

---

* Famously, France has no equivalent for our term "winemaker." A vigneron is more a winegrower; the wine is not made so much as coaxed into existence.

Nature offers different deals in different places. The patterns of wind, wave, light, and life that define a region come through in the plants and animals that grow there. If you want to understand the world—if you find joy in its diversity—then those patterns are worth paying attention to. Another example: In New England, a tree developed a system for dealing with long, cold winters by using changes in barometric pressure to pump clean, sweet sap up to its crown in the earliest spring, getting a head start on the season, and early humans discovered that they could boil away the water in the sap to make a syrup. In the central Mexican highlands, a tree took advantage of the endless growing season, fertile volcanic soil, and abundant rains to produce the richest, most valuable (in terms of calories—nature's currency) fruit in history. New England never could have produced an avocado tree, and Michoacán never would have been right for the sugar maple, no matter how ingenious the farmers and plant breeders. The two foods are natural outgrowths of their environments, and tell us something fundamental about life in those regions—which, in turn, tells us something fundamental about life, period.

THE REIGN OF TERROIR

The term *terroir* has been used by different people in very different ways, and there is still a lot of confusion about what it includes. For example, locavores tend to get enthusiastic about terroir as a means for promoting local foods, but regionalism, tradition, and terroir are not the same thing. Manhattan clam chowder, Montreal bagels, and Seattle coffee are not examples of terroir. Cajun gumbo is, as it's a dish that evolved to celebrate the best of what the land had to offer (crayfish, sassafras leaves, and so on). And though tradition is often a good indicator of terroir, especially in Europe, where they have had centuries to work out which agricultural products do best in a given place, terroir need not be traditional. Some of the best

American wines come from new and surprising places with no grape-growing history.

To understand how the idea of terroir has morphed, why it has such power, and why it is only now being embraced in America, it helps to know the history of the concept, which is undoubtedly as old as agriculture itself, or possibly older. Did early hunter-gatherers notice that the shellfish near the mouth of a bay were saltier than those near the head, or that the fruit in the south-facing valley was bigger than that on the shaded, north-facing slopes? How could they not? From there, it's an easy path to detecting increasingly fine distinctions from increasingly specific locales, and then to endlessly debating their respective merits.

Although the French get credit for concretizing the term, they certainly have no monopoly on the concept. The Greeks of 2,500 years ago favored wines from the Aegean islands of Chios and Thásos. The Thasians even had rules governing the production and distribution of their wines that are not unfamiliar to today's French appellations. The Thasians dried the grapes they used to make wine and boiled the must to produce a high-alcohol, sweet, nearly black wine of excellent repute. The wine could not be watered down before shipment (as was done with many other wines). The amphorae that carried the wine (also made on Thásos) even had to be of a uniform size. As a rule, the Greek and Egyptian wine trade stamped any amphorae with the location and vintage of the wine it contained. People cared.

As with so many other aspects of Greek culture, the Romans inherited the Greek's appreciation for the provenance of food and expanded on it. They favored oysters from Bordeaux and wines from the fabled vineyards of Mount Falernum, between Rome and Naples. They even differentiated between the prized high-elevation vineyards, the middle slopes, and the lesser wines from the base. At a banquet in 60 B.C. celebrating his military triumphs in Spain, Julius Caesar was honored with Falernian wine from the legendary vintage of 121 B.C. Surprisingly to our modern palate, Falernian wine was white, sweet, and strong (Pliny observed that it was "the only wine that takes light when a flame is applied to it"), and it was allowed to oxidize to a deep amber color over many years. It would have been more like sherry than what we think of as table wine.*

If the concept of terroir was alive and well in ancient Rome, it still took the French, with their fondness for regulations and hierarchy, to systematize it. In the Middle Ages, many of the best vineyards in Burgundy were carefully worked by Cistercian monks, whose standards were impeccable. They made their best wines from the Pinot Noir grape, and Burgundy wine developed quite a name, thanks to their efforts. Yet the name was also being sullied by other producers in Burgundy who were making inferior wines from the less delicious but more prolific Gamay grape. In 1395 the monks successfully convinced Philip the Bold, duke of Burgundy, to issue a decree stating that the Gamay grape was "very bad" and must be ripped out of all the vineyards in the region, and one of the most successful brands in history was protected.† With a single grape variety being used in all the best parts of Burgundy, and with the monks having fairly standardized production methods, a perfectly controlled experiment had been arranged. The remaining differences in the Burgundy wines had to be ascribed to the only variable that remained—the land.

Over time, certain regions of France developed fine reputations for their wines, and some of these areas even became synonymous with the wines. Champagne is the most famous example, and in fact the Champagne vignerons were the first to seek name protection from the French government, in the early 1900s. Champagne is

---

* It can be startling to discover how thoroughly tastes have changed through the ages. The Greeks and Romans favored sweet wine over dry, sometimes added resin as a preservative, and always cut their wine with water, even seawater.

† The Gamay grape slunk off to the southern part of the duchy, where it turned out to be very good for making Beaujolais.

the most northern wine region in France—a full ninety miles northeast of Paris—and that had always been its burden. Like other wine regions, it would harvest and press its grapes in the fall, then let the juice ferment over the winter. But the winters are so cold in Champagne that the yeast would go into hibernation before the fermentation process was complete, then restart in the spring once the temperatures warmed up. The result was wine that was still fizzy when it was served, which the French considered about as attractive as we view sweet cider that has gone fizzy in the fridge. After failing for centuries to solve the fizzy problem, the Champagne houses decided to promote it instead. In this they were much more successful, and by the fin de siècle Champagne had a firmly established identity: It was sparkling white wine, de rigeur at celebrations.

Of course, lots of other places could produce a sparkling white wine if they tried, and they did, calling it "champagne," which to many people was synonymous with sparkling wine. Thus the Champagne houses desired to protect their brand. They made a good case. Their region had a unique climate and an unusual chalky soil created by marine organisms sixty-five million years earlier. It couldn't be "Champagne" unless it came from Champagne. The government agreed.

After Champagne, numerous other wine-growing areas of France lined up to protect their famous names, too. This was codified, beginning in the 1930s, with the development of France's government-run appellation system, which mapped all the wine-growing regions and demarcated which wine producers could use which names. At first, an appellation was defined purely geographically: A wine couldn't be called Chablis unless its grapes had been grown within the boundaries of the Chablis appellation. Later, to refine the identity of each appellation, the rules were expanded to cover raw materials: A wine couldn't be called Chablis unless its grapes had been grown within the Chablis appellation and were 100 percent Chardonnay.* Today, in continuing efforts to regulate quality, the rules sometimes cover everything from allowable yields to aging techniques. Starting in 1990, they also expanded beyond wine to protect everything from Camembert cheese and Bresse chickens to Corsican honey and even Puy lentils. Italy, Spain, Portugal, Switzerland, and Germany all have adopted similar systems.

While the appellation system began as a guarantee of quality, it became part of the national soul—a map of the flavors of France. The identity of the regions and the products became fused, and the regulations made sure it stayed that way. They made official what had become clear over the centuries: When it comes to food and wine, terroir is king. Laying it out cartographically appealed strongly to what Karen MacNeil in *The Wine Bible* calls "France's near obsession with geography." Appreciating—and labeling—the regional character of wines, foods, and even people is deeply ingrained in the French character. Perhaps it is ingrained everywhere that regional traditions have solidified over many centuries.

Yet these traditions, as codified in the appellation systems of Europe, can also be stultifying. Because the ingredients and techniques for making things like Champagne and Roquefort cheese are set by law, nothing changes. Innovation is rare. It's reassuring to know that Roquefort will always be Roquefort, but it's also predictable.

In America things are different. Perhaps because we have less history, because we are immigrants and our connections to the land aren't so rooted in family ancestry, we are less interested in what the land has been or has meant and are more excited about what it can *do*. If our terroir is immature, it's also youthful, with all the energy

---

* Of course, the rules had no power outside France, which is why American grocery shelves used to be stocked with jugs of domestically produced "chablis" and "burgundy." In general, American wine labels have always emphasized the producer and the grape and downplayed the place—a good indication of our value system. At last, this is beginning to change.

and exuberance that brings. If you want to tour the museum of old terroir masterpieces, go to France and Italy. If you want to visit the galleries where new artists are trying new things, look around America.

Indeed, something extraordinary and unprecedented is happening. You see it in more and more food markets, farmers' markets, and restaurants: a spontaneous upwelling of passion for beautiful foods and the way they are made. Most observers thought that the artisan food movement would come and go, that people would tire of the expense and inconvenience and return to the supermarket. They didn't understand that the trend was answering a deep, pent-up desire. "Everywhere here it's flipping back," said Mateo Kehler, a visionary cheesemaker you'll meet later in the book. "You go to central Illinois, corn desert, and there's all kinds of little organic farms popping up. The locavore movement is incredible. Six years ago we had a really hard time selling cheese in Vermont. People had to read about it in the *New York Times* first. It's changed radically and quickly. It's pretty exciting." Though this passion feels new, it began, like so many other contemporary trends in American society, with the seismic shifts of the 1960s.

The phrase *goût de terroir*, or "taste of the earth," first showed up in the 1600s, when it was meant more or less literally. Modern-day terroirists are often surprised to learn that for most of its history, *goût de terroir* was considered a defect. As late as 1964, Frank Schoonmaker's *Encyclopedia of Wine* describes it as "a characteristic, unmistakable, almost indescribable, earthy flavor, somewhat unpleasant, common, persistent . . . Superior wines rarely if ever have much of this, which if once recognized, will not easily be forgotten."

The early sixties, of course, were the tail end of a long period when "earthy" was not a plus. Technological progress in the twentieth century had, for the first time, made it possible for many people to leave the farm, and leave they did. Aspiring to an urban life of more refined tastes—the kind that previously had been available only to the upper class—the Western middle class sought to distance itself from its rough and rustic past, embracing refined white bread, uncallused hands, transparent accents. Unsurprisingly, they valued wine that, like themselves, seemed to have risen above its earthy roots.* For its part, the upper class was no more enamored of earthy wine than it was of an earthy middle class. No wonder *goût de terroir* had negative connotations. It was like saying, "You can take the wine out of the country, but you can't take the country out of the wine."

My, how things have changed. In the United States, characteristically, the reaffirmation of the countryside came from a rebellion against government, first in the back-to-the-land movement of the forties and fifties, and then in its love child, the sixties. From naked hippies on Tennessee communes to virtually naked vegetables on plates served at Berkeley, California's Chez Panisse, a new veneration of the land and the simple life arose. Earthy was in.

Yet, in a way, it didn't take. Sure, we reminisced about our Bohemian youth and went to Chez Panisse for a special treat, but meanwhile our diet and lifestyle were getting farther and farther from any connection to place. We lived in cookie-cutter suburbs and ate at Chi-Chi's. Even if we were part of the minority who still cooked regularly, we used supermarket ingredients that, in the process of being moved around the world, had had their identity whitewashed as completely as any participant in the witness protection program.

And it wasn't terribly satisfying. I believe that our recent interest in the terroir of wine—and, by extension, of local food—is simply one manifestation of a much more fundamental desire. Maybe you

---

* And not just wine. As you'll see in my chapter on maple syrup, for example, the lightest, most ethereal syrups—the ones with less flavor—were always the favorites of Vermont farm families.

have to be disconnected from the earth for a generation or two to truly appreciate the profundity of being connected to it.

Or maybe you just have to be burned enough times by the current system. As Mateo Kehler put it, "the whole industrial food system is failing. It's hugely successful on one level, and on another you've got salmonella-tainted tomatoes and *E. coli* spinach." When a single *E. coli*–laden hamburger bought at Sam's Club, as documented by the *New York Times*, contains fresh fatty edges from Omaha, lean trimmings from old cows in Texas, frozen trimmings from cattle in Uruguay, and heated, centrifuged, and ammonia-treated carcass remnants from South Dakota, maybe it's time to start paying attention. Maybe it's only natural to feel that a single food should come from a single place and taste like it.

Today, the amazing proliferation of farmers' markets, local food networks, and artisanal products testifies to our unease with the industrial system. Food safety is a valid reason to pay more attention to the origins of our food, but it's probably not the best reason. Rather than acting out of fear, many of us are acting out of love. Food has always helped to define our lives and anchor us to a particular time and place on this planet. To love food that is real and distinctive—that could not come from anywhere other than where it does—is to love the myriad and dazzling ways that life has adapted to the many landscapes of Earth. It is to rebel against the flat meaninglessness of sprawl.

Say I'm hooked on the gingery spiciness of sourwood honey, which can be made only from a tree found in some fast-disappearing Carolina forests. That attaches me to those forests in a very tangible way, and girds my resistance to any proposal to bulldoze those forests and throw up another housing development and Walmart. Places are not interchangeable. I hope the amazing fruits and fish, the cheeses and wines I profile in this book will make that obvious. Learning about them and seeing the places they come from have given me a lot of joy, as well as a whole new way of reading the American landscape.

We crave food with stories, as evidenced by those handwritten signs explaining the pedigree of seemingly every apple, cheese, and bottle of wine in Whole Foods. This can seem a little precious to conventional food buyers. "Don't fall for the marketing!" they protest. "Why must food have a story? It's just food."

But that's just it. The fact that we can even entertain a phrase like "it's just food" emphasizes what a strange time we live in. Because until the advent of the modern grocery, every food had a story. Anonymous food is not the norm; it's the aberration. Whether we are buying it from the farmer at a market, or growing it ourselves, or, further back, gathering it ourselves, food comes heavy with history and meaning.

When most of us were more or less responsible for getting our own food, whether farming or foraging, reading the landscape was essential to survival. Understanding how it worked, and how to work with it, was no elitist activity. At the core, our interest in terroir is an enduring desire to partner with a landscape, survive on it, and live well.

At some level, our survival still depends on somebody knowing how to nurture the many living things we depend on. Most of us have outsourced this knowledge to thousands of rural people we will never know, but that doesn't mean we are any freer from the earth. It just means we can no longer make the connections. Ultimately, that's what meaning is—grasping the connections between things.

We are some of the first people in history not to have built-in connections to the land we inhabit, not to be able to take comfort and pleasure in its verities. Paying attention to terroir is one of the best and most enjoyable ways to reestablish the relationship. It can teach us much about who we are, why we like what we like, and how we go about living on this earth. It can allow us to rediscover a romance that is exhilarating, fortifying, and real.

IT'S THE INGREDIENTS, STUPID

In recent years, I've had the opportunity to judge a few *Iron Chef*–style competitions, and I've realized something about myself. I don't like fancy food. When the entrée arrives in a gravity-defying tower that topples at the first tentative touch of my fork, you've lost me. When tweezers are employed in the assembling of the dish, I get the heebie-jeebies. When dinner is a guessing game to determine exactly what one is eating, the fun is gone. There are two distinct traditions running through gastronomy, and I am securely in one camp.

One tradition can be traced to Antonin Carême, France's "King of Chefs and Chef of Kings." Carême, the father of haute cuisine, cooked for royalty and the richest of the rich in early-nineteenth-century France. He was famous for cakes modeled after pyramids or other ancient architectural feats and unbelievably complex recipes that took days to prepare. A typical ingredients list for a dish served at an 1817 banquet at Brighton Pavilion: 20 vol-au-vent cases, the diameter of a glass; 20 cockscombs; 20 cocksstones (testes); 10 lambs' sweetbreads (thymus and pancreatic glands, washed in water for five hours, until the liquid runs clear); 10 small truffles, pared, chopped, and boiled in consommé; 20 tiny mushrooms; 20 lobster tails; 4 fine whole lambs' brains, boiled and chopped; 1 French loaf; 2 spoonfuls chicken jelly; 2 spoonfuls velouté sauce; 1 tablespoon chopped parsley; 2 tablespoons chopped mushrooms; 4 egg yolks; 2 chickens, boned; 2 calves' udders; 2 pints cream; sauce Allemande; salt; and nutmeg.

Today, the heirs to Carême's throne are the molecular gastronomists, with their dehydrated black-currant foam and liquid ginger spheres. This is dinner theater, with the chef as performer whipping up paradoxical concoctions designed to awe. The focus is on the chef, and people pay obscene amounts of money for the privilege of eating foods designed by the master (though rarely cooked by him).

I have no interest in this food. (I'm not a big fan of dinner theater, either.) But when a beautifully fragrant pear or a bowl of
Rhode Island razor clams is set before me, I get crazy happy. This is
the ingredients-forward tradition of Alice Waters and Peter Hoffman and generations of good home cooks before them. The cook's
role is still vital, to be sure, but the goal is to let the nature of the
beast (or beet) shine through. To me, that's where the real enlightenment lies, and that's the focus here. This book includes a few recipes, usually fairly simple preparations that highlight, rather than
hide, the terroir of the ingredients. Each chapter also includes resources on the best way to score said ingredients.

I've arranged the chapters to loosely follow the order of foods
you might eat over the course of a day—a very good day. What
would breakfast be without maple syrup and coffee? Then, after a
midday repast of apples, honey, *moules frites*, and a variety of edibles
gathered from the northern forest, it's on to a seafood dinner: oysters for starters, followed by salmon with an avocado garnish. Accompanied, of course, by a variety of wines. A cheese course bridges
the evening to a dessert of—what else?—chocolate.

But don't feel that you need to consume these chapters in any
particular order. I myself favor fish for breakfast and eggs for dinner.
Go for whatever looks good. Trust your tastes. Enjoy the sampler.

And a sampler is what it is. I've chosen subjects in which the
connection between place and taste is obvious and the story is compelling, but I've only scratched the surface. Why are the onions in
Vidalia County so sweet? Why are Ossabaw Island hams so rich?
The list is endless. We are only beginning the process of learning
what works best where. Might apples from the Yakima desert be
better than those from New England? Might cool San Benito
County produce better wine than hot Napa Valley? The frontier is
wide open, and I look forward to exploring it and hearing the latest
dispatches.

You'll find certain motifs running through these chapters.

Mountains pop up again and again. Many foods, across all sorts of categories, seem to develop a particular intensity when raised in the rarified air of the highlands or otherwise stressed. *Slowness* is another recurring theme. It's almost as if goodness can only accumulate so fast in a thing, no matter the production tricks. Which explains the steady tension between quality and quantity: Artisans constantly battle the siren song of higher yield. On a lighter note, yeast plays a role in creating half the foods and drinks in this book. Gourmets are to yeast as remoras are to sharks: just happy to be along for the ride. Sex rears its head with regularity in these pages, because most of our calories come from "repurposing" other organisms' reproductive energy. The realms of food and sex have been blurred on this planet for millions of years. Just ask a flower.

Ultimately, these threads point to some commonality between plants and animals we tend to think of as being utterly unalike. I used to get annoyed by wine writers who would describe a wine flavor as, say, "raspberry," until I learned enough chemistry to realize that it really is the same compound. We tend to think of each type of fruit, vegetable, animal, or fungus as being completely unique, but DNA is DNA. No matter how far removed we are from our common microbial ancestors, we all face similar challenges. We're all working from the same pool of materials. Nature has only so many aroma molecules in her bag of tricks, only so many ways of combining carbon, hydrogen, and nitrogen atoms. So if a cheese smells fishy, some dairy protein has been broken down into the same molecule that turns up in fish protein. Berries, apples, and maple leaves all independently discovered the same compound to turn themselves red. A wine can taste appley when it's full of malic acid, the tart acid found in apples, and creamy when this acid transforms into lactic acid, the dominant acid in milk. The same essence is found in Yirgacheffe coffee, Darjeeling tea, and Chanel No. 5. It's not a metaphor; it's the deep structure of life.

In the Church of the North Woods

HIGH-MOUNTAIN MAPLE SYRUP, VERMONT

APRIL IS THE cruelest month, stirring dull roots with spring rain, but March is wicked sweet. In Vermont, a day comes in early spring when the sun flares bright and the air smells of earth once again. The snow turns from diamond dust to taffy and the land relaxes. From up and down the hills—shy at first, then insistent—comes the *tink, tink, tink* of shiny drops falling into tin buckets. Doctor, come quick; the patient has a pulse.

Many people believe that maple syrup flows in the veins of sugar maples. If only. Sap flows in the trees, and, as generations of bleary-eyed New Englanders could tell you, it is a long, long way from sap to syrup. Forty to one, to be exact. If you have forty gallons of sap, you must boil off thirty-nine gallons of water to yield one gallon of maple syrup. That's why maple syrup is so expensive and why the syrup market is dominated by artificial products containing not a drop of real maple. What you are paying for in the genuine artifact is a terrific amount of fuel, along with somebody's long nights in the sugarhouse tending the sap as it boils.

Most sugarmaking is a small-scale enterprise. People tap their own trees, maybe their neighbors' with permission. (And permission, in exchange for a gallon or two of syrup, is easy to come by.) This has created a terroirist's dream: thousands of geographically unique, unblended varieties of a single product. Long before coffee and chocolate marketers ever thought of promoting single-estate foods, before single-vineyard wines were common in California, Vermont was full of single-sugarbush syrups.*

Not that anyone except a few locals ever paid attention.† Who sits down on a Sunday morning, pours a glass of maple syrup, and savors it with the newspaper? Most syrup is conveyed to our mouths atop steaming forkfuls of pancake. It's hard to notice any nuances amid the fusillade of blueberries and vanilla. But if you do sip your way through a few "syrup flights," you quickly realize that maple syrups are wildly different once you get beyond that great bear hug of sweetness. Some are more buttery than others, some are more smoky. Some taste thin, some spicy. Some are nutty, some malty, some just a little bit salty. These differences result from the sugarbushes' bedrock, soil, slope, microclimate, and genetics, as well as from the sugarmaker's methods.

No matter what their differences, however, all sugarmakers are using the same tree: the sugar maple. For, although a 40-to-1 sap-to-syrup ratio may sound like an insane amount of work, the ratio is even worse with other trees. You can make syrup from the sap of all sorts of trees (birch syrup is an Alaskan specialty), but most have less than 1 percent sugar in their sap (that's a 100-to-1 boil). Sugar maples are the sweetest, with 2 to 3 percent sugar, though it varies with the individual tree. A few standouts have twice that. Though sugar content changes from year to year (old-timers say that a summer drought produces sweet sap the

---

* A sugarbush is a stand of forest used for maple syrup production. Some have been thinned of everything except sugar maples; some are left in a fairly wild state.

† It's amazing how many people don't know what actual maple smells like. For years, Manhattan was occasionally enveloped in a mysterious aroma that everyone described as smelling like "maple syrup." In 2009, the city finally tracked the fragrance to a flavor factory in North Bergen, New Jersey, that uses fenugreek seed in its products. Fenugreek releases a sweet, pungent smell that might smell mapley to those raised on Aunt Jemima. To those who know the real thing, it isn't even close.

following spring), a "sweet tree" will be relatively sweet year after year.

All that sugar was made by the tree over the previous summer and stored in the trunk during the fall. Sugar is the basic fuel for plants, just as it is for animals. All life craves it. Trees make theirs in their leaves through photosynthesis, using the sun to power tiny green factories that scramble carbon dioxide (CO_2) and water (H_2O) to produce sugar ($C_6H_{12}O_6$) and oxygen (O_2). Here is the basic formula: $6CO_2 + 6H_2O + light\ energy \rightarrow C_6H_{12}O_6 + 6O_2$. Trees release the oxygen they produce (good thing for us animals) and use the sugar to fuel their growth and metabolism. Once the growing season is over, they store their leftover sugar, like a battery, to power the first leaf-building of spring.

Maples have a second innovation that allows them to get a jump-start on the season. While other trees store water between their cells, maples store carbon dioxide gas. During New England's sloppy spring, temperatures rise above freezing during the day, then fall back at night, turning dirt roads into mud soup. Those warm days also thaw maple trees. The gas in them expands, creating pressure. The first parts of the maple to thaw are the upper twigs. As gas expands in them, it can't go down the tree, because the thicker parts are still frozen, so it is forced out the twigs. When the thicker branches thaw an hour or two later, their gas moves up the tree to equalize the pressure. (Again, it can't move down, because the trunk is still frozen.) Eventually, later in the day, the same process occurs in the trunk.

Then night falls, and the temperature drops. The exposed twigs freeze first. Water freezes on the walls of the cells, like frost on a windowpane. The gas contracts, creating negative pressure that pulls up gas and water from below. The process continues as the tree freezes from top to bottom. The trunk, the last to freeze, creates the strongest suction, but, since everything above it is frozen, it pulls up water from the still-thawed ground, via the roots.

By following this daily cycle of thawing and freezing, the maple tree acts like a gigantic pump, sucking tremendous amounts of water from the soil up to the tops of its twigs. As the water passes through the roots and trunk, it dissolves the sugar stored there, and sweet sap is delivered to all parts of the tree before the growing season has even begun. During the day, when the air is expanding and dissolving in the sap, the pressure inside the tree rises higher than the ambient air pressure, so sap will push out of any opening, like beer out of a keg.

Famously, really nasty days—sleet, blustery gray skies—make for the best sap runs. You need a warm temperature to thaw the sap, but then you want a nice low-pressure storm system to move in, because that creates a significant gradient between the trees' inner pressure and the atmospheric pressure, and the sap gushes forth— "gush" being a relative term. Sugarmakers dance for joy if they fill their three-gallon buckets in a day. A typical tree produces enough sap to make about a quart of syrup per year.

Before humans had tapped their first maple tree, squirrels had already figured out that sap would ooze out of wounds in a tree, evaporate, and leave behind a sweet and sticky residue. It didn't take humans long to observe the addicted rodents and postulate that they were on to something good. Algonquins inserted hollowed-out sumac stems into holes in the trees and hung birch-bark buckets to collect the sap. Colonists upgraded to metal taps and buckets. In most small-time sugaring operations, little has changed. If you cut down an old New England sugar maple and slice up its trunk, you will see the dark, inch-long scars of past tap wounds, sometimes a hundred in a single tree.

Good syrup can be made only in the early spring, when the trees are still mostly dormant. Once a tree becomes active, it infuses its sap with bitter and astringent compounds destined for its buds. Most other species of tree, which lack the freeze-thaw pump, have sap that is bitter as soon as it starts flowing. Sun-loving species, in particular, have a strategy of leafing out early to outcompete other such opportunists.

Stately sugar maples won't stoop to such antics. They take the long view, and that leisure makes their syrup especially fine. A climax species of the northern hardwood forest, sugar maples grow in the understory of a young forest of colonizing trees and then slowly take over. Extremely shade-tolerant, they have no need to be the first to leaf out. They take their sweet time producing buds. (They take their sweet time doing everything; sugar maples can live three hundred to four hundred years.) This means that, for those extended weeks of early spring, only sugar maples have flowing sap with that miraculous formula of high sugar content, a few flavor compounds, and nothing nasty. You could say that the rich taste of maple syrup is the taste of waking up without urgency. No wonder we've paired that flavor with lazy Sunday mornings.

Eventually even sugar maples must think about leaf production, flowering, and other matters of survival. Once the days get consistently warm, their sap gets rank. And that's why the Greater Northeast (a triangle running from Michigan to New Brunswick to West Virginia) has the only suitable terroir in the world for maple syrup. You need that staccato spring of thaws and freezes to prime the pump, that tantalizing warmth that gives way to a foot of snow.

Sugaring can be delight or torture, depending on whether March is in lion or lamb mode. Lions predominate. Sometimes a nor'easter sweeps through, leaving three feet of cottony snow and necessitating snowshoes to access the sugarbush.* On the other hand, there are days when the sun blazes, the temperature soars to fifty, the snow clears, and sugaring becomes a bug-free walk in the woods. You might even get your first sunburn of the year. I once spent a glorious evening in the woods gathering sap from 270 buckets with

---

* Legendary sugarmaker Burr Morse's tip for proper snowshoeing form: "Walk like a little boy with a load in his pants."

some friends and their three daughters, ages four, six, and nine. The girls worked hard, hugging pails and managing to fill collecting buckets while losing only a little sap. When I poured a thick stream of sap into the main collecting bucket, they leaned in, opened their mouths under the sap waterfall, and let it splash all over their faces. Childhood. The snow was gone and the woods were the brown and tan colors of last year's leaves—syrup colors, actually. The setting sun peaked through the trunks and silhouetted small and large figures scattered through the woods. Time went all gooey.

But when you sugar for a living, time stays rock hard. The biggest innovation for sugarmakers was the switch from buckets to plastic tubing, which started in the 1970s and now dominates most serious operations. Instead of hanging a bucket beneath each tap, you run the tap straight into a 5/16-inch tube of blue plastic (the color reflects UV rays). Each little capillary tube feeds into a larger artery, and the whole network runs downhill to a collection tank. A tubed sugarbush has an incongruous spiderwebby look to it, with electric-blue lines zigzagging through the snowy woods, but it can feel pretty miraculous to stand near the collection tank and listen to an entire hillside's worth of sap thundering into it.

Not that tubing doesn't have its own quirks. Moose will, on occasion, plow right through tubing. More than one moose in Vermont is undoubtedly festooned with an antlerful of blue garlands at this very moment. Squirrels will chew through even well-cleaned tubing to get at the sap. (An earlier movement to clean tubes with a diluted bleach solution was abandoned when it was found that squirrels adored the salty bleach residue.) Buckets also attract squirrels, of course, but the worst that can happen is the occasional drownee.[*]

---

[*] Old joke: What's the difference between a Vermont sugarmaker and a New Hampshire sugarmaker? When a Vermont sugarmaker finds a drowned squirrel in a bucketful of sap, he'll look left, look right, then toss out the squirrel and save the sap. When a New Hampshire sugarmaker finds a drowned squirrel, he'll look left, look right, then *wring out* the squirrel and save the sap.

I appreciated the beauty of tubing one day while working with Paul Limberty, a curly-bearded thirtysomething who lives off the grid with his wife and young son on eighty acres of forest in Vermont's Green Mountains. You have to navigate miles of dirt road to find him. In March, only four-wheel-drives need apply. Sugar maples dominate his hardwood forest, nestled in an alpine valley that's been called Happy Hollow since prohibition, when the local farmer ran a still in the area. Paul has two thousand taps in his maples, running right up to the ridge at 2,100 feet, making it one of the highest sugarbushes in the world. "I hope to get up to three thousand taps," Paul told me. "I think that's pretty much the limit of a one-man operation."

I'll say. As we walked up his vertiginous sugarbush on a drizzly March day, slipping through an inch of wet snow, Paul explained that in addition to running the tubing and boiling the syrup, he also manages the forest and cuts all the firewood for the evaporator—a staggering twenty-eight cords per year, burned up in a few weeks of spring.* He is also at the Burlington Farmers' Market every week, selling beautiful bottles of the golden-amber fruit of his labor.

Because he's a one-man operation, Paul can do things no large-scale sugarmaker could imagine. For instance, he tastes every single barrel of syrup that comes off his evaporator. He jots down a few tasting notes in his log. And when he hits a batch that is especially excellent, that has particular complexity and intensity, he pulls that barrel for his certified-organic Private Reserve line. A bottle of Dragonfly Sugarworks' Private Reserve contains the essence of the life force of a single day in a high-mountain maple grove, created with renewable energy from the same land.

---

* For comparison, I heat my house almost entirely with a woodstove and use four cords per year.

On the windowsill of Paul's sugarhouse sits a glass bottle of every batch of syrup he's made during the year. The general progression is from lighter to darker, but every now and then, because of unusual weather conditions, a light run will come in the middle of the season. Paul consulted his notes, then pulled down a pale gold bottle and opened it. "Try this one," he said.

I did. Wow. It tasted like somebody had melted a pad of sweet butter in it. It was rich, creamy, and sweet but not cloying, with the woodsy notes I rarely find in lighter syrups and none of the burnt aftertaste of darker syrups. This was the kind of syrup the old-timers waxed poetic about.

How can he get such rich flavor? Thank that high-mountain sugarbush. Most sugarbushes are found on gently rolling hills or valley floors with limestone bedrock. There, the trees get plenty of water and rich, alkaline soil—hog heaven for a maple. They make loads of sap with high sugar content—just what a sugarmaker wants, right?

Well, yes, but not necessarily what the customer wants. All maple syrup is boiled to the same concentration—about 67 percent sugar. Below that, wild yeasts can ferment the syrup. Above it, sugar crystals will begin to precipitate out of solution. So no matter what the sugar content of the sap, the sugar content of the final syrup will be the same. It's just a matter of how much you have to reduce the sap to get it there. And that's where our 40-to-1 ratio comes in. Typical maple sap has to be concentrated forty times to become syrup. High-sugar sap might need to be concentrated only thirty times—a real boon to the sugarmaker in terms of his time and fuel consumption.

But Paul's sugarbush is different. Up on that two-thousand-foot peak, bedrock erupted frequently. Trees grew straight out of the rock. The bedrock was all schist and gneiss, with lots of quartz in it. No farmer in his right mind would have embraced it. "This land is really only good for one thing," Paul said. "Maple. There's nothing else you could do out here." And it is far from ideal for maple. "The soils are thin and acidic. There's very little soil at all. The trees get hammered by wind. They're fighting for life all the time. They are very slow growing. It's definitely a struggle, especially in a drought year."

That struggle means the trees can't make as much sugar as maples living a cushier existence, and it shows up in his ratio. "I think I'm around sixty-to-one," he told me. His backache (better cut a few more cords, Paul) is our good fortune, because in addition to the sugar, everything else in Paul's sap is being concentrated sixty times. By the time his sap becomes syrup, the levels of certain minerals, amino acids, and other flavor compounds might be twice as high as that of a high-sugar-content sugarbush.

Wine aficionados will already see the obvious parallel. The greatest wines come not from flourishing vines but from stressed ones. Here is Paul Lukacs in *The Great Wines of America*: "Mountain wines are different. Thin ground on steep slopes yields small but concentrated crops, so wines grown in such sites tend to taste firm and fierce, with tight tannins and concentrated flavors." Or Master of Wine David Bird: "In well-drained poor soil the vine is forced to develop a large root system which penetrates deep into the sub-soil in search of moisture and nutrition, and in so doing it picks up an abundance of minerals that find their way into the grapes." No doubt, in their survivalist search for water and nutrients, the deep roots of the Happy Hollow maples are also picking up an abundance of minerals.

I asked Paul whether it felt like a struggle to work in such a rough, isolated environment, but he shook his head. "It's all fun," he said. "Sometimes when you're rushed and you're losing stuff in the snow, or you fall off a ten-foot cliff, it's not so great. But I couldn't be happier out here. It's peaceful, quiet, and the views are awesome."

MAKING THE GRADE

Until the Civil War, you didn't see much maple syrup around. Most maple sap was boiled down all the way to maple sugar,* a golden, fudgelike product that was one of our main sweeteners until cane sugar from Florida and the Caribbean became commonplace. The best maple sugar is made from the first sap runs of the season, which are high in sucrose (table sugar) and crystallize beautifully. Back when the market wanted maple sugar, those first runs, which produce a very light syrup called Fancy, were the money crop. Later runs are lower in sucrose and higher in fructose and glucose (as are honey and high-fructose corn syrup), sugars that don't granulate as easily. These later syrups, which are darker colored and stronger flavored, make lousy maple sugar—and thus were kept for the home table. Naturally, generations of farm children pined away for the fancy stuff that was sold off to the city.

Eventually cane sugar undercut the market, and maple producers switched from sugar to syrup, marketing it as a specialty product. But to this day, most multigenerational sugarmaking families still have a reverence for Fancy. In addition to tradition, Fancy is the epitome of the sugarmaker's art. Anybody can make the late-season treacle, but pulling off a batch of super-delicate Fancy requires skill, experience, and luck. You have to use the first sap runs of the year, which are higher in sugar content and thus require less boiling, because the longer you boil syrup, the darker it gets. And you have to boil right away, because if sap sits, microorganisms flourish in it, and these "impurities" are what make the syrup dark and strong. Some years produce no Fancy syrup at all.

Of course, nobody really cares except the handful of remaining maple sugar manufacturers and the old-time New Englanders

---

* Which is why the process is called *sugaring* and a grove of maples isn't called a *syrupbush*.

who continue to go to great lengths to keep flavor *out of* their syrup. Until recently, they even charged more for it—a bizarre situation, since most everyone who didn't grow up in a sugaring family prefers the rich, chewy, darker grades. Today all grades usually cost the same.

The state of Vermont, which leads the country in maple syrup quality and quantity, grades syrup by color and flavor. It used to call these grades A, B, and C, until somebody pointed out that B and C sounded inferior. Unfortunately, in an attempt to incorporate some old traditions, it made the new system byzantine. We now have Fancy, Medium Amber, Dark Amber, B, and Commercial. Fancy is the color of vegetable oil, Medium Amber the color of honey, Dark Amber the color of Amontillado sherry, and B the color of iced tea. Commercial, which has the color and flavor of motor oil, can't be sold retail and is shipped by the barrel to the packaged-food industry for products "made with real Vermont maple syrup."

In a typical year, the first sap runs of the season will be used to make Fancy syrup, then later runs will be used to make progressively darker and stronger grades as the syrup gets more caramelized. Caramelization is one of those unlikely tricks that reminds you that the world is magical and mysterious. It's the flavor equivalent of using a prism to transform white light into a rainbow. In this case, the prism is heat, which breaks an odorless sugar molecule (sucrose) into a rainbow of delightful aroma compounds. Hundreds of buttery, fruity, nutty, and floral molecules (yes, the same ones found in those actual foods) appear from nowhere and come zinging out of the pan. Dumbledore, eat your heart out.

For this wizardry to occur, sucrose must be broken down into fructose and glucose, the two simple sugars it is constructed from. Unlike sucrose, which tends to keep to itself, fructose and glucose love to share electrons with neighboring molecules and create new molecules in the process, which is the heart of the whole caramelization process. Fructose will caramelize at 220 degrees Fahrenheit, far cooler than sucrose (which needs to reach 340 degrees). Lots of fructose means lots of caramelization.

To make caramel, you mix table sugar and water and boil it. As the liquid cooks down, it gets very hot, turns brown, and undergoes its remarkable metamorphosis. Making maple syrup is like making a gigantic batch of caramel. But because maple syrup doesn't get reduced as much as a caramel sauce, it doesn't get hot enough to break down most of its sucrose. To fully caramelize, the sucrose in maple sap must already have been split into fructose and glucose.

For this service, we can thank the silent partners in the syrup-making process: bacteria. Not everybody wants you to know this. I once received a panicked, deer-in-the-headlights stare when I asked a Vermont tourism official if it was true that microbes were responsible for the flavor of maple syrup. He didn't want to lie to me, but he didn't want to confirm it, either. But it's true, and it should be celebrated. Given its sugar content, sap is a tremendous environment for microbes. As soon as it pours out of a tree, they'll colonize it and eat the sugars. But in order to digest sucrose, they use special enzymes to split it into fructose and glucose.

Fancy syrup—made at the beginning of the season—has little flavor other than sweetness because it has little in it other than sucrose. That early in the year, with temperatures barely creeping above freezing, there are few bacteria around—nothing to transform the sucrose into flavorful fructose. And, with the trees not yet biologically active, there are no additional flavor compounds in the mix. The flavor of Fancy is simply the lightest of caramels—delicate to some, bland to others.*

Just a few more days of springtime, however, and things start to get interesting. Bacteria start to do their thing, increasing the

---

* Paul Limberty defends it: "I find that the complexity of flavor in Fancy is greatest. I can taste more things in Fancy than I can in Dark Amber. Some days it's got a hint of vanilla; other days it's more buttery tasting."

fructose level of the sap and also contributing the amino acids (the building blocks of protein) they themselves are made of. More amino acids come from the trees as they begin to add hormones to their sap. Amino acids add nitrogen and sulfur to the carbon, hydrogen, and oxygen of the sugars, and when this mix gets cooked down, a whole new remarkable chemical reaction takes place. Known as the Maillard reaction, it is responsible for the irresistible complexity of chocolate, coffee, and roasted meats.

In Medium Amber syrup, just the slightest hint of savory Maillard flavors appears. Medium Amber is a big butterscotch bomb—gentle, rounded, caramel at its peak.

With an extended stretch of warmth, the syrup turns to Dark Amber, the most balanced of the grades. It's still as buttery and warming as a crème brûlée, but now intrigue is creeping into the mix. Underlying the caramel is a layer of woodsy flavors—walnuts and sherry and a delightful hint of bacon. Those darker, savory flavors mingle with the caramel to form the essential combination of flavors we think of as "maple."

Toward the end of the season, with biology bursting forth from every hill and dale, sap is a veritable soup of bacteria and tree amino acids, and the syrup turns to Grade B. If you want to understand the essence of the Maillard reaction, taste a Grade B syrup, which has a much more challenging suite of flavors. The sweetness is still there, but it's tinged with the flavors of coffee and burnt toast. Dark beer. Fried peanuts. The first hint of bitterness has crept in. The assertive flavors of Grade B are ideal for a salad dressing or a marinade, but, to me, a little indelicate for pancakes, to say nothing of straight up. Still, people with complex, adult tastes—people who like their movies ambiguous, agonizing, bittersweet—usually claim Grade B syrup as their favorite.

By the time a sap run reaches Grade C, the flavor is skewed toward the molasses end of the spectrum. This is the result of the Maillard reaction gone wild, with sulfur compounds taking over and creating onion aromas and significant bitterness from the burnt caramel. The sweetness is just enough to trick you into thinking poison palatable. "There's some really bad-tasting C out there," Paul Limberty said. "It's like getting hit in the leg with a hammer."

Sometimes the end of the season is marked by a sap flow known as the "frog run." A warm breeze blows in from the south and the day gets downright balmy. As evening comes and the sugarmaker hauls his sap to the sugarhouse and begins the night's boil, a choir starts singing. The spring peepers have awakened. From every wet spot in every field, these tree frogs start to call. You can't see them, so it feels as if the marsh itself is singing. At first it's a fragile, uncertain sound, but with warmer nights it becomes cacophonous and bacchanal, as the frogs' blood sugar starts to rise. If you stand in the midst of a peeper swamp, the sound does something vertiginous in your eardrum, whuffling as if a tiny bird were trapped inside. From across the darkening meadows, it sounds like distant sleigh bells ringing, as if some forest god is drawing near.

The land has awakened. The maple sap is filling with amino acids that the trees have made in preparation for budding. A weirdly fruity, fake-chocolate, Tootsie Roll flavor known as "buddy" appears.* Soon it will turn intensely bitter and chemical, the trees' way of saying, "Enough." Time to quit sugaring for the year.

THE SUGARHOUSE

From the time of the colonists, the standard way to render maple syrup has been to boil the living hell out of the sap. Don't try this on your stove unless you hate your wallpaper. The clouds of steam need an escape route. Settlers boiled it outdoors in cauldrons, with a tarp over the pot to keep anything from blowing into it. Eventually

---

* In the Northeast this flavor is considered a defect, but in the South, where molasses and sorghum have always figured prominently, people like it.

the tarp became a real roof, walls were added, and the sugarhouse was born. Function has imposed a distinctive form on the building. It looks like a small, rustic Cape Cod cottage with an extended cupola. The sides of the cupola fold down to allow the steam to escape.

Boiling sap in a cauldron or pot is painfully slow because there just isn't enough surface area. Evaporation can only occur from the very top layer. But if you spread the sap over a wider area, you increase the evaporation and decrease the boiling time. Hence the modern evaporator, a fairly elaborate and expensive contraption. If it's wood-fired, one end of the building will be filled with firewood. The other end has a pipe running from the evaporator, through the wall, to the collecting tank, which is generally perched on a covered outside shelf where it can be easily filled.

A typical midsize evaporator has a four-by-thirteen-foot series of stainless steel pans, about four feet off the ground. Underneath is a giant cast-iron firebox, like an enormous woodstove. It's called the arch (because the heat and flame is "arched" through flues beneath the pans before going up the chimney), and, though they all used to be wood-fired, today the high-tech versions use propane or oil.

One sugarmaker told me he's skeptical of the modern systems. "It just feels weird to be in a sugarhouse and not smell the wood smoke," he said. "Maple syrup is good at picking up flavors; some of that smoke must get into the aroma of the syrup. I've been in some sugarhouses that were filled with that burning-oil smell. You couldn't stay in the building without feeling sick. How does some of that smell not get into the syrup?"

Another shortcut is the use of reverse osmosis (RO) machines. RO machines force sap against a fine screen through which only pure water can pass, meaning they can separate water from sap without the need for boiling. This can save sugarmakers a tremendous amount of fuel (and shrink the carbon footprint of syrup), by significantly reducing the amount of boiling time needed to make syrup, but it doesn't produce maple flavor. Sugarmakers can benefit from an early round of RO, but they must balance it with boiling time. Raising the sugar content through RO from 2 percent to 6 or even 10 percent is probably fine, but some sugarmakers take RO beyond 20 percent, at which point the sap hardly boils for any time at all.

Whatever the fuel, all evaporators work similarly. Fresh sap from a holding tank is fed into the large back pan, called the "flue pan," where it is vigorously boiled. This is where most of the steam is cooked off. A channel at one corner of the flue pan feeds into the front pan, where the syrup follows a labyrinth of linear channels, thickening all the time, to the point where it can be drawn off. As the level in the front pan drops, more syrup feeds in from the flue pan.

Fresh sap has a clean pumpkin smell, like the inside of a jack-o'-lantern; it's cool and moist and vanishingly sweet. There's nothing "mapley" about it. Even when it starts to boil on the evaporator, you can breathe in the steam from the flue pan and detect little maple essence. It's a wet and green smell, like trees in the rain. But if you let your nose travel along the snaking alleys of the front pan, you can trace the evolution of the aroma. You detect toasted nut in lane one, then brown sugar as you curve into lane two, then roast beef and bacon and earth kick in as you head toward lanes three and four and the finish line.

High above the evaporator rises the cupola. The white steam writhing up the open ceiling and out the cupola has an uplifting effect. You expect a choir to break out. The evaporator is the bubbling organ, the sugarmaker wielding his sugar scoop the organist. In these little churches of the north woods, the faithful gather to take communion, a little taste of the god of spring.

Any time steam is billowing from the cupola of a sugarhouse, it means somebody's there in the warmth and steam with time to kill. This invites the unscheduled drop-by—an endangered pillar of healthy communities. If fresh snow is on the ground, people will scoop up bowlfuls and top it with hot syrup to make taffylike "sugar on snow."

My favorite sugarhouse to visit belongs to Craig Line, a photographer by trade and something more than a hobbyist when it comes to sugarmaking. Line makes syrup in Maple Corner, a tiny hamlet that became famous a few years ago when the men of Maple Corner, to raise money for their community center, posed nude for a calendar. The calendar made the *Today* show and went on to sell hundreds of thousands of copies. In March, however, nude men are few and far between in Maple Corner, while buckets and tubing are ubiquitous.

Craig's primary sugarbush consists of 660 taps on a southwest-facing slope, all feeding through tubes into a 750-gallon metal collection tank perched twenty feet above a nearby dirt road. A PVC pipe runs from the tank to the edge of the road and ends in a spout seven feet off the ground. Craig parks his pickup, which holds a 325-gallon plastic tank in the bed, directly under the spout and runs a flexible tube from the spout into the tank. In minutes he can have a full load of sap ready for the sugarhouse.

Of course, anyone else could collect this sap, too, so Craig keeps the handle to the valve with him. Still, this didn't stop a rival sugarmaker from once splicing into Craig's main line and redirecting the sap to his own collection tank on the other side of the hill. The denouement was a screaming match in the snowy woods.

What I like about Craig's sugarhouse are its clean, classical lines, its soaring cupola, its orientation toward the late-day sun, and its chummy neighborhood. After a long winter of being cooped up indoors, people can't wait to gather, to see that it's all happening again. During one typical March evening, the local garbageman swung by with his children, followed by several other neighbors. Everyone sampled the still-warm syrup. Craig loaded more wood into the arch. Then the chair of the town selectboard appeared with his young daughter, who immediately stepped up near the pan to watch the bubbles. In a nod to tradition, a bowl of pickles sat on the side table—a sour counterpoint to the syrup. We discussed maple cocktails: Vodka? Bourbon? The Maple Shooter—half syrup, half brandy—received much support. Like ice fishing, the pace of sugar-making lends itself to drinking. Beer and bourbon are at their best in the sweet steamroom of the sugarhouse. But most everyone agreed that the smoky smells of wood and maple call out for a peaty single-malt Scotch.

As the light faded, a thin, white-haired figure came trundling up the path, bearing a mixed six-pack. It was the editor emeritus of *Vermont Life* magazine, a man who commands popelike reverence in the state. He climbed the steps to stand beside the evaporator, enrobed in swirling steam, then leaned over the pan, breathed deeply, and smiled. "First crop of the year," he said.

RECITES

MAPLE CRANBERRIES

Of any dish likely to have appeared at the real first Thanksgiving supper, my money is on this one. Plymouth is both cranberry and maple syrup country. A pot of this, a wild turkey, some squash or corn, and a big fat pipe of something to smoke, and you've got a celebration on your hands. This is as easy as it looks, and so good that it will free you forevermore from the tin chains of canned cranberry sauce. The tart cranberries offset the round, roasty, caramel maple flavors beautifully, and the color is memorable. I make this on the tart side, but you can add more maple or sugar to taste.

Serves 4 (but my son will eat the whole pot)

1 12-ounce package fresh cranberries
1 cup maple syrup (preferably Dark Amber or Grade B)
peel of 1 orange, in strips (optional; not native American, but tasty)

1. Rinse the cranberries and pick out any debris.
2. Combine the cranberries and maple syrup and orange peel (if using) in a medium pot and cook over medium heat, stirring regularly, until the cranberries pop and the juice and syrup combine into a sauce—about 10 minutes. The berries should be soft with pleasantly chewy skins. Turn off the heat. Remove the orange peel. Let cool slightly before serving.

MAPLE-DEGLAZED VENISON MEDALLIONS

Another ur-American dish. Each fall my neighbor Chris blows away a phenomenal number of ungulates, and over that two-month stretch a series of cuts appears on my doorstep in descending order of desirability: first the celebratory tenderloin, then backstrap, then flank steaks, then stew meat, then burger. It's all good, but the tenderloin is like a revelation, with little forest spirits singing around my head as I eat. If you can't get your hands on venison, pork tenderloin works fine, too (just don't expect to hear the forest spirits).

Serves 4

2 tablespoons olive oil or duck fat
1 venison or pork tenderloin (about 1½ pounds), sliced into inch-thick medallions
salt and pepper
½ cup maple syrup (preferably Dark Amber or Grade B)
½ cup chopped green onions

1. Heat a large skillet over medium heat until hot. Add the oil or fat.
2. Season the medallions with salt and pepper and sauté them in the pan until seared on one side, about 1 minute. Flip them with a spatula and sear them on the other side for about 1 minute.
3. Remove the medallions from the pan and place on a serving plate.
4. Add the maple syrup and green onions to the pan. A nice loud sizzle should go up, and the syrup should immediately start bubbling. Push the green onions around the pan with a spatula, scraping up the browned bits, until they're wilted, maybe 30 seconds. Pour the hot sauce over the meat and serve.

RESOURCES

DRAGONFLY SUGARWORKS

www.dragonflysugarworks.com

802-434-6502

To identify the best syrup in the country, I convened a panel of experts for a blind tasting. Then I invited their parents, too. My star member was a twelve-going-on-twenty girl named Maggie. She'd been disappointed in me for years as I turned up at her house for dinner bearing six varieties of oysters, or fresh wasabi root and weird sharkskin graters. "Rowan," she'd say, "when are you going to write about something *good*?"

Well, how do you like me now, Maggie?

Maggie liked me fine, which was more than could be said for all the syrups. One she labeled "fine," another "thin but sweet." One syrup received a "bleck," and for another she simply wrote, "That's shit." But one syrup received a perfect 10. Beside her score she wrote, "That is awesome, my friend. Yuuuuuuum!" It was Dragonfly Sugarworks' Dark Amber, and it received perfect scores from multiple kid and adult judges, including me. Try a variety of grades, and ask if the Private Reserve is available.

FIFIELD'S SUGARHOUSE

802-333-4467

Winner of numerous Best of Show contests, Fifield's tiny sugarhouse is festooned in more blue ribbons than Secretariat's stable. Fifield's sugarbush is located in the town of Thetford Center, considered the top maple terroir in Vermont.

MORSE FARM MAPLE SUGARWORKS

www.morsefarm.com

800-242-2740

Famous and venerable source of maple syrup and maple stories.

VERMONT MAPLE SUGARMAKER'S ASSOCIATION
www.vermontmaple.org
An excellent source for learning about maple and finding sugar-makers. The best way to explore maple terroir is to visit during the Maple Open House Weekend in late March, when most sugarmakers are boiling and offering tastings in their sugarhouses.

The Fresh Young Thing

GEISHA COFFEE, PANAMA

THE BIDDING BEGAN at $3 per pound. It was 2:30 in the afternoon of May 29, 2007. The event was the Best of Panama specialty coffee auction. The top specialty coffee roasters in the world were competing, online, for a unique coffee known as Esmeralda Special. At 2:37 the price jumped to $5 per pound, then at 2:38 it jumped to $10. Even that was a formality. Most coffee sells on the global commodity market for less than $1 per pound, but Esmeralda Special was no normal coffee, and there was reason to believe that the price would go much higher.

At 3:28 the bid leaped to $15 per pound. At 3:32 it hit $22, a resonant number. It had just surpassed the at-the-time unfathomable price set by Esmeralda Special in its coming-out party at the 2004 Best of Panama auction. In 2004, the best coffees in the world wholesaled for $2 to $3 per pound. The second-most-expensive coffee in the 2004 Best of Panama auction went for $2.53. Esmeralda Special sold for $21. It had already swept the Best of Panama and Rainforest Alliance cuppings, as official coffee tastings are called, where judges were blown away by its intensely floral aromatics. The cup was a scintillating kaleidoscope of jasmine, citrus, and bergamot. It received almost perfect scores. Famously, Don Holly, quality-control manager for Green Mountain Coffee Roasters, turned to a reporter from Reuters and commented that he had just seen "the face of God in a cup." Neither he nor any of the judges had ever tasted a coffee like it. Which made sense, because, until then, no coffee like it had ever existed.

In a span of less than ten minutes, the bid for the 2007 Esmeralda Special leapfrogged from $22 to $25 to $27 to $30 to $35 to $40. Then the participants took a twenty-minute hiatus to catch their breath.

Esmeralda Special comes from high atop the Hacienda la Esmeralda estate in Panama's lush Jaramillo region. The farm was an unruly hodgepodge of coffee trees of various varieties planted by various owners through the years when it was sold in 1996 to Price Petersen, an American who had been dairy farming in the area since the 1970s. Price's son Daniel was interested in the specialty coffee business and hoped to transform the farm into a producer of high-quality beans. He set about cupping coffee from every corner of the farm. At an altitude of about 4,500 feet, he found a group of strange-looking coffee trees. They were tall and scraggly, with long, thin leaves and large gaps along the branches between the nodes where the red coffee fruit, known as cherries, appears. Each coffee cherry, which resembles a cranberry, contains two seeds, which are what we call beans. The beans are separated from the fruit pulp, dried, and roasted to produce coffee. Daniel thought he detected something highly unusual—a hint of that jasmine—in the coffee from those scraggly trees. But the flavor was hit-and-miss. Because higher altitude usually translates to finer flavor in coffee, Daniel theorized that growing the trees higher on the farm might help to bring out that flavor. He had just the spot in mind: a remote, little valley that was exposed to the brutal Pacific storms that slammed into the Panamanian mountains. The valley was sunny, but notably cool, with winds that occasionally exceeded sixty miles per hour. Daniel had noticed that the trees were quite hardy, and he wondered if they might not just survive the harsh microclimate of that valley but also actually thrive in it. By 2004 the trees were established in the valley and bearing fruit. And the coffee he made from their beans knocked his socks off.

At 4 P.M. bidding on the 2007 Esmeralda Special resumed,

and things got serious. Within minutes the price was up to $50, causing an hour-long hiatus in bids. They had now matched the record-shattering 2006 price. Could it go higher?

Yes. Within a minute it went to $55 and then $60. Records were broken again. At 6 P.M. it hit $85 per pound. Over the next half hour, a furious battle between two syndicates representing the hardest of the hard-core coffee roasters drove the price to $99.99 per pound.

In the Hollywood version of the Esmeralda Special story, this would be the moment when the computers exploded, showering fireworks on the bugged-out bidders and auction house. In reality, no computers exploded. They just became useless. There was no place to insert bids higher than $99.99 per pound.

At the time of their 2004 triumph, the gawky coffee trees in Hacienda la Esmeralda's far-upper valley were a mystery. No one knew what they were or where they had come from. Physically, they were very different from Typica and Bourbon, the two varieties responsible for most gourmet coffee. After much sleuthing, the Petersens established their origins. The trees were a variety called Geisha.* One of the countless wild varieties native to Ethiopian forests (like coffee itself), the trees had been sent to a coffee research lab in Costa Rica in the 1950s because of their disease resistance. There they remained until the 1960s, when Panama, searching for a tree resistant to the coffee leaf rust fungus, imported the Geisha from the lab. But Geishas proved to be low-yielding. At the time, quality was an afterthought in coffee; amazing beans didn't command much of a premium. And beans were blended across farms, regions, and even countries, making it virtually impossible for any one type to stand out. Yield was all that mattered. Geishas were quickly thrown on the compost heap of coffee history. The only survivors

---

* The variety was originally named "Gesha," after the Ethiopian town it came from, but, predictably, over time the name mutated into "Geisha."

were those on forgotten farms that hadn't modernized. When Daniel Petersen made an all-Geisha coffee from a high-altitude region, he was doing something no one had ever done. And, in his matching of plant and terrain, he happened to strike gold. It was as if, in a world where all anyone knew was Cabernet Sauvignon and Merlot, he had wandered into Burgundy's Côte d'Or and decided to see what would happen if he planted a few acres of a weird little grape called Pinot Noir.

At 9:55 in the evening, the 2007 Esmeralda Special auction resumed by conference call. The offers came swiftly: $101, $105, $110, $115, $120, $125. At 10:09, a bid of $130 per pound on the lot of 500 pounds of coffee—a total of $65,000—was made by a consortium of seven gourmet coffee roasters in the United States.[*] No one bid again. The entire 2007 harvest of Esmeralda Special was theirs.

THE UNBEARABLE LIGHTNESS OF ROASTING

The nutty price of the 2007 Esmeralda was driven by scarcity. The hauntingly lovely fragrance was a factor, of course, but only 500 pounds of the stuff was available, all as one lot. In 2008 and 2009, as more Esmeralda became available, and as a couple of other Panamanian farmers found Geisha trees on their land (now that they knew what to look for), the price dropped to "only" $105.25 and $117.50, respectively. Future prices will certainly drop more, because after Esmeralda Special's debut in 2004, the Geisha gold rush was on, and now those new trees are beginning to produce.

The more important point of the Esmeralda story is that there was a specialty coffee auction at all. Even as late as the 1990s, when Starbucks had seemingly raised the bar for gourmet coffee, quality

---

[*] The Roasterie, Intelligentsia, Willoughby's Coffee and Tea, Zoka Coffee Roaster and Tea Company, 49th Parallel Coffee Roasters, Groundwork Coffee Company, and Klatch Roasting.

beans earned just a few cents more than regular beans on the wholesale market. Without George Howell, the Best of Panama auction would not have taken place, nor would the similar auctions that are held in every coffee-producing country in Latin America. It was Howell who conceived and cofounded the Cup of Excellence, the first specialty coffee tasting and auction, in 1999. A quality-coffee pioneer, Howell developed a taste for good coffee in the 1960s in Berkeley, California, where Alfred Peet was roasting some of the first good coffee beans in the United States.* When Howell moved to Boston in 1974, he discovered that the city was drinking the same stale, brown dishwater as the rest of the country† and set about to change that. He started a cafe called the Coffee Connection, which, by the time he sold to Starbucks in 1994, had expanded to twenty-four locations throughout the Boston area.

By then Howell thoroughly knew the coffee industry and recognized its problems. An old-fashioned commodity industry, built on the backs of third world farmers, it was dominated by importers who kept prices extraordinarily low, abetted by governments. For example, Howell told me that in Colombia "the farmer is viewed as a unit of industrial production. Screw the individual and any desire he might have for aesthetics or craftsmanship or anything like that. And screw the environment. It all goes, in the name of high productivity."

With no reward for quality, farmers concentrated on producing higher quantities by growing disease-resistant, high-yield varieties, and they often picked many green, unripe cherries. Howell had seen too many coffee farmers give up on quality, and too many go out of

---

* When Starbucks started in Seattle in 1971, Peet's Coffee and Tea handled all the roasting until Starbucks acquired its own roaster.

† Believe it or not, Americans were pretty coffee-savvy in the old days. Most towns had local roasters in the nineteenth century, and Americans usually ground their own beans. Around World War II, however, metal cans of ground coffee became ubiquitous.

business entirely. Working with the United Nations, the International Coffee Association, and the U.S. Agency for International Development, he focused on getting farmers a decent price for their crop. But he feared that the ethereal-tasting coffees he loved so much might disappear. The introduction of fair-trade practices helped ensure a better price for farmers, but it did nothing to improve the quality of the beans. So Howell decided to set up a series of blind cuppings to find the best coffees in Latin America and then auction off the winners to the burgeoning specialty market, which was exploding in the wake of Starbucks' success.

To do that, first he had to educate the jurors. "The first day of Cup of Excellence would be calibration," Howell told me as we sat cupping coffees in his Acton, Massachusetts, roastery, within ambling distance of Walden Pond. "For the first cupping, we'd choose eight coffees: some that were defective, some that were good, and one masterpiece. They'd cup those eight blind, then we'd sit down and discuss. Why did this one get an eighty-five? Why did this one get a ninety-five? Then we'd go back and cup them again. The majority got it very quickly and came out of that being good basic cuppers—as long as you pointed them in the right direction. Which meant paying attention to two things: sweet cup, which is related to ripeness—not sugary sweetness, but the way that nuts can be sweet—and clean cup, which is the processing. Those two things are the key criteria. Don't even worry about whether it tastes like tangerine or blackberry or something else."

In order to have any kind of meaningful tasting, Howell also had to fix some bad habits that had slipped into the coffee industry. "Back in '99, when Cup of Excellence started, what had been a universal code of how you sample roast had been destroyed," he said. Coffee beans must be roasted at around four hundred degrees Fahrenheit to develop their flavor. A ten-minute light roast highlights the natural acids and aromas in the beans. A fourteen-minute medium roast begins to break down these compounds and replace them with nutty, caramel, and pot roast flavors. At a full eighteen-minute dark roast, the beans' intrinsic flavors are destroyed and a generic charred flavor dominates.

Traditionally, beans were roasted lightly for cupping. But in the 1990s, Howell told me, "a new wave of companies said, 'I'm going to sample roast my coffee the way we roast it in production.' That's nuts. It's like cooking a tomato before you sample it to see if you want to buy it. People were sample roasting at different levels. This was created to a certain extent by Illy, which was doing an espresso roast, and Starbucks, which was roasting it *really* dark. That leaves this amazingly bitter aftertaste in your mouth, and there's *no way* you can pick up the defects or nuances as much. Dark roast is a sauce that you're adding to coffee." Howell mentioned a famed coffee personage who would invariably choose the darkest roast during blind cuppings. "He'd say, 'Ooh, I really love this coffee,' and I'd say, 'Of course you do; it's the darkest.' And I'd take him back and show him the grounds. He was buying the roast instead of the beans."

It seems to be a peculiar quirk in the American character, mistaking strength for quality. Not so in Europe. "The farther north you go in Europe, the lighter the roast," Howell notes. "It's a matter of economics. The poorer the quality of the coffee, the darker the roast." A dark roast can disguise the defects in bad beans. "In southern Italy, Spain, Portugal, the places that used to be really poor, it's all dark roast. As you go north, Germany, Switzerland, Scandinavia, it's light roast, because they're buying the best. France is the exception to that rule because their colonies were in all the wrong places. In West Africa and Indochina, it's all low-growing Robusta.* Now, why the West Coast went all dark I don't know. They just took the quality pyramid and turned it upside down. I'll never figure that out."

---

* A deeply inferior species of coffee tree.

But to me, it's obvious. Why go to the trouble of sourcing expensive, finicky good beans and trying to blend them into a consistent profile when you can buy cheap beans, roast the hell out of them, and give Americans something that can cut through the cream and sugar in their lattes? It's the taste of charcoal—70 percent of a dried coffee bean is cellulose—but it's an undeniable presence. Howell agreed with this idea. "Dark roast attacks. It's instantly recognizable, and it's strong. It's best hot, and it goes downhill as it cools. You start to notice all these grungy notes. Light roast is the exact opposite. It's kind of weak when it's hot, and as it cools, you start to taste more and more.* That's one thing I say to people right away: Don't judge the coffee while it's steaming hot. You get the aromatics, and that's about all. The cooler the coffee, the more you taste everything."

And when buying beans, you want to taste everything. "Cup of Excellence did more than just teach people about cupping. It taught them how to sample roast," Howell said. "It *always* has to be light. I insisted on that in all these competitions, and it introduced a new generation to that concept." That new generation included the buyers for the post-Starbucks wave of coffee companies, who tended to be what you might call "Lonely Planet" entrepreneurs—countercultural thirtysomethings with a lot more interest in social and environmental issues than their predecessors had; with a willingness to rough it in third world backwaters for a chance to establish direct relationships with farmers; and, above all, with an interest in sourcing coffees with unique terroirs. A serious art collector in his midsixties, Howell has a vibe that's decidedly more cultural than countercultural, but he is the godfather of this movement. "I found this huge jump when we did Cup of Excellence with companies that just started in the '90s, like Intelligentsia and Stumptown. They

---

* You might conclude from this that light roasts make sublime iced coffee, and you'd be right.

were ready for it. *Whoom!* They just picked up the ball and ran with it. They're less light in their roasts than I am, but they're headed that way."

Which explains the proliferation of single-estate, wildly individual coffees we are seeing today. Esmeralda Special may have been the apotheosis of George Howell's effort to give coffee farmers the incentive to grow great beans, and no other has approached it in price, but now there are scores of coffees in the Americas earning $10 or $20 per pound for their growers, instead of the 50 cents per pound they may have been earning a few years ago.

I asked Howell if he thought we were in a golden age of coffee. He shook his head. "We're still in the dark ages. Maybe we're at the doorstep of a golden age. I don't know." Too many world-class coffee farmers still teeter on the edge of economic ruin. Howell pointed out that an average bottle of wine costs $10, and that for an equal amount of coffee to sell for the same price, the beans would have to cost $125 per pound. "Coffee has not reached the noble-beverage stage of wine and tea. They've had a few thousand years, whereas coffee is five hundred years old at best. We're just getting started."

Howell actually fears that we might plunge deep into another dark age. The coffee crisis continues. Farmers who can't get a specialty price for their coffee are switching to vigorous and productive hybrids that look and taste like dirt, but the world coffee market doesn't care. The poor-quality Robusta's share of the market is 40 percent and growing, most of it destined for emerging markets such as Russia and China. Meanwhile, Robusta-Arabica hybrids, which are as productive as Robusta but taste a little better, have become extremely popular. For the most part, the only farmers who haven't switched to the hybrids are the ones who couldn't afford to. The great beans' last strongholds are in the high tropical mountains of East Africa and the Americas—a result of the quirks of both biology and history.

GOATHERDS AND GEISHAS

Since its inception in the lands surrounding the Red Sea five hundred years ago, coffee has stood in opposition to tea. While both end up as steaming liquid in a cup, and both pack a heady caffeine punch, a veritable gulf separates the two, and it comes down to function. One starts life as a leaf, and the other as a bean. A leaf gathers sunlight. Its whole orientation is upward, toward the heavens, the realm of illumination and clarity. I like to think of tea as concentrated sunlight. Coffee is a different story. It's a seed, and seeds head downward, to the earth, the realm of reproduction. There can be little argument that, in most coffees, these lusty, earthy qualities find their way into the cup.

Even the foundational myths for each beverage bear this out. The standard story for tea goes like this: Siddhartha Gautama, the future Buddha, retreated to the forest to meditate and form his central ideas. To his frustration, he found himself getting sleepy and unable to concentrate. As luck would have it, however, he was sitting beneath a tea tree. He ate some of the leaves and magically found himself able to stay awake through eight full days of meditation. Buddhism was born.

The myth for coffee is a little different. One day an African boy observed his goats nibbling the red berries of a strange bush. The boy noticed that after they ate the berries, his goats had an extra bounce in their step, a little more rowdiness than usual. *Hey*, thought the boy, *I want to get me some of that, too*. He did, and whammo, a new addiction was born.

Could the differences be more stark? One drink awakens your higher chakras, the other your inner goat. One reaches its apotheosis in the Japanese tea ceremony, where aesthetics and delicacy are refined to new heights, all in the name of enlightenment. After hours of silent contemplation, moving through a series of rooms, sitting just so, making exactly the right remark about a clay pot or a wooden whisk, you are rewarded with a thin cup of frothy green tea. Nowhere else has so much been made of so little. But that's the point. Psych yourself up to see eternity in a handful of tea dust and you're pretty much set to make the best out of life. Somehow it just wouldn't work if, at the end of their ceremony, the Zen monks passed around double mochaccinos.

Coffee drinkers have no time for contemplation. Whether it's Turkish men arguing loudly around a table while sipping thimble-fuls of black mud, Italians knocking back an espresso in a stand-up bar while dodging their mother and their mistress, or Silicon Valley entrepreneurs brewing another pot while burning through venture capital, coffee drinkers always seem to be on the verge of losing control of their lives.

Yet there's an upside, too. Politically and artistically, coffee has been stirring the pot for centuries. The Age of Reason and the French Revolution are just two of the new ideas birthed in cafés.* I've never encountered a writer's block that two cups of java couldn't explode. Forget god in a cup; coffee is a muse in a travel mug.

Given a choice between a life of Zen quietude and a lock-jawed, all-night jag, it's a no-brainer for most of us, which helps explain why coffee has been vanquishing its venerable rival on all fronts for five centuries and is now, after oil, the most traded com-modity in the world. Like the ingenue who eclipses her mentor onstage, coffee is the fresh young thing we can't get enough of.

Coffea arabica, the species of coffee tree that produces all good coffee, originated in the forests of east Africa, where it still thrives in the understory. I suspect our primitive ancestors were intimately familiar with its cherries. Perhaps this explains the affinity we feel for coffee. We were once ingenues taking the world by storm, too.

Yet we certainly weren't making coffee in prehistory, or even in

---

* Bars, in contrast, foment loud revolutionary talk that dissipates in a fog by morning.

ancient history. African tribes crushed raw beans and mixed them with fat as a stimulant, but otherwise the fruit pulp was the main draw. Today, a drink is still made from it. Coffee's big break came in the 1400s, when Arab slave traders brought African slaves and their beans across the Red Sea to Yemen, where the practice of boiling the crushed beans in water soon arose. This is the muddy Turkish coffee still drunk throughout the Arab world.*

By the 1500s, coffeehouses had sprung up from Mecca to Cairo. Coffee was celebrated as a catalyst of freethinking, and periodically banned by the authorities for the very same reason.† The coffee tree didn't expand beyond the Arab world until the early 1600s, when an Indian saint named Baba Budan smuggled the beans to India, from where the Dutch carried them to Indonesia. From there, beans were brought to the greenhouses of Amsterdam and Paris in the early 1700s. Then, in 1723, Gabriel Mathieu de Clieu, a French naval officer, carried a single tree to the Caribbean island of Martinique. That the tree survived the journey is a miracle. It endured storms, an attack by pirates, a shipmate's attempt to kill it, and a shortage of drinking water (de Clieu gave most of his to the plant). Soon millions of coffee trees were growing in the New World.

This history is essential to understanding the great coffees of the world, because two key things happened during this multi-century journey. The original coffee that came out of the high forests of Ethiopia was adapted to the fully tropical, mountainous conditions there: lots of rain and temperatures that never dipped below forty degrees Fahrenheit or soared above ninety. During its two-hundred-year layover in arid Yemen, it maintained its water requirements

---

* One 1610 English visitor described the drink as "blacke as soote, and tasting not much unlike it."

† King Charles II tried the same thing in England in 1675, with about as much impact as Rudy Giuliani's ban had on jaywalkers in New York in the 1990s.

(the Yemenis irrigated), but it changed in other ways as the Yemenis selected for certain characteristics. It lost its resistance to the many fungi and diseases that thrived in humid tropical forests, and it lost its floral notes.

The variety of coffee tree that made the journey from Yemen to Indonesia to the New World is called Typica, and it is the source of many of the best coffees in the world today. Until recently, its only competitor was Bourbon, a cousin that traveled from Yemen to the African island of Réunion (then called Île de Bourbon) in the 1700s, thence to Brazil in the 1800s. Today many of the finest Bourbons come from El Salvador and Guatemala. While both varieties produce sweet, clean cups, Typica makes more finessed and fruity coffees, while Bourbon leans toward creamy nuttiness.

Yet Arabicas are problematic coffees. The globe-trotting species has passed through so many genetic bottlenecks that it now suffers from an incredibly narrow gene pool, and the typical accompanying lack of vigor. This is why the Geisha variety was brought to Central America in the first place. And it explains why the great plumes of jasmine and soursop rising from a cup of Esmeralda had never before been sniffed in the Americas. That smell, previously detected only in the high Yirgacheffe Valley of Ethiopia, is the smell of ancient wild coffee. And the only other place in the world so hospitable to it is the moist, tropical highlands of Latin America.

"THE WINE OF THE TROPICS"

The quality of coffee correlates with altitude. The higher the beans grow, the better the coffee tastes. This is more than just a general principle; in many places, coffees are graded based on their altitude. For example, in Guatemala, the eight grades begin with Good Washed at 2,300 feet and rise to Strictly Hard Bean (SHB) at 5,250 feet. The thin air of the mountains, and the strong diurnal swings in temperature, make for beans that are denser, less porous, and more refined in flavor. Even good Arabica beans display a muddiness when grown at 2,000 feet that becomes earthy around 3,000, nutty around 4,000, and suddenly explodes with liveliness around 5,000 feet. That's where the fruitiness becomes apparent—citrus, berry, or floral, depending on the variety and the roast. It's one of those rare examples where terroir terminology becomes literal: Beans from flatter areas taste flat, while the exalted coffees, the ones with the elevated and uplifting aromas . . . well, you get the idea.

Because coffee trees can't survive temperatures below forty degrees, the only places they can cut it at 5,000 feet are the true tropics—Latin America, equatorial Africa, and Indonesia. Precious little real estate fits the bill, and most of it is steeply sloped and fairly inaccessible. Such areas tend to be fairly unproductive and inconvenient, but that's turned out to be a blessing in disguise for the specialty coffee industry. Such undesirable farms are typically held by the poorest farmers, who can't afford to buy the new hybrids. They are the ones still growing Typica and Bourbon, the heirloom varieties. Politics has played a role, too. El Salvador and Guatemala are still filled with Bourbon thanks to the chaos created in the 1980s by their civil wars.

For now, the mountains of Guatemala, Nicaragua, El Salvador, Costa Rica, Panama, Colombia, Peru, and Ecuador continue to harbor tiny farms that grow brilliant coffees on unique pockets of land, and it is the mission of George Howell's new company, Terroir Coffee, to promote them. He comes at it partly out of concern for the well-being of the farmers, but ultimately out of reverence for the finest examples of what he calls "the wine of the tropics."

Over the course of one highly caffeinated day, we tasted our way through some of Howell's favorites from across the Americas. It took some getting used to the roast. If you're used to dark roast or even medium, light roast can be virtually unrecognizable as coffee. Gone are the bitter, burnt notes of French roast, which is fine with me, but also missing are the toasty caramel, chocolate notes, and mouth-filling body I've always enjoyed in coffee. The problem seems to be that both drinks are called "coffee" when they taste virtually nothing alike. Anticipation is a huge part of food enjoyment, as anyone who's ever sipped a mug of coffee while expecting tea, or vice versa, has discovered. Instead of the creamy comfort drink I knew, I was drinking something thin and tart, without the slightest trace of bitterness,* that smelled like flowers and dried figs and pasilla chilies. Was this coffee?

In America, this is an uphill battle that only Howell has chosen to fight. Other than its espresso blends, everything Terroir Coffee sells is light roast. Even Stumptown, Intelligentsia, and the other hard-core roasters sell a variety of roasts to please as broad a market as possible. But Howell refuses to damage any of the aromatics in the masterpieces he painstakingly imports.

And maybe there's hope for the rest of us. Although it took me a little while to adjust, adjust I did. Within just a few days of drinking these light-roast coffees, I began thinking about them all the time. I went to bed anticipating my cup the next morning—something I'd never done before. I began having sudden little mouth hallucinations at random times during the day, when I'd experience a flash memory and my mouth would water at the thought of the coffee's acid kiss.

These coffees can be broken into geographical belts. "I think you get a Central American profile," Howell said, "that really goes from Guatemala down to Panama. You get a variance within a certain spectrum, and the varieties add dimension to it. Then you get the Andean flavor profile, with variance there. Brazil's separate. And then you get the African profiles."

---

* This can be confusing for people who have never really paid attention to their palates. "It's amazing how few people know the word *sour* anymore," Howell mentioned to me. "Dark-roast drinkers will tell me my coffee is bitter, and I'll say, 'No, you mean sour. I'll accept sour.'"

Perhaps the classic Central American profile comes from La Minita, a 700-acre coffee estate at 4,500 feet in the Tarrazú region of central Costa Rica, an hour south of San José. Nearly two million bushy coffee trees line La Minita's jagged, misty hills in neat rows of terraces, taking advantage of what comes very close to the ideal climate pattern for coffee. The dry season lasts for months, until the plants are wilting, and then come the "blossom showers"— heavy rains in the afternoon that disappear by sunset. After a week of such blossom showers, the plants recharge and burst into bloom. The hills of Tarrazú become laced with billions of white, honeysuckle-like flowers. Then the rains must hold off until the fruit has set and the flowers fall. Interspersed sun and showers are needed throughout the seven-month growing season, yet the rains must stop before the harvest, otherwise the flavor of the beans will be diluted.*

What struck me about La Minita was the absolute clarity of the flavor. Smooth, balanced, and sweet, it had none of the stale flavors I'd always thought were part and parcel of coffee. La Minita's location is partly to thank. Its high, west-facing slopes catch plenty of afternoon sun, as well as just enough rain at just the right times. And its climate, moderated by both the altitude and the cooling influence of the rivers that run through the valleys at the base of its mountains, never gets hot enough to mar the beans. But the coffee's irreproachable flavor is also due to the incredible care taken in the harvest. No other coffee estate has such high standards. Each tree is handpicked up to five times over the few weeks of harvest season, with only the ripest cherries being gathered each pass. Even so, more than 70 percent of the cherries picked are culled and sold as lower grades. The taste of La Minita is the taste of pure coffee ripeness.

"Back in the eighties," Howell recalled, "Bill McAlpin, La

---

* Too much rain can also cause the fruit to ripen before the seed—the inverse of the situation with wine grapes, where too much sun is the culprit.

Minita's owner, was the first one to teach me how to cup. Back then none of us knew how to do it. Bill said you're looking for clean cup and that's it. He had five coffees, three samples for each, for a total of fifteen cups on a circular table. He said pick out the best one, and tell me why. I failed that first test. Then he said pick out the cleanest one. I thought, *windowpane . . . clarity*. And I picked out the La Minita right away. That was a major adrenalin rush! That kept me in the business."

From the misty highlands of Guatemala, near 6,000 feet, came La Soledad, a coffee filled with orange marmalade scents and the darkly fruity note of dried chilies. "That's very Guatemalan!" Howell said excitedly. "We got this roast just right." Then he cocked his head and aerated the coffee in his mouth. "Maybe just a knick darker. Just a *tad*." It was more complex than the La Minita, more aromatic, yet not as clean.

A Colombian, also grown at 6,000 feet in the Nariño region on an organic farm called Villa Flor, was a complete departure.* This was the Andean flavor profile: the sweet, fresh, green astringency of raw sugarcane, both tropical and refreshing. There were notes of persimmon and walnuts, along with a hint of what Howell calls "barnyard"—comparing it to the flavor found in certain red wines—a little of which can be a good thing. "To me, these are the Burgundies of the coffee world," Howell said. "Brighter, very delicate, but now you get more clear-cut fruit notes. It has a lightness like the Burgundies. Sometimes you get a little bit of a wintergreen note. That's the closest I've been able to come. There's apple in it, too. It's a beautiful coffee." The top Colombian coffees, grown in the high valleys between Andean ridges, possess a unique microclimate. Air streaming off the Pacific hits the wall of the Cordillera Occidental and drops much of its moisture as rain. The mountain

---

* I know, I've tiptoed beyond the bounds of even Greater North America, but the contrast helps to illuminate the unique Central American coffee profile.

valley receives almost no rain, but as the air mass hits the Cordillera Central, it is squeezed just hard enough to release gentle rains. Villa Flor occupies the west-facing slopes of this second range.

And then there was the Esmeralda of Panama, angelic in its lightness and purity. Jasmine, lavender, nutmeg, papaya, lemon. After cupping all the Esmeralda microlots blind, Howell hadn't liked the ultra-pricey Reserva as much as the less-expensive coffee from the Mario Carneval lot, which he felt had a sweeter, mouth-filling flavor, and that was what we were drinking. It seemed to be made of finer stuff, like a sylph from the mountaintops. I mentioned the "God in a cup" line to Howell, and he winced. "I hate that," he said. "It doesn't do any favors for either party." I had to agree. With its whispers of flowers and African forest nurseries, it was more like the smell of bright, dangerous, and irresistible new thoughts.

RECIPES

THE PERFECT CUPPA JOE

It won't matter how stupendous coffee beans are when they reach you if they get mistreated in the brewing process—which almost all of them do. A few simple rules can greatly improve the typical cup. So instead of accompanying this chapter with some unlikely recipe for coffee ice cream, I thought it would be more useful to lay out the ground rules for carrying those fascinating coffee aromatics all the way to the final cup.

- An obvious but often overlooked point: Use only fresh coffee. Buy roasted beans in a sealed, airtight bag with a degassing valve (to release the carbon dioxide the roasted beans continue to generate). Beans will stay fresh in such bags for about three months. The best companies put the roast date right on the bag. Once opened, the beans will stay fresh for only ten days, so buy your coffee in small quantities. Store the beans in a cool, dry place, but not in the fridge or freezer.

- An obvious but even more often overlooked point: Use good-tasting water. Only 1.2 to 1.5 percent of your coffee is bean solids; the rest is water, which has a huge impact on flavor. If you don't like drinking the water, don't use it for making coffee, either.

- A spinning-blade grinder (the kind most of us use at home), in which the beans sit in the well with the blades as they spin, creates a variety of grain sizes, depending on how many times each grain comes in contact with the blades. This leads to uneven extraction and some sediment in the cup. In a burr grinder, however, the beans travel linearly through the spinning wheels, like in a tiny mill, and are ground to a uniform size.

- Never pre-grind your beans. Ground coffee goes stale within hours.

- A French press requires a course grind to keep the grains out of the coffee. Invariably, some sediment slips into the cup, creating a more muddy brew with more than 2 percent solids. Some people like it; some don't. Brew coffee in a French press for about five minutes.

- A drip pot is even more problematic. "The home coffeemaker cannot produce great coffee," Howell said. "It just can't." Home machines heat the water to only 185 to 190 degrees, which tends to overemphasize the sourness of the beans. The ideal temperature of 200 degrees or so is achieved by only one machine (according to both Howell and *Cook's Illustrated*)—the Technivorm, a Dutch model that retails for $250. If that is too steep, consider boiling the water manually, letting it sit for about fifteen seconds, so it reaches about 200 degrees, then pouring it over the grounds in the filter. (You can also buy a new version of a one-cup filter cone that has a spiral design that keeps the grounds agitated as the water swirls around and down, extracting more flavor.) Surprisingly, experts prefer white paper filters to the "natural" brown ones, which are less processed and leave more of a cardboard taste in the coffee. (Mesh filters let more sediment and oils pass through, giving a French-press-like brew, and require a coarse grind.) Drip pots and filter cones require a medium-fine grind, and it should take about five minutes for all the coffee to pass through them.

- In my experience, brewed coffee loses its verve within ten minutes, and tastes noticeably stale or cooked within twenty. Use a thermal carafe that keeps the coffee hot without heating it, and brew only what will be drunk right away.

- Sorry, espresso fans, but drip and French press coffee better capture the nuances of a particular terroir. (Although espresso, at four times the concentration, delivers more total flavor per sip.) The tiny grains and intense pressure used in the espresso-making process greatly exaggerate any acidity in the coffee, meaning that good espresso blends must have the acidity (along with other delicate flavors) roasted out of them or must use lower-elevation beans with "flatter" flavors. When I want to appreciate the intrinsic beauty of the bean, I go for drip coffee. When I'm in the mood for personal service, I go for an espresso, savoring the deft handwork as the barista coaxes the crema from a well-pulled shot.

- The true obsessive may want to invest in an ExtractMoJo, a device Terroir Coffee developed that includes a handheld refractometer, which analyzes the percent of dissolved solids in your cup of coffee, and a software program, which then calculates the amount of coffee and water needed to achieve the best possible cup for your home machine's brew temperature. As Howell explained it, "You can typically extract about 30 percent of the solids from a coffee bean before you hit pure cellulose. But above 22 percent, you start to get bitter off-flavors. I call it chewing tobacco. Harsh. Below 18 percent, you're underextracting. Between 19 and 20 percent, you hit the sweet spot." While he was showing me the device, a new employee walked by cradling an armful of new equipment.

  "If you hang out with these guys," she warned me, "you need a grinder, a Technivorm, a scale—"

  "Don't forget the MoJo!" Howell chimed in.

  "A MoJo," she continued, "and beakers to make sure you get the right amount of water."

  Howell laughed. "That's about a thousand bucks!"

RESOURCES

COFFEE REVIEW

www.coffeereview.com

Kenneth Davids, the Robert Parker of coffee, started this site in 1997. It is the place to find an objective guide to the best coffees in the world, all rated on a one-hundred-point system. It's also the best single source of in-depth and well-written information on coffee.

GREEN MOUNTAIN COFFEE ROASTERS

www.greenmountaincoffee.com

888-879-4627

A big company that acts like a small one, GMCR sells a variety of single-origin coffees as well as its many blends and wildly successful single-serving K-Cups. The company is a leader in sustainability and fair-trade issues. A few of its coffees score with the best on the Coffee Review site and are a steal.

INTELLIGENTSIA

www.intelligentsiacoffee.com

888-945-9786

The pride of Chicago (and now Los Angeles), Intelligentsia has a stellar reputation for sourcing great coffees and for promoting direct trade with farmers. It has fewer offerings than some other sites, but Geoff Watts, Intelligentsia's famous coffee buyer, chooses with extreme care.

STUMPTOWN COFFEE ROASTERS

www.stumptowncoffee.com

503-230-7797

Stumptown, which dominates the coffee scene in Portland, Oregon, prides itself on selling some of the most prized and expensive coffees in the world. Among others, it has exclusives on some of the most coveted microlots of Esmeralda Special ($95 for eight ounces). Stumptown sells mail-order beans and has cafés in Seattle and New York City. Its Web site has a nice guide to coffee varietals.

TERROIR COFFEE
www.terroircoffee.com
866-444-5282
Terroir offers incredibly exacting single-estate coffees with an emphasis on light roasts that bring out the aromatics in the beans. It's the most uncompromising coffee company in the western hemisphere.

Eat Me

NEW ENGLAND CIDER AND
YAKIMA VALLEY APPLES

I GET MY HOOCH from Terry Bradshaw. It goes like this: One gusty October day, when the air is shattering crisp and yellow birch leaves careen across the road like goldfinches, we know it's time. My son climbs into the back of our old red Ford pickup, and we maneuver it under the century-old apple trees in our backyard. My son reaches up, gives the tree branches a shake, and hard little red-and-green apples, along with a few leaves, hail down into the bed. A surprising number bounce out. We try to gather these escapees, but really, in New England in fall, time is short and wild apple supplies are not, so soon we are cruising back roads and visiting our neighbors' yards, and their kids are climbing through the apple trees and shaking their arms and legs like conga players, and the apples keep raining down with satisfying thumps.

Judging by the red-cheeked faces, there is nothing closer to heaven than being ten years old and riding in the back of an old pickup with apples piled around your knees, the rosy smell filling your head as you creep along toward the next tree. The hillsides are red and orange, punctuated by sharp, green spruce triangles, and the air is wistful with wood smoke. Fall is fruition. Things are ending and deepening as the epicycles of the years spiral into the coils of our lives.

You can eat these apples, and we do, but they aren't what you'd call out-of-hand apples. Too small, too sour, too much skin, too many scabby bits—they were never really intended for eating. Instead, they have a higher calling.

We bring our apples to Terry Bradshaw, who has a press and a little operation called Lost Meadow Cidery. Terry has a beard and bushy eyebrows and a ponytail and unnervingly blue eyes. If he were in a werewolf movie, you'd have no trouble picking out the werewolf. He has never played football. Weekdays, he is Horticultural Research Guy for the University of Vermont; weekends, he unleashes his creative juices.

Terry does not have a liquor license. He simply fills up your container with the juice that he presses. If said juice should happen to transform into booze back at your place, well, so be it. Of course, it always does. After burbling quietly in glass carboys all winter in my cellar, it has metamorphosed into piss-clear, low-alcohol cider by spring. By summer it will be bone dry, dominated by puckery tannins and acids, as the yeast digests the last sugars, but in spring there is still enough lingering sweetness to balance the drink and evoke the apples that were.

That's my apples, anyway. And my friends' apples. All coming from nameless trees of uncertain origin. Somebody planted these trees with a particular intention, but those plans have been buried by the sediment of time like so many cellar holes. Accessibility—truck-friendliness—drives our selection of apples more than flavor, and the resulting cider is an exhilarating crapshoot. There is no bad cider, as far as I can tell, but there are a few challenging ones.[*]

Terry's cider is a spirit of another sort. Most of the juice Terry sells comes from apples he and others have painstakingly selected. The names are not ones you're likely to find in the produce section of Walmart: Ellis Bitter, Major, Liberty, Big Yellow Bittersharp, Little Yellow Sweet, Kingston Black, Aromatic Redstreak, Foxwhelp,

---

[*] It should go without saying that I'm talking about hard cider here, not the thick brown sludge sold in supermarkets. Before pasteurization, sweet cider was an ephemeral product, since it spontaneously became hard cider with the help of wild yeast.

Yarlington Mill, Chisel Jersey, Dabinett, not to mention local crab apples.

The Big Yellow Bittersharps and Little Yellow Sweets you won't find in any horticultural catalog anywhere. They come from a local forager named Chris, who has become something of an apple sleuth. Chris keeps his life simple enough that he can take advantage of good things when they come. One of those things is the October apple bonanza. In fall, Chris spends days cruising back roads and fields in his old Saab, an open wine bottle jammed between his legs,* gathering forgotten apples. He does this because he can't stand to see premium product left to rot by the side of the road. "A lot of these apple trees were chosen because they made the finest cider," he said to me. "It's as if wine went out of fashion and people stopped picking the grapes in Napa." Chris's best finds get worked into Terry's premier blends.

A good, dry cider is a poignant mix of sugars, tannins, acids, alcohol, and aromatic compounds. It usually requires a blend of apple varieties—sometimes twenty—to achieve balance. Some apples supply lots of sugar to make the alcohol. Some provide aromas of nutmeg and clove. Some are so tannic that biting into them is like sucking on a green banana; yet this astringency becomes refreshing in the final cider. Kingston Black, a legendary British variety, has long been hailed as one of the only apples that can make a good cider on its own.

The general profile of a dry cider is similar to that of an extremely sharp white wine, maybe a Grüner Veltliner—sour, green, racy, almost salty. But white wines don't have the tannins that ciders do. Tannins are defensive compounds, invented by plants to discourage certain animals from grazing on them. They work by being bitter and by linking together proteins in our skin and saliva, interfering with lubrication and drying out the surface of the

---

* Turns out it's filled with water; Chris is deeply suspicious of plastic.

mouth.* The result is the rough, puckery feeling we get from tea, chocolate, red wine, and apple skins.

So a cider has the astringency and bitterness of red wine and the acidity of white wine, with about half the alcohol, which gives a lighter body to the drink. Add in a unique suite of aromas created by the yeast-apple interactions—flowers, citrus, soap, and mice are sometimes cited—and you have an acquired and grown-up taste. Most people, who have been conditioned to expect a very narrow range of flavors in their alcohols, have not acquired it.

Once you do, however, you can't let it go. I eagerly anticipate a new cider, with its weird wafts of pear and musk and the way it makes my lips sandpapery. It's also a spectacular accompaniment to food. Cider sharpens the tastes, scours the palate, and enhances whatever you're eating. It captures the essence of a family farm on a crisp October day—the hay barn and the animals and the orchard—in a way that no wine can.

It also makes you tipsy, of course. This should not be overlooked, and certainly wasn't by America's early colonists, who depended on apples for their hooch. At first, Europe's grains and grapevines withered in the New World, but its apples took to the country like they'd found the promised land. In a way they had: The Colonies had a climate more similar to the apple's ancient Kazakhstan home than to Europe's Gulf Stream–moderated one.

But even if the apple had never in its ancient past encountered a climate like that of Maine or Pennsylvania, it probably would have adapted pretty quickly. The reason is that apples do not "come true" from seed, any more than your children "come true" from you. Take a McIntosh apple from a tree, plant any of its five seeds, and you won't get a McIntosh tree. You'll get a tree with some genes from its mother, which made the apple, and some from its father,

---

* This protein-linking ability is also why tannins were the original *tanning* agents for hides.

which sent its sperm-packed pollen winging over on the back of some bee during the spring bloom. In fact, since changes in just a few genes can make for a very different apple, you will probably get a tree that produces apples shockingly different from those of its parent. The vast majority won't pan out as eating apples (or "dessert apples," as they're called in the trade), but every apple still carries five potential superstars in its core.

If you like the apples produced by a particular tree, and you want to make more trees that produce the same apples, you need to clone that tree so that its offspring will have identical genes. No problem. While we are only starting to get a grasp on cloning animals, with trees it's a cinch. You take a new twig from an existing tree and graft it onto the rootstock of some other apple seedling that's been cut down. The two parts of the new tree will have entirely different genes, but fruit characteristics are controlled only by the twig part; the root genes stick to their tasks of gathering water and nutrients and passing them up to "headquarters."

Grafting is why we are able to create apple varieties. Every variety, from Red Delicious to Lady, began as one sexually produced, individually unique seed. (Note that even on the same tree, different seeds can have different fathers and be as different as any other half-siblings.) This seed managed to grow into a tree that happened to make apples that somebody found exceptional enough to clone. Then those clones were cloned, and so on.

Of course, if the only new apple trees that got made were all clones, we'd never see a new variety, and the apple would be incapable of adapting to new conditions. Fortunately, enough happy accidents continue to occur in the hedgerows of the world's orchards. All this gene swapping ensures that, of all the individually unique apple seedlings sprouting every year, more than a few will be tough bastards. And that is the apple way.

Eric Bordelet, France's premier cider maker, insists that what gives his Argelette cider such depth and complexity is the terroir of his orchard: schist and granite. Poor soil, in other words—virtually identical to the mountain soil that I found makes for the best maple syrup. In so many organisms, a challenging environment seems to foster character.* This is never more true than it is for the apple. Apple trees don't just endure adversity; they thrive on it.

And there you have the essence of the apple. It's a resourceful survivor, embracing the kind of brutal northern climate that would make a grapevine wither and a peach cry. It's the fruit that made America bearable. When the geese flew, and the temperature dove to levels you'd never imagined in merry old England, and the local natives decided maybe they didn't want to share Thanksgiving with you after all, at least you had lots of long-lasting fruit (as much as a ton per tree) sitting in your root cellar and several barrels of cider to take the edge off your misery.

What I call the Greater Northeast—the "sugar maple triangle" from Michigan to New Brunswick to West Virginia—still bears witness to what the apple was able to accomplish in foreign territory. Every fall, when the fruit appears, I suddenly realize how many of the trees that line the area's dirt roads and regrown forests are apples. Working hand in hand with people, its preferred partner, the cider apple transformed the landscape, expressing a different terroir in each region, one that was novel but always a great match.

The first chapter of Michael Pollan's *Botany of Desire* nails this Asian native's core Americanness:

> Whenever a tree growing in the midst of a planting of name-
> less cider apples somehow distinguished itself—for the har-
> diness of its constitution, the redness of its skin, the excellence

---

* Some organic-cider makers believe that a little insect pressure triggers a response in the trees that brings out the flavor in the apples. (The same claim is
  made by a grower in my avocado chapter.) While such blemished fruit wouldn't
  do well in the produce aisle, it's perfect for cider.

of its flavor—it would promptly be named, grafted, publicized, and multiplied. Through this simultaneous process of natural and cultural selection, the apples took up into themselves the very substance of America—its soil and climate and light, as well as the desires and tastes of its people, and even perhaps a few of the genes of America's native crab apples. In time all these qualities became part and parcel of what an apple in America is.

In other words, American apples are not English apples, because America is not England. Americans and American apples reinvented themselves, and their country, in tandem. This is ongoing. As Pollan relates, the changing face of apples in America mirrors our evolving tastes and desires. From a riotous diversity of form, color, and flavor, reflecting the multitude of needs we asked the apple to meet—food, dessert, refreshing drink, inebriator—the apple tree suffered a biodiversity crash in the nineteenth century, brought down by the temperance movement. The campaign to chop down every cider tree drove cider underground and impoverished the drink in a way it is only now recovering from. The apples that survived the purge were the ones that could legitimately claim to be for eating, not drinking. Most of the tannic, astringent apples disappeared, replaced by apples with abundant sugars and enough acid to keep things interesting.

It was a disaster for the few remaining cider aficionados, but even then the country was full of uniquely American varietals, with new ones occasionally still popping up in orchards. Jonathan, McIntosh, Northern Spy, and Red Delicious all originated as orchard accidents during this era. Most farmers were still grafting their trees from a neighbor's, so most varieties remained regional. The apple continued to reflect the character of American farms: small, diverse family affairs.

RED MEANS GO

As the twentieth-century wave of consolidation and industrialization swept American agriculture, it took many an apple with it. From more than fourteen thousand varieties of apple listed by the U.S. Department of Agriculture in 1905, we are down to less than one hundred. Old varieties were left to be swallowed by the encroaching forest as family farms closed their doors. Large-scale growers focused on cloning whatever apple would bring the highest price nationwide. In the process of chasing that highest price, by the late twentieth century commercial apple growers were putting their eggs in just a handful of baskets, and one in particular.

In 1872 a seedling tree that produced lovely and tasty red-striped fruit was discovered in an Iowa orchard. Cuttings were made, and in 1895 the first Red Delicious apples hit the market. They were immediately popular, and grew more so as various bud mutations through the twentieth century produced apples that were redder and redder. It turns out that, given a choice, people overwhelmingly go for the reddest apple. So growers kept selecting for the reddest. They were not, however, selecting for the tastiest. Eventually, Red Delicious apples eclipsed fire-engine red and reached a color imaginatively described by the industry as "midnight red." And most are virtually inedible, with dry flesh and thick skin. Good-tasting apples have small, tightly packed cells that break apart at first bite, spilling their juice in all directions. Red Delicious have cottony, dry cells with too much air in between.

This has not been lost on the industry, but until recently, it didn't care. The mealiest Red Delicious outsold the tastiest McIntosh. Why not give the people what they want? Not so long ago, three quarters of the apples grown in America were Red Delicious, which has been called "the best-selling and worst-tasting apple in America."

Even its grading is based on color. To qualify as U.S. Extra

Fancy, the top grade and only one you're likely to see fresh in stores, a minimum of 66 percent of the surface of a Red Delicious, Empire, Jonathan, Winesap, or other red variety "must be covered with a good shade of solid red characteristic of the variety." And that's just the USDA standard; industry standards are skewed even further toward the red end of the spectrum.

You'll notice that the apple standards do not mention flavor. And there you have the tragedy of the U.S. apple industry. Apple growers get paid based on how *red* their apples are. Large growers have optical sorters—of both the human and mechanical varieties—that cull apples that aren't red enough from the sorting lines.

Our preference for red fruit is built-in and shared with most other animals. As the purest contrast to green, red is the natural choice for plants that want their fruit to stand out against a leafy backdrop. Plants like to keep their fruit green and inconspicuous until their seeds are mature. Only then do they transform it into an irresistible beacon: Starches get converted to sugars, enticing aromas waft through the air, and skins turn red. The plant is turning on the lights in the store and putting its best wares in the display window. Over the eons, we've learned to read the signs. Green means stop; red means go. It takes more than a few decades of tasteless red apples to recondition us.

In addition to attracting animals, the redness in apples helps protect them from sunburn. The red is created by anthocyanin, the same pigment that turns raspberries, grapes, and fall leaves red. Just as we generate tanning pigments in our skin in response to sunlight, fruits generate anthocyanins in theirs.* The more sunlight that hits an apple in summer and fall, the redder it will be.† It will also be bigger and sweeter, since sunlight is the energy that the apple tree

---

* Anthocyanins are also tannic, which is why many animals avoid apple skins.
† To make the bottoms of their apples red, many orchards unroll strips of reflective foil beneath their trees.

captures with its leaves, via photosynthesis, and turns into food energy: sugar. An apple is a well of sunlight. And there you have condition 1 for growing the perfect apple: maximum sunlight.

But there's more to it. Apples are native to the mountainous forests of Kazakhstan and Kyrgyzstan.* All domestic apple trees still have at least a faint genetic memory of life in these boreal forests. There, the sign that winter was coming was cold. When night temperatures dip into the forties, apple trees know it's time to sweeten up the fruit, turn it red, and get it out into the hands, mouths, and gullets of animals. And that's perfect-apple condition 2: cold nights.

Already we can eliminate a good chunk of North America. Mexico and the southern United States just don't get cold enough. Even California's Central Valley, stone fruit capital of the universe, isn't right. Apples will grow there, but they won't get that sweet or that red.

During the summer growing season, Canada and the northern United States have the longest days and coldest nights, and this is where you find most apples—though usually not perfect ones. Apple trees love the Northeast, for example. They grow on every old homestead and in many commercial operations. But while the summer days are long in the Northeast, they aren't necessarily clear.

Don't let the tourism board know I told you, but the Northeast gets no more sun than the notoriously rainy Pacific Northwest. It's an extremely damp place. That's fine with the apple trees, but it's also just dandy with a rogues' gallery of fungi and pests that love apple trees, especially apple scab, the fungus responsible for those scaly blemishes on untreated trees. I won't bore you with the list of nasty things sprayed on conventional apples to keep them cosmetically

---

* These wild apple forests still exist, and sometimes I fantasize about making cider in them in fall, though certain regrown Vermont forests are so thick with settlers' old apple trees that they probably make a decent stand-in.

perfect; suffice it to say that you want to choose organic apples. Yet it is maddeningly difficult to grow unblemished organic apples in a wet environment. Which leads us to the Zen-koan-like perfect-apple condition 3: water without rain.

To summarize, perfect apple terroir is somewhere with long, sunny summer days, cool nights, and ample water that comes from somewhere other than the sky.

Do I have such a place in mind?

I'm so glad you asked.

HIGH, DRY, AND SWEET AS PIE

The next time you're in Seattle, grab a car and drive due east. In about an hour you'll hit the foothills of the volcanic Cascades and start to climb. Climbing with you will be all that wet air surging off the Pacific. (North American weather generally travels west to east, a huge factor in the climate differences between the two coasts.) As that water-rich air is squeezed up into the mountains, the moisture comes out as rain, just like a wet sponge being squeezed. In your car, you climb through soaking evergreen rainforest, your wipers slapping away as you fight carsickness through the hairpin curves.

And then, suddenly, you crest. The heavens part, and a treeless cowboyscape of sagebrush, dun buttes, and blue sky stretches to eternity. Wrung out by the great grasp of the Cascades, the air that reaches Eastern Washington's Yakima Valley is bone dry.

Until the late 1800s, not a whole lot lived in the Yakima Valley beyond a handful of desert plants. The exception was the well-watered corridors of the rivers that drained the Cascades and Rockies, eventually merging with the mighty Columbia and heading for Portland, Oregon, and the Pacific. Then the government began a massive public works project, digging a series of canals and pipes to bring that water to the far corners of the valley.

The basalt soil of the Yakima Valley is extremely fertile. It owes this fertility to massive volcanic eruptions fifteen million years ago, which filled the entire valley with one of the largest and deepest lava flows in the history of the planet. That was followed about fifteen thousand years ago by one of the world's largest floods, when glacial Lake Missoula, in the vicinity of Montana, burst the ice dams holding it back and scoured half of Idaho, Washington, and Oregon, depositing rich sediment throughout the region.

All that fertility was just a tease, since the area received zero rainfall. The few inches of precipitation came as winter snow. But once irrigation was in place, the sagebrush steppe became the greatest, and most counterintuitive, apple-growing region on the continent. With warm days, cool nights, and a good two hours more summer sun per day than California, the Yakima Valley can grow bigger, sweeter, redder, more unblemished apples than anywhere else.

Craig Campbell's grandfather moved from Saskatchewan to Tieton, a high plateau on the far western edge of the Yakima Valley, in 1920, a couple of years before the water arrived. He knew it was coming, and he knew what that meant. He planted his first orchards and hauled his own water to them, a good eight hundred feet of altitude above the river, until the irrigation arrived. "We have the oldest water rights in the valley," Campbell told me. "The rest of the lower Yakima Valley could dry up, and we'd still get water."

The Campbells have always been a little ahead of the game. Not long after Craig Campbell took over the family orchard from his father, the Washington apple cart was overturned by two tremors. First, a famous *60 Minutes* broadcast in 1989 labeled the growth-regulator alar, commonly applied to apples, as a likely human carcinogen, triggering a massive campaign against its use. With Meryl Streep leading the charge, apples became guilty until proven innocent.

At the same time, massive orchard plantings in China were

starting to bear fruit. "At that time Washington was growing so much fruit for the Pacific Rim," Campbell's wife, Sharon, recalled, "and then China came on and took away that whole business." Today China dominates the apple business, with more than 60 percent of world production. The second-place United States is a speck in China's rearview mirror, with 6 percent, two thirds of which comes from Eastern Washington.

With the international market disappearing and the domestic market spooked, Craig Campbell made the decision to switch to organic farming. He'd been considering it for some time, partly as a way to get off the Red and Golden Delicious bandwagon and start focusing on the many tasty varieties being developed, but the alar reaction convinced him that a tipping point had occurred in the market. "We had to replant the whole farm," Sharon said. Harmony Orchards became the first organic grower in the area. "When we started, we'd go to dinners in Yakima, and people would say, 'Really? Why you doing that?' It's a real philosophy. Craig is very conscious of the history. He feels like it's a gift that his grandfather came here and that his father was here. His mother hated it out here, his sister hated it, but Craig could never get enough. It was a good place to be a boy. He never had a toy tractor; he had a real John Deere." From an initial five acres, the Campbells now have more than two hundred acres of apples, pears, and apricots in organic production.

And what acres they are. On a crisp day in late September, the Campbells took me through their orchard. At an altitude of two thousand feet, it is one of the highest in the country. It is also quite remote. "They didn't think too much of the Campbells in the twenties," his business partner likes to joke. Wander a hundred yards beyond the edge of the orchard and your shoes poke over a crumbling precipice that falls to the Naches River.

But the Campbells love their edge-of-the-abyss orchard. "This is truly the end of the Yakima Valley," Craig said. "This is where the

water stops. We've got a golden eagle nest around the corner. There
are quite a few goldens along the river. It's pretty neat to see those
things roaming around."

The draw for the Campbells and the eagles is the same: steady
winds that come howling down Mount Rainier, channel through
the river valley, and tear across their butte. "It's actually beneficial.
We get more of a differential swing up here because of this cooling
that comes out of these mountains every night," Craig said. "It'll be
ninety during the day and maybe forty-five at night. That's what
sets us apart up here. An apricot that's just orange in Pasco [at 383
feet above sea level] will get a red cheek on it up here because of the
cool nights. But some days, with all this damn wind up here, you
think, God, it'd be nice if it didn't blow."

I suggested making lemons out of lemonade and throwing up
some wind turbines. After all, Eastern Washington has some of the
largest wind farms in the country. But he winced at the idea. "We'd
have to put it on these rock buttes, and I don't know about tearing
them up to put one of those things in. If we're farming here on land
that's been farmed before, that's one thing. But putting in wind and
tearing all this up? I couldn't do it. This takes so long to make. It's
an arid climate. Things don't happen very fast here. Better to leave
it as is."

With so little ground cover, the geological processes that
shaped the area are particularly hard to ignore. A ghost from the
ancient past came calling in 1980, when Mount St. Helens erupted
and covered the Yakima Valley in an inch of ash. "That was a pretty
interesting time," Craig told me. "In Yakima it got dark, and the
streetlights came on. It felt like the end of the world. At the time,
our pears were about the size of your index finger. The ash scratched
them up. At first we thought we were wiped out. But that year we
wound up growing some of the best apples ever. There was a little
fertilizer in that stuff. The white ash is still laying out on these
buttes. It didn't melt and go away. It's part of the history here."

We stood looking across the chasm at the pronghorn-colored flanks of Mount Clemmons. Craig, who is soft-spoken, lean, and fit, likes to go for epic mountain bike rides in those hills. He pointed out how what looked, through my Northeasterner's eyes, like a dead landscape was very much alive: lichens on the basalt rocks and withered plants with deep taproots that would come alive in the spring and paint the hillsides white and gold. And he explained that, even without windmills, the wind was doing invaluable work for him: "We have a lot less insect pressure here than orchards do down in the valley. There's nothing upwind of us except sagebrush and mountains, so we're not infested with other people's problems. The wind comes down this canyon every night and blows until about four in the morning. Codling moths fly at night. We kinda blow them down to the neighbors."

The full-desert climate—four inches of precipitation per year, all of it snow—northern latitude, and camphor-scented wind make for a strangely ideal apple oasis. The usual suspects that like to plague apples—apple scab, mildew, and the like—aren't adapted to the sage-steppe landscape upwind of the orchard. For years, USDA inspectors have been intrigued by the remarkably low level of insect pests—particularly aphids and pear psylla—at Harmony Orchards, even compared with other orchards in the valley. They suspect that spiders, ladybugs, and other predators that live in the native environment move into the orchard to feast on the aphids and psylla, naturally controlling the population. Additional pest control comes from the rows of Lombardy poplars planted as windbreaks thirty-five years ago by Campbell's father after he saw a similar technique used in New Zealand.* Poplars harbor poplar

---

* The idea is to slow the wind just enough that it won't bruise the fruit. The poplars also are responsible for Harmony Orchard's symbol: a gigantic, New Agey spiral of poplar trees, planted by Craig and Sharon in 2004, that must have caused even more consternation among their straight-laced neighbors than the switch to organic farming.

aphids—a big draw for local predators, which move on to the orchard aphids for their next course.

The biggest challenge remains codling moths, some of which manage to hang on despite the wind. Craig places mating disruptors throughout the orchard. These plastic strips, which are twisted around apple branches, emit intense female sex pheromones. Like an explosion in a Chanel factory, the oversaturation of feminine odors in the air makes it difficult for the males to find any actual females.

It's about the most stress-free life an organic apple tree could have, and it makes an important point about terroir: Mimicking nature is not always the goal (as Europe's winemakers learned long ago). Sometimes, like William Faulkner, a thing achieves its best expression in its native landscape. Sometimes, like Cormac McCarthy, it has to head west to find itself.

A single look at Harmony Orchards' newest plantings would be enough to subvert any old-fashioned notions about what's "right" or "good" for apple trees. Twenty acres of Ambrosias in clean green rows perch at the edge of the chasm, with brown Mount Clemmons looming behind. At first glance, you might not guess they are apple trees. The trees are ten-foot spindles trellised together in long rows with wide alleys in between. Instead of significant branches, little stubs stick out from the trunks. The trees won't be allowed to get any bigger. And they crank out the fruit.

"This is the new modern orchard," Craig explained. "Our whole goal is to get the big limbs out of these trees and keep the fruit balanced. It's so important to get the sunlight into the center of the tree for spur development and fruit next year. If you close these trees in, then the center dies and the tree moves up toward the sun. We don't want tall ladders here." The benefits were obvious. "In four growing seasons, this orchard is fully grown. It's just these walls of fruit. The pickers love it."

To me, it resembled a gigantic vineyard. I plucked a fat apple from one of those pink walls and bit into it. It was explosively crunchy. It was loud. Atomized juice misted my face. High-altitude apples have a smaller cell structure, which keeps them extra firm, even in storage. The crispness of the nights is translated into their flesh, the mountain sun and cold turning their cheeks as pink as a kid's. In the fall, Craig purposely underwaters them. "A little stress isn't a bad thing at all," he noted. "It'll bring on your sugar and your flavors. You don't want to get those things too fired up, or they don't finish out right."

Ambrosias are one of the new darlings of the apple world. The original tree was discovered in a British Columbia orchard in the 1990s. The surrounding trees were Red Delicious and Golden Delicious, but this hybrid had grown up unnoticed in one of the orchard's rows. It wasn't unnoticed by the pickers, however; they always stripped it clean for their own uses. Eventually the orchard owners discovered it, grafted some trees, and the Ambrosia variety was born. It's a sweet apple with a great depth of flavor, a relatively low acidity, and a beguiling perfume. It's one of the few apples I know that carries the apple blossom scent all the way to the finish line.

Most of the intoxicating flavors in apples show up at that finish line, late in the season, so Harmony Orchards color-picks each orchard multiple times, taking only the ripest fruit each time. And, since the cold nights are what trigger the anthocyanin production, and even the organic market prefers red fruit, they wait as long as possible. "If this had more bright red, it would be a more desirable apple at retail," Craig said, pulling a greenish Jonagold from a tree. "These retailers, they push this red thing." He shrugged and looked out across the parched steppe. "We're always chasing color here."

I tried to picture it from the air, as the golden eagles must as they shoot past—the spiraling poplars and the neat walls of red, the landscape coming alive in pattern and color as the desert explodes in sugar and the apple continues to reinvent itself in the boundless West.

RECIPES

MAPLE-CARAMELIZED APPLES

Here I am, cooking with maple syrup again. But here's why: In apple cookery, you want to bolster the fruitiness of the apples with savory, buttery caramel richness, and since maple syrup is already caramelized, it gets the process off to a smashing start. It's also more foolproof than using sugar. Any time you cook with apples, use a firm and tart variety, such as Honeycrisp, Jonagold, Pinova, or good old McIntosh or Granny Smith. Some heirloom varieties, such as Ananas Reinette and Belle du Boskoop, can be heavenly. I tend to eat this as is, maybe with a little vanilla ice cream on top, but if you want to fancy it up, bake it in puff pastry and call it a tart.

Serves 4

4 tablespoons butter
¼ cup maple syrup
6 apples, peeled, cored, and sliced
½ teaspoon cinnamon
pinch freshly grated nutmeg
zest and juice from ⅛ lemon

1. Heat the butter and maple syrup in a skillet over medium heat until bubbling.
2. Add the apples and cinnamon, toss to coat in the butter-syrup mixture, and cook, stirring and turning the apples occasionally, until they are browned and soft but not mushy, about 6 to 8 minutes.
3. Turn off the heat, add the nutmeg, lemon zest, and lemon juice, and stir. Let the dish cool enough that the sauce thickens, then serve.

APPLES WITH MISO DIP

Think of this sweet, salty, savory dip as a Japanese version of apples and peanut butter.

Serves 1 to 2 as a snack

2 heaping tablespoons sweet white miso
1 tablespoon honey (apple blossom, basswood, or another herbal honey are excellent)
zest and juice of ¼ lemon
chopped mint or toasted sesame seeds to garnish (optional)
2 apples, peeled, cored, and sliced in wedges

1. In a small saucepan, mix the miso, honey, and lemon zest and juice. Heat over low heat, stirring frequently, until the sauce turns glossy and begins to bubble. Add a little water (or cider) if necessary to make it smooth, but the dip should be thick enough to cling to the apple slices; it will thicken as it cools.
2. Scrape the mixture into a small dip bowl, garnish with the mint or sesame seeds (if using), and serve surrounded by the apple wedges.

RESOURCES

FARNUM HILL CIDER

www.farnumhillciders.com

603-448-1511

Many people believe that Steve Woods's ciders are the best in America. They are made in the classic Old World style, meaning they have lots of bitter tannins, tart acids, and fascinating aromatics. Here is Amanda Hesser in the *New York Times* on Farnum Hill's Extra Dry: "An aroma of cherries and melon that seem to leap from the glass. It is dry and distinct with a pleasant sharpness reminiscent of bitter oranges." Frankly, I don't know what she's talking about. My notes on the same cider read: "Dandelions, straw, saltines." The one thing we agree on is that it's excellent with food. Retailing for twenty to thirty dollars a bottle, Farnum Hill's Kingston Black Reserve is the priciest, and most sought-after, cider in the country.

HARMONY ORCHARDS

www.harmonyorchards.com

Harmony Orchards grows some of the top organic Red Delicious apples in the world, but it is becoming known for its more adventurous varieties. If you buy an organic Lady apple (those plum-size beauties, usually green with one red cheek, first grown by the Romans, making them the oldest cultivar in existence), chances are it came from Harmony Orchards. My Harmony favorites include the dusty-pink Ambrosia, sweetly perfumed with shades of violet, rose, and lilac; Pinova, a new German variety with an intense pineapple flavor; the sweet and snappy Honeycrisp, with, yes, a honey nose; and spicy Jonagold which, according to Sharon Campbell, is "the perfect applesauce apple." Harmony Orchards' twelve-apple December gift box is beautiful to behold.

LOST MEADOW CIDERY
www.lostmeadowvt.com

Terry Bradshaw offers squeezes of his own unique blends of cider apples: Kingston Black, Hubbardston Nonesuch, Sweet 16, Liberty, Ellis Bitter, Ashton Bitter, and a whole lot of things growing wild in the Vermont woods that don't even have names. He's even worked "Rowan Russets" from my backyard into the occasional mix. There's a brand-new blend each week in the fall, and you have to show up in person to get some. Terry's blog is a fascinating peek into the world of cider science and lore. His 2007 Kingston Black Special Reserve, a silver-medal winner at the Great Lakes International Cider and Perry Competition, is the best cider I've tasted. It's dry and crisp yet full-bodied, with a prickle of carbonation to keep it light on your tongue and enough tannins to make it pleasantly rough against your lips.

TIETON CIDER WORKS
www.tietonciderworks.com

Surprisingly, for an area that dominates apple production, Eastern Washington is still new to the cider game. Its innovations have been in the realm of production, not product. Red Delicious still dominates, with just a handful of other dessert apples making up the bulk of the rest: Granny Smith, Golden Delicious, Fuji, and Gala. All make cloying cider. The hearts of artisan cider production are Oregon and New England—places with a more traditionally gloomy northern European climate and, perhaps not coincidentally, places that have always appreciated the tart art of bile.

Now Craig and Sharon Campbell are once again shocking their neighbors with a new seventy-five-acre orchard of aromatic heirloom cider apples like Ashmead's Kernel, Esopus Spitzenberg (Thomas Jefferson's favorite), and Gravenstein. "Out here, people don't know the first thing about these old varieties," Craig Campbell told me. "No one in the state of Washington's even heard of

Ashmead's Kernel. It's an ugly apple, but I think it's excellent." The cider apples are mixed with a sweeter apple from their other orchards, in a recipe they are still perfecting. "We wanted the Ambrosia to work so badly," Sharon Campbell said, "but the pH was too sweet. But the Ladies work. And the Pinova is *really* good." Their first ciders came on line in 2010.

Mother Nature's Little Black Book

VARIETAL HONEYS OF NEW ENGLAND,
NORTH CAROLINA, FLORIDA,
THE SOUTHWEST, AND CALIFORNIA

*I*F NOT FOR sex, there would be no honey.
       I don't mean human sex, though honey has certainly played various supporting roles in that through the ages. I mean flower sex. Flower sex is one of nature's more brilliant schemes, and honey is its by-product. If a certain postcoital suggestiveness lingers in honey, I believe this is the reason. "It's the sweetness," you say. "It's the texture." But no. Because corn syrup never got anyone in the mood.

For the first few billion years of life on Earth, all sex took place in the ocean. In a nice, watery medium, individual creatures can simply release their sperm or eggs into the water and let the match-making take place on its own. That's the way it still works for everything from seaweed to shellfish to snook. But five hundred or so million years ago, life clawed its way onto land and the game changed. In the air, unprotected sperm and eggs dehydrate almost instantly. This is no problem for terrestrial animals, who learned to cozy up to each other and make the handoff without exposure to the killing air. But plants, rooted in place, couldn't cozy up. They needed to figure out some long-distance way to swap genes.

Early plants, like the conifers, stuck to a variation in what they knew, letting the wind work for them the same way the water and tides had worked for their ancestors. They wrapped their sperm in protective capsules, like little spaceships, so it could survive the journey through the interstellar reaches of air, and made those capsules so tiny that they would fly on the lightest breeze. They launched these capsules, called pollen, by the billions, counting on sheer numbers to ensure that at least a few lucked into a receptive ovary. Each scale of a pinecone, for example, bears an ovule awaiting a lucky pollen visitor.*

This wind pollination dominated the sex life of plants for hundreds of millions of years. It worked well, and still does, as many people's sinuses can attest. Pine trees, ragweed, and other wind pollinators are doing just fine, spreading their seed far and wide. But around 140 million years ago, some plants got a brand-new idea. Instead of all this random, cast-your-seed-to-the-winds nonsense, why not enlist the animals to help? After all, insects were already flitting to and fro all over the plants, munching on them and living on them. Why not make them do something useful?

The advantage of getting insects, instead of wind, to carry pollen from one plant to another is that it's a direct connection. Your "hit" rate is astronomically higher, which means that you can make fewer sperm and invest more resources—more bytes of memory, in a sense—in each one. And that means you can produce offspring with a lot more functionality.

But how do you do it? How do you convince an insect to come to you, pick up some pollen, and deliver it to another plant just like you?

You bribe it, of course. A hundred and forty million years ago, these clever plants invented a gadget that would get an insect's attention, give it a reason to come calling, dust it with pollen once it arrived, and pick up any pollen that had been attached to the insect by a previous plant.

It's called the flower.

The shape, color, and aroma of flowers represent 140 million years of market testing to determine what characteristics insects

---

* The shape of a pinecone improves its odds of attracting gentlemen callers by creating a wind vortex that helps to capture passersby.

find attractive. The fact that we find these same characteristics attractive is no surprise, considering how many genes we share with bugs.

But beauty alone won't compel a bug to visit a flower. From time immemorial, free food has been the way to draw customers to your booth. Flowers give away nectar—sugar water that they produce in tiny wells, called nectaries, tucked at the base of their petals. This is what bugs are after, but to get to it, they have to push through a forest of pistils and stamens that are, not coincidentally, in the way. The stamens, the male part of the flower, end in pads of pollen that rub off on a bug as it pushes through to the nectar. The pistil, the female part in the center, captures pollen that may already be on the insect from a previous encounter and connects it to an egg in the center of the flower. The fertilized egg then becomes a seed, and good sex has been had for the umpteenth trillionth time.

With this killer app, the flowering plants took over the world. With the exception of a few ferns and coniferous forests, they now dominate terrestrial life on the planet. And right along with them, a certain type of insect evolved to take advantage of what they had to offer. It developed superb vision and smell (the better to find flowers), memory unmatched in the insect kingdom (the better to return to flowers), a fuzzy body (for collecting pollen), and an internal tank (to be filled with nectar). And it developed such a passion for nectar that it could cross-pollinate up to five hundred flowers a day.

Which is why more than one entomologist has referred to bees as "flying penises." In the process of going about their business of gathering food, bees impregnate entire meadows, fields, and orchards, sowing the seeds of the next generation.

It makes perfect sense that we tend to think of flower scents as "sweet," because they truly are signifiers of sweetness. We usually think of the sweetness coming later, with the fruit, but it's already there in those little nectaries, as every bee knows. A wildflower meadow, or a cranberry bog, or a blooming apple grove is full of sugar—the basic fuel that powers all life—and bees are extraordinarily adept at wringing the sugar from a landscape and collecting it in their hives.

Some bees lead solitary lives. Others, like bumble bees, live in small ground-nesting colonies of a hundred or two. Only honey bees developed a fully urban lifestyle, forming colonies of forty thousand individuals that work together to store as much food as possible. That's why, while you can find a few thimblefuls of honey in a bumble bee nest, you can often extract a hundred pounds of honey from a honey bee hive.

The nectar given away by most flowers has a sugar content of 10 to 20 percent—about the same as fruit juice. If bees stored this in their hives, it wouldn't last long. Wild yeasts would quickly go to work on those sugars, and soon the bees would have a hive full of mead (honey wine), which would make for a hell of a party but a dysfunctional colony. To stabilize their food supply, the bees begin dehydrating nectar as soon as they bring it back to the hive. First they pump it in and out of themselves, one drop at a time. Then they pack it into their hexagonal cylinders of beeswax comb and fan it with their wings. When the moisture content drops under 20 percent and the sugar content rises to 70 percent, it has been transformed into the syrup that we call honey. The bees have done exactly what sugarmakers do to maple sap: concentrated it enough that no microbes can grow in it (sugar is a natural preservative) but not so much that it crystallizes.

To keep honey in its syrupy state, bees add enzymes that break apart the sucrose in nectar into the simple sugars fructose and glucose. Fructose and glucose are more soluble in water than sucrose is, so they stay liquid at higher concentrations—and liquid is much easier for the bees to work with. The goal is utility, but it has a serendipitous effect on flavor, because, as with maple syrup, fructose and glucose react much more readily with other molecules than sucrose does, creating all sorts of flavor molecules. Fructose also registers more quickly on the tongue than sucrose, tastes sweeter and more refreshing, disappears faster, and enhances fruit flavors. Combined with honey's natural acidity, this makes for a delightfully fruity, slightly tart, amazingly complex syrup—nature's best sauce. Because raw honey isn't heated, it has just a touch of maple syrup's caramel flavor but a great variety of fruity, floral, spicy, and herbal notes.

A pound of honey represents the concentrated nectar contributions of four million flowers. Some call it "the soul of a meadow," which is lovely, but I think of it more like a little black book, a record of who was putting out in a particular place and time. Was the fireweed rioting purple in the California hills? Was the goldenrod blanketing New England fields in its late-summer glow? You can tell from the honey.

The reason you can tell is because nectar is much more than simple sugar water. Each nectar is a unique mixture of different sugars, acids, minerals, and aromatic compounds, leading to a unique flavor. The range is wide, which only makes sense. We speak of "honey" as if it is one thing, but honey is really a category of foods made by bees using plants of all kinds. There are as many honeys as there are fruits, and they are just as diverse.

A honey bee will fly about three miles on a recon mission, and a hive will take advantage of whatever floral resources it can find, so most honey is sourced from a mixture of flowers. Like a fruit smoothie, it has a middle-of-the-road flavor. It might be sold as wildflower honey, but even clover honey, the most popular in America, is usually a blend, with clover being one of the dominant flowers. And even wildflower honey from the same hive will change with the seasons, as different flowers come into bloom. A hive might make a light spring honey from apple trees and acacia, then a dark fall honey dominated by goldenrod and knotweed. Numerous other flowers will contribute minor notes.

Although blended Scotches are more balanced, single malts are more interesting and command premium prices. So it is with honeys. A single-varietal, or monofloral, honey can display wild flavors beyond the reach of the dull honeys filling plastic bears in the supermarkets of the world. But getting a monofloral honey is no easy task. Beekeepers can't control what their bees do outside the hive (or even inside for that matter); all they can control is the environment their bees work in. If a beehive has but one type of flower within its reach—and all previous honey has been removed from the hive—it will fill its comb with pound after pound of single-source honey.

That situation is rare in wild areas but common in those with agricultural monocrops, which is where most monofloral honeys are created. Apple orchards, orange groves, and cover crops such as clover or alfalfa all make excellent monofloral honeys. Maine's vast wild-blueberry fields and Florida's tupelo-lined swamps present "wild" opportunities for monofloral honeys. The Carolinas have a late-blooming tree called sourwood that makes a beautiful honey, and beekeepers there have long followed the practice of clearing the summer honey from their hives in anticipation of the sourwood bloom. California, with its abundance of microclimates, produces more unusual honeys than any other area.

For years I've enjoyed tasting honeys wherever my travels have taken me. Like wine and cheese, it's one of the best ways to gain a little insight into the local terroir. And, because so few honeys make it into distribution (and because they last indefinitely), it's a perfect souvenir of anywhere you've visited. One of the best honeys I've tasted is made, strangely enough, in Ginza, the heart of Tokyo, home to ten-story department stores and strobing neon billboards. It's also home to the Ginza Honey Bee Project, which seeks to prove that honey bees can be successfully raised in urban environments. The palace and gardens of Japan's emperor border Ginza, so I suspect the emperor is contributing more nectar to the Ginza Honey

Bee Project than he knows. The honey is thinner than others I've had, as clear and delicate as honey can be, with the light yet saturating fragrance of rosewater.

One recent summer, I decided to broaden my honey palate as much as possible and see how American honeys would measure up against the world's finest. It would have taken me years to track down bottles of all those honeys. Fortunately, I knew someone who had already done the legwork.

THE RED QUEEN

Marina Marchese puts honey on everything. Buttery blueberry honey on her yogurt and mapley knotweed honey on her waffles and pancakes. North Carolina sourwood honeycomb on her toast and bitter chestnut honey on her Gorgonzola. She likes gallberry honey on her fried chicken and lavender honey in her salad dressings. She cooks her food extra plain to make a neutral canvas. "I don't season; I drizzle," she told me as we sat in her Connecticut garden on a steamy August morning, watching her bees wake up. "I could do it all day." She poured goldenrod honey into an espresso and handed it to me. The sun was just climbing over the hill that rims the eastern edge of her garden, but the ten red beehives on the hillside were still in shadow. As the first foragers of the day issued forth on their sorties and rose into the air, heading west, their bodies caught the sun and glowed like little golden fairies.

A bee found our bottle of honey and searched for a way inside. Then it nuzzled Marina. Then it flew back toward the hives. "She's going to get her friends," Marina said. "She'll be back in about ten minutes."

Bees follow Marina like small children. The founder and sole proprietor of Red Bee Honey, which sells single-varietal domestic honeys and honey-based cosmetics at boutiques and gourmet shops in Connecticut and New York, she spends much of her time bottling honey. "It can be a very sticky situation!" she said, hinting at certain disasters in the kitchen that serves as her bottling room. "I can't even tell you." She also anoints herself with her own honey facial creams and beeswax salves. You can hardly blame the bees.

Marina Marchese looks and acts like you'd expect someone named Marina Marchese to look and act. The dark hair and olive skin are pure Italy, the accent lightly Brooklyn. Picture Marisa Tomei's big sister in a bee suit. She's proud of her Italian heritage and had her honey awakening while traveling the Amalfi coast. "In Italy, they treat honey with the same respect they give wine and olive oil," she said. Her company is named partly for the red cottage that serves as her home and office and partly for her feisty Neapolitan grandmother, who once expressed her anger at some relatives by throwing red paint on their car. Marina's cottage is lined with paintings of bees from her past life as an artist. A lovely trapezoid of honeycomb rests on her mantle. Her sofa and armchair are upholstered in a red bee pattern she found somewhere online.

As the sun rose and the day warmed, the sparse trail of bees flying west thickened into an undulating ribbon of gold. A few bees detoured toward us. Marina's dog, a redbone coonhound named Honey, snapped at one. I poured more espresso and watched other bees cruise the garden, a splash of fecund chaos amid the Waspy lawns of Weston, Connecticut. What other house in town, I wondered, had a well-tended circle of goldenrod? A dozen chickens bustled around a pen, pursued by a testosterone-addled rooster. Oregano, thyme, and mint were in full bloom—a concession to the bees. Marina believes the herbal nectars keep them healthy. ("They really love the cilantro. Who knew?") A carpet of Japanese knotweed oozed down the hillside like kudzu. Old bocce balls peaked out from the weeds. We sipped our coffee and watched the bees, which had a lot more energy than we did.

We were still recovering from the previous evening's honey binge. When I'd arrived, Marina showed me her storeroom, which was lined with dusty, crusty jars of honey from all over the world. "How many do you want to try?" she asked. I explained that I didn't think I could handle more than about ten without going into shock. She quickly pulled down twelve domestic jars.

"That's probably plenty," I said.

"But what about sourwood?" she asked. "Have you ever tried North Carolina sourwood?"

I hadn't.

"What about autumn olive from West Virginia?"

Nope.

Saguaro cactus? Cranberry? Mesquite?

Somehow, when we sat down at her wooden table, we had twenty-four jars, all from the United States. And after I'd tasted them all—the basswood and the raspberry and the black locust and the tupelo—and was resisting the urge to slide out of my chair, curl up on the sticky floor, and fall into a sugar-drunk slumber, she popped up from her chair and said, "Ready for the internationals?"

Thus twelve more jars appeared, from a Chilean ulmo honey to an Italian chestnut so bitter that no amount of Pellegrino could expunge the taste. Afterward, I went back to Marina's guest cottage to collapse.

The United States has the most astonishing variety of honeys of any country—about three hundred at last count. Everyone seems to know this except for us. "My best customers are not Americans," Marina said. "Most of the ones who really understand honey are foreigners—Hispanics, Europeans, people from any country but America. They have such a tremendous respect and passion for honey. In Europe, they talk about it like it's gold. I'll never forget the first time I went to the honey show in England. One of the judges said to me, 'I'm really jealous of the United States. You have so many different honey varieties. Here in England we have maybe four or five. How come you don't have a honey show?' And I asked myself, 'How come we *don't* have a honey show?' We have such an amazing collection of honeys, but you don't see them in stores. If you go into gourmet food stores, you'll see honeys from Europe, but not local ones."

This is a mystery to me, because, with few exceptions, the domestic honeys blew away the internationals. Chilean ulmo honey, which previously had been recommended to me as the greatest in the world, had the unmistakable bouquet of a Tire Warehouse. Lavender honey reeked of camphor. Bitter, mineral chestnut honey was even more disappointing than chestnuts themselves. Marina also forced a Greek rhododendron honey on me, which made me suspect that she was trying to kill me. In 400 B.C., a Greek army retreating from Persia stumbled upon a cache of rhododendron honey on the shores of the Black Sea, gorged on it, and was seized by convulsions and vomiting for hours. I suffered no convulsions, but I didn't love the honey.

By comparison, humble clover, the most common honey in the United States, was a revelation, its rich flavors unfolding over time. Marina agreed: "Clover is amazing! You forget how good it is. It's kind of spicy and a little grassy." There are numerous species of clover in the United States, so the flavor can vary quite a bit. (A southwestern clover honey that we tasted had nowhere near the richness of Marina's Pennsylvania clover.) The best clover honeys are made from sweet clover.*

Our next honey, alfalfa, underlined clover's goodness. The alfalfa had a simple hard-candy sweetness to it, without other interest. You may as well pour corn syrup on your food.

A Maine blueberry honey, on the other hand, was every bit as good as the clover, yet quite different. It was amazingly buttery, with a clear nose of blueberry—a rarity, since most plants' honeys bear little resemblance to their fruit. "Blueberry is always my favorite," Marina declared. "It's luscious—like velvet."

---

* See my chapter "Little Truths" for more information on sweet clover.

Raspberry honey was lighter and less smooth, with a berrylike tartness on the finish. Cranberry also had a tart, fruity finish, but a less-refined flavor than the other berry honeys. Tulip poplar was like cassis, all currants and liqueur. Basswood—a tree sometimes called the "honey tree" because, when in bloom, it can be a white, lacy mass of bees—had a distinctly medicinal quality to it. It reminded me of gin. Some people don't like basswood honey, but I find it iconoclastic and memorable, and I always look forward to reacquainting myself with it.

With some excitement, Marina produced a goldenrod honey, a new discovery for her. "This is one of my all-time favorites," she said. "It's super-flowery, like French perfume. People are blown away by it. Yet no one knows it." I could see what she meant about the perfume. It was both floral and musky—a little animal lurking under the flowers. It has always surprised me that goldenrod honey isn't better known; since goldenrod is the last wildflower to bloom in profusion in the Northeast, it has saved many a beekeeper from disaster. Its strength of flavor also makes it one of my favorite mead honeys.

Buckwheat honey is wildly popular in some circles. Famously dark and strong tasting, it appeals to people who feel that all food should be intensely flavored. The darkness comes from buckwheat nectar's high protein content, which allows the Maillard reaction[*] to take place, giving buckwheat honey a savory, toasty quality. To me, buckwheat honey tastes like malted milk balls—great, if that's your kind of thing.

Tops among the Northeast honeys was black locust, an important springtime honey tree throughout the East. It's also a major honey tree in France and Italy, where they call it acacia. This jar was

---

[*] A chemical reaction that occurs when proteins and sugars are combined, creating roasted aromas. (Think of sugar-cured bacon.) See my maple syrup discussion, page 29, for more information.

right from Connecticut, and it was nearly clear, with a stunning honeydew nose. "Like fruit salad," Marina said. "My honey always has this taste in the spring."

And that ended our honey tour of the Northeast. Marina and I marveled at how few of these honeys ever make it onto store shelves in the region. Then we pointed our palates toward a region with a much stronger honey tradition: the Southeast. In parts of the South where rural culture has endured, unique honeys are not only harvested but also enthusiastically embraced.

Sourwood, which comes from understory trees of the piedmont forests, is one such iconic honey. North Carolina is particularly known for it. Marina's jar was dark and red-tinted. "Do you taste anise?" she asked. I did, but what I really tasted was gingerbread—sweet, warm, pungent, with spicy molasses notes.

Next we tried tupelo honey, which also had a bit of a tongue-twanging molasses finish, but its color and flavor were much brighter than sourwood's, leaning toward the cinnamon end of the spice spectrum. Tupelo is the most famous and expensive honey in the country, selling for about twice the going rate of other table-grade honeys. Van Morrison may have had a small hand in this, but tupelo's reputation originally rested on its reluctance to crystallize. Scarcity also keeps the price high: Tupelo trees grow only in the swamps of southern Georgia and the Florida Panhandle; the Apalachicola River marks the heart of their range. To many, the taste of tupelo is the taste of the Southern swamp itself.

Florida is particularly rich in distinctive honeys. Besides tupelo, the state's northern forests produce gallberry honey, while the southern forests produce palmetto. Gallberry, with its minty nose, is particularly attractive. But Florida's most alluring honey, and my personal favorite, is orange blossom. The citrus industry used to dominate central Florida, but development and a series of freezes have driven it south. Today, introduced diseases threaten to put the nails in the industry's coffin. Until then, seek out any bottle you can find, because no other honey captures such floral essence. If you've ever walked through a blooming orange grove and inhaled that narcotic, dreamy scent, you'll be whisked back there by your first taste of orange blossom honey. I've also had avocado honey from Florida (let me save you the trouble) and Brazilian pepper, a muddy-tasting honey sold for commercial blending purposes.

Continuing our honey tour of the States, Marina and I arrived in the Southwest desert, home to dazzling and unusual honeys. Huajillo, a tough little shrub of the Texas scrub country, is a famous honey plant. Stories abound of explorers finding caves and hollow trees filled with clear huajillo honey—"white gushers." Today, it's an increasingly rare treat. The old-timers talk of huajillo honey's surpassing delicacy. More appealing, to me, was catclaw honey, made from a desert shrub that one field guide describes simply as "one of the most despised southwest shrubs." Nice. The eponymous thorns are the reason for such animosity, which I suspect fades in those who know the delightful honey derived from the plant. Buttery and thick, it's the desert analog of blueberry honey.

Although some cacti are bat-pollinated (good luck getting honey from a bat), others rely on bees. Saguaro honey, with its riesling-like hints of petrol, was particularly intriguing. Mesquite, the state tree of Arizona, supplies a lot of nectar to Arizona's bees (many of them killer bees). Marina and I tasted a Sonoran Desert blend of mesquite, catclaw, ironwood, saguaro, and god knows what else, which, alas, tasted like ham. Perhaps the beekeeper had been overzealous with his smoker.

California's unique climate gives it, unsurprisingly, unique honey terroir. I've stumbled upon some amazing varietals, including star thistle, sage, vetch, and manzanita. The cream of California honeys is fireweed, which is nearly clear and has the most evanescent lily of the valley perfume.

Before I left, Marina made me anoint myself in honey-lavender cream and something called Rescue Salve, a blend of honey, pollen, and propolis. I rubbed some on my hands. I began to feel rescued. A few bees nosed me hopefully, following me all the way to my car.

THE SHINING DRINK

Put yourself in a prehistoric era, when it was unusual to come across anything sweeter than a few berries in late summer, and it is easy to understand why honey has always been associated with magic. For many millions of years, there was nothing else like it on the planet. Now, in your prehistoric diorama, allow some rain to fall. Let that rain fill a hollow in a tree trunk where bees have stored their honey, or an animal-skin bag that hunter-gatherers have filled with honey. The watered-down honey loses its natural antiseptic power, and wild yeasts begin to work on its sugars. Soon, when the sweet drink is sampled, the magic of the honey has been taken to a new level.

Meadheads put a lot of stock in this "magic-bag theory," citing it as proof that mead—honey wine—was mankind's first alcoholic drink. There is some logic to this argument; honey was available long before grains were cultivated, much less malted, and before grapes were domesticated. So far the archaeological record is coy. The oldest residue of an alcoholic beverage discovered so far was in nine-thousand-year-old Chinese potsherds. The residue contained honey, grapes, and hawthorn fruit. Likely the fruit and its wild yeasts got the fermentation started, and the more concentrated sugars of the honey accelerated the fermentation, increased the alcohol, and improved the flavor.

Many ancient cultures considered mead the crème de la crème of alcoholic drinks. The Egyptians were devoted mead drinkers by 2500 B.C., and the Greeks not long after that. Mead's scarcity—there wasn't that much honey to go around—probably cemented its status as the drink of privilege. The lower classes drank beer in

Egypt and what must have been harsh wine in Greece.* Even the Romans added honey to improve their lesser wines, or they fermented the honey with the wine. The ultimate compliment for a wine was that it was "honey-hearted." In our age of ubiquitous sugar, we value dryness. But when sweet wine was difficult and expensive to make, sophisticates sought it. If you want to taste with a classical palate, steer clear of sugar for a month and then sip a sweet mead.

Spurred by Roman expansion, wine eclipsed mead in the Mediterranean. Wine science left mead far behind, and wine culture followed. But Northern Europe, where grapes struggled, remained the bastion of mead.† Evidence of spiced meads has been found in cauldrons in Germany and Britain dating to 1000 B.C. Mead thrived across Britain, Germany, Poland, and Scandinavia. Beowulf drank it throughout the Norse saga bearing his name, pausing only to battle monsters and hang their limbs from the rafters of the mead hall, and Thor, Norse god of thunder, showed his manhood by downing three tons of "the shining drink" in one long Valhalla night. Mead is a drink with lineage.

But its popularity suffered a blow in 1066. The Normans conquered England, bringing with them Mediterranean culture, including good wine. Anglo-Saxon affinities fell out of favor. Squeezed between cheap, plentiful beer and delicious, prestigious French wine, mead found no market. Other than areas such as Poland, where wine never gained traction and mead still holds primacy, and Ethiopia, where *tej* (honey beer) is ubiquitous, mead survived only as a novelty. It was what you made with the sweet water left after boiling a honeycomb to separate the last bits of honey from the beeswax.

---

* The Greek tradition of adding resin as a preservative lives on in retsina.
† The Germanic tribes who encountered Caesar and his legions would have nothing to do with wine, which they feared would make men effeminate.

Mead began to pull out of its thousand-year rut when Charlie Papazian published his paradigm-shattering *Complete Joy of Home Brewing* in 1984. It inspired a whole generation of Americans, including me, to home brew, but it also featured an appendix that sang the praises of mead, promoted the highly suspect but undeniably romantic notion that the word *honeymoon* derives from an ancient tradition of supplying the bride and groom with an ample supply of mead to sweeten the new marriage, and had a recipe for Barkshack Ginger Mead. Quite a few of us were smitten with the idea—if not the actual product. I brewed mead for my wedding, and it was not a success. Honey ferments much more slowly than beer wort, but I didn't know that at the time and bottled the mead long before it had finished fermenting. It kept going in the bottle, and the pressure kept building. Those lucky enough to actually open a bottle were hosed by a six-foot geyser of foam that smelled like rotten fruit. Others simply had the bottles explode in their hands on first jiggle. One bottle went off under the driver's seat of my car, where the smell settled in for life.

Mead's original revival was driven by people like me and by the Renaissance Faire crowd, who love to cavort in chain mail with frothing pewter mugs of the stuff. Many people have been turned off the drink by bad experiences with these poorly made, cloyingly sweet examples. In recent years, however, this school of meadmaking has given way to serious craftspeople making seriously dry meads.

"What's the meadmaker's objective?" asked Gordon Hull, who specializes in dry, Champagne-style meads at Heidrun Meadery, in the shadows of the redwoods of Arcata, California. "Is it to recreate the meads of our ancestry? Should we be faithful to traditional meadmaking recipes and produce meads that mimic those of an Elizabethan court? Or a Viking drinking hall? I do think there is a niche for this style of meadmaking. There is another approach, though, in which the meadmaker focuses on the characteristics of the raw ingredients and applies whatever techniques are at his disposal to express those qualities. My objective is simply to reveal these tremendously fascinating and varying flavor characteristics of honey."

It isn't easy to do. Sugar can mask some of honey's stranger scents. But rather than see honey's unusual flavors as a drawback, Hull considers them the point. "Honey aromatics are subtle," he said. "To reveal them I need to eliminate other olfactory components that get in the way. Sweetness is great for hiding off-flavors, but it also obscures the good flavors we do want, like the floral aroma of, say, orange blossom. This is why I focus on dry meads."

Honey's erotic pedigree is exposed in dry meads. With the sugar removed, what remains is the chemical poetry of a prehuman world. Experiencing it is like eavesdropping on the ardent murmurings between flower and insect.

Hull makes his meads in small batches—usually less than fifty cases—and uses strictly varietal honeys, working with artisanal beekeepers in California. "I prefer my honeys raw and unfiltered, loaded with bee parts and beeswax and never heated," he said. From these honeys he makes eight different meads, including avocado blossom, orange blossom, star thistle blossom, and sage blossom. "Interestingly, funky-tasting honeys sometimes make the best meads," Hull noted. "For instance, I'd been warned by meadmakers for years to stay away from avocado honey because of its bitter, vegetal qualities. But, as it happens, the avocado-blossom mead is among my most popular varietals, and I drink it regularly myself."

Why Champagne style? Hull believes bubbles best present the flavors: "We have these delicate aromatics in mead, but we need to deliver them to the nose. Carbon dioxide is a great vehicle for this. Those tiny bubbles extract aromatics from within the wine as they travel through it, aerating those aromas and delivering them to your nose. What a great phenomenon! No wonder the French invented Champagne."

The first bottle of Heidrun mead I tasted was California Orange Blossom. Order a glass of sparkling wine and have your waiter detour through a blooming orange grove on his way to your table, and you'll get a sense of the drink. There's a floral echo, a tropical mist that is very different from the steely austerity of Champagne. It's almost unfortunate that Heidrun's bubbly is automatically compared to Champagne, because the two are very different experiences. One epitomizes northern France and the flourishing of beauty, art, and culture in a gray climate; the other is pure California seduction. Champagne tastes like winter in Paris; Heidrun Orange Blossom mead tastes like spring.

RECIPES

CHICKEN CIRCE

I've never understood why honey has a reputation as the wimpy stuff Granny puts in her tea. Perhaps Winnie the Pooh is to blame. Regardless, with its exotic, erotic allure, honey is a very grown-up ingredient. Its culinary apotheosis has been in the Middle East, and I always associate it with the eastern Mediterranean: Homeric Greece, Africa, Turkey, the biblical lands. When combined with the region's "three Cs"—cinnamon, coriander, and cumin—it casts quite a spell. This is the kind of dish that Circe might have used to seduce Odysseus's crew. You can also make it with lamb, beef, or pork (and believe me, the temptation was strong to call it "Circe's Swine" and suggest it's what Circe did with the crew after transforming them, but honestly, I prefer it with chicken), but the cooking time will increase significantly. If you're making it with boneless chicken breast, cut the cooking time (and flavor) in half. If you can find pre-served lemons, they add a fantastic touch; if not, an extra squeeze of lemon juice is fine. You want to use a robust, spicy honey here, such as tupelo, goldenrod, lavender, or thyme. Serve the dish with rice or couscous and some bitter braised greens to offset the sweetness.

Serves 4 to 6

2 tablespoons extra-virgin olive oil
2 pounds boneless chicken thighs
salt and pepper
1 14-ounce can chickpeas, drained
½ cup honey
3 cloves garlic, peeled and minced
1 tablespoon ground coriander
1 tablespoon ground cumin

½ teaspoon ground cinnamon
1 cup chicken stock or white wine
½ cup preserved lemons, chopped (optional)
½ cup kalamata olives, pitted and roughly chopped
zest and juice of ¼ lemon
1 cup chopped walnuts, toasted (optional)
½ cup fresh mint, chopped (optional)
½ cup fresh cilantro, chopped (optional)

1.   Heat the olive oil over medium heat in a skillet large enough to hold all the ingredients.

2.   When the oil is hot, dust the chicken with salt and pepper and add it to the pan. Brown it on one side for a couple of minutes, then turn it and brown the other side.

3.   Add the chickpeas to the pan, then drizzle the honey over the chicken and chickpeas. Add the garlic, coriander, cumin, and cinnamon and stir for about 1 minute.

4.   Add the stock or wine, the preserved lemons (if using), and the olives. Cover the pan, reduce the heat to low, and simmer, stirring occasionally, until the chicken is tender—about 20 minutes. Turn off the heat.

5.   Add the lemon zest and juice and stir. Let the chicken sit for a couple of minutes.

6.   Plate the chicken over couscous on individual dishes or a serving dish and drizzle the sauce over it. Garnish with the chopped nuts and herbs (if using) and serve.

BERRIES IN THEIR OWN HONEY

Few honeys taste like the fruit of the plant they were gathered from. Blueberries and, to a lesser extent, raspberries are the glorious exceptions. The affinities in the honey help bind the berries, literally and figuratively, into a cohesive dessert. And the herbs brighten the sweetness with poignancy. A dollop of crème fraîche is lovely, but not essential.

Serves 4 to 6

2 cups raspberries
2 cups blueberries
3 tablespoons blueberry or raspberry honey
1 cup chopped fresh mint, basil, or a mix of the two
1 cup crème fraîche (optional)

1. Combine the berries in a bowl, drizzle with the honey, toss, and sprinkle with the herbs.
2. Divide the berries among individual serving bowls and top with a spoonful of crème fraîche (if using). Serve immediately.

RESOURCES

Look for honeys that are raw and unfiltered. Most commercial honey is heated and filtered of its tiny particles of pollen, propolis, and beeswax, which act as seeds for crystallization. The resulting product stays liquid on store shelves much longer. But the process also removes a lot of flavor, which is why people who have tasted only mass-produced honeys don't have an inkling of honey's potential.

HEIDRUN MEADERY

www.heidrunmeadery.com
877-HEIDRUN
Heidrun was the faithful goat of Odin, king of the Norse gods. Odin avoids feasting with the other gods, for fear of being poisoned, and instead takes all his nourishment from the mead that springs from Heidrun's teats. "What could be more irresistible than a sparkling golden wine made from honey?" asks Heidrun's meadmaker, Gordon Hull. "Someone has to make sure this is available to humanity, and I'm glad to do it." Some recommended meads are the California Orange Blossom (off-dry, perfumed, and tropical), the California Avocado Blossom (dry with a slight hoplike bitterness), and the Ventura County Wildflower (dry and herbal).

MARSHALL'S FARM NATURAL HONEY

www.marshallshoney.com
800-624-4637
Legendary Bay Area beekeepers, Spencer and Helene Marshall, provided me with my first tastes of star thistle and manzanita honey.

MENDOCINO QUEEN HONEY

www.mendocinoqueenhoney.com
707-459-6335

Mendocino County's finest terroir turns up not in its wines but in its honeys. The profusion of unusual flowers in the Mendocino, California, wildlands makes for honey that is complex and strongly floral. Patty Rede and Matt Crawley keep their hives in wild areas, away from pollination, so what you taste in their honey is truly the taste of the land. This changes with the seasons. Their late-summer honey comes from pennyroyal, wild chicory, star thistle, and button-bush. The pennyroyal, in particular, provides a piercingly clear and refreshing lemon note; it's one of my all-time favorites. Their spring honey includes nectar from camas, vetch, and meadowfoam, which gives a cotton-candy-like fragrance. Meadowfoam's small white flower, which blooms en masse in early spring, can make certain western fields look like somebody whipped them into a meringue.

PITCAIRN ISLAND HONEY
www.government.pn/shop/honey
The best foreign honey I've found is also the most exotic. It hails from Pitcairn Island, the volcanic crumb in the South Pacific in-habited by the descendants of Fletcher Christian and the other mutineers from the H.M.S. *Bounty*, along with their Tahitian wives. Remoteness is Pitcairn Island's defining quality. After the mutiny, Christian sussed the South Pacific for the place least likely to be found; Pitcairn Island won. About fifty people live on the is-land now, their only three exports being stamps, honey, and the In-ternet domain .pn. The island is apparently as much a honey bee paradise as it was a mutineer one, and today its thirty hives produce a thousand jars a year of organic honey from the abundant mango, lata, passionflower, guava, and rose apple flowers that wreath the island. Most honey tends to have a heavy flavor, adding depth and body to dishes and drinks, but Pitcairn Island honey is extraordi-narily bright, with a nose of coconut and papaya and citrus. Unlike any other honey I know, Pitcairn's really captures the essence of the tropics. A taste of it provides tantalizing hints of the erotic al-

lure that made Christian want to ditch his day job and embrace the South Pacific. The honey can be ordered by mail, though you'll have to wait up to five months, depending on when the next mail boat is scheduled.

RED BEE HONEY
www.redbee.com
877-382-4618
Connecticut's Red Bee Honey has a great selection of monofloral honeys from throughout the United States, plus body care and apitherapy products.

SAVANNAH BEE COMPANY
www.savannahbee.com
912-234-0688
This Georgia company is a good source for tupelo, sourwood, and other Southern honeys.

TROPICAL BLOSSOM HONEY COMPANY
www.tropicbeehoney.com
386-428-9027
For seventy years the McGinnis family has focused on producing and selling only Florida honeys, and they are the best source for the state's finest varietals: orange blossom, tupelo, gallberry, and palmetto.

UVALDE HONEY
www.uvaldehoney.com
830-261-5263
Huajillo honey from Uvalde, Texas, the self-proclaimed "Honey Capital of the World."

Spud Island

MOULES FRITES ON PRINCE EDWARD ISLAND

*F*ROM THE AIR, the munchkin province of Prince Edward Island looks like it nicked itself shaving. Out of its stubbly spruce woods and smooth fields, blood-colored streams empty into the sea. Even if you haven't flown in from Kansas, when you walk off the plane, you feel a bit like Dorothy stepping out of her dull gray house. When they made PEI, whoever handled the color saturation didn't let reality get in the way of artistic license.

It starts with the red earth. PEI is a low island of gently rolling hills in the Gulf of St. Lawrence, the massive, fish-rich estuary where the St. Lawrence River spits the water of the Great Lakes into the sea. Millions of years ago, the river continued over what is now PEI, depositing the sand it had excavated along the way. Then the seas dropped and PEI emerged from the waves. As one islander put it, "We're a sandbar that grew trees."

By the time those trees grew, PEI was no longer a sandbar. As that sand was compressed under the weight of additional sediment, the intense pressure forced the individual silica grains closer and closer together. Eventually they grew close enough that the iron atoms in the water trickling through the grains could act like bridges, attaching to two grains at once and gluing them together. What had been sand became sandstone. Then the iron oxidized. Like an old pickup, PEI sits atop a crumbling undercarriage of red rust.

If PEI's primeval Acadian forests were still intact, the only place you'd notice this would be on the thick red Crayola line of cliffs rimming the island. The contrast with the blue sea and the grassy cliff tops is surreal—Ireland meets Mars. But long ago the Scotch and Irish immigrants to PEI realized that the place was perfect for another plant they knew well.

Potatoes like lukewarm days, cool nights, regular rain, and soil that is neither too acid nor too sweet. They prosper in cold, wet northern climates, producing far more food per acre, and more vitamins, than any grain, which is why potatoes were the salvation of northern Europe after they were brought over from the Andes. PEI's gentle fields, bathed in the moderating influence of the sea, are potato heaven. Those Acadian forests spent ten thousand years tilling the earth into the excellent soil the first settlers encountered. Not all plants thrive in such rich, thick, heavy clay soil, but potatoes root around in it like pigs in slop. They love nitrogen fertilizer, too, so PEI farmers lay it on thick.

"Spud Island," as locals call PEI, became one giant potato field a century ago. Today, this tiny island of small towns and churches, which you can circumnavigate by car in a few hours, devotes a hundred thousand acres to potatoes—and grows 30 percent of Canada's entire production.

Having such an abundance of spuds leads to experimentation. Most meals on the island are anchored by fries or mashed potatoes, but islanders also do some odd things with the tuber. They like *poutine*, fries covered with brown gravy and cheese curds—which is not to be confused with *poutine râpée*, a kind of potato dumpling filled with pork. They'll throw almost anything on top of a base of fries. Ground beef, onions, peas, and gravy is "chips with the works." I pronounced it "shepherd's pie" and received a glare from a local. When I had dinner at an Indian restaurant in town, the curry was draped over fries instead of rice. A potato vodka distillery recently opened on the island. Its signature product smells like mosquito coils.[*]

---

[*] The molasses-based local moonshine, however, is excellent.

In September, when the potatoes are harvested, the raw land bleeds into the sea. Of course, this is a problem for agriculture everywhere, but when your fields are in Idaho, you never see the dirt eroding into the Columbia River, much less the brown river emptying into the Pacific hundreds of miles away. In tiny PEI, the sea is always in sight, or just over the ridge.

Just as nutrients on land—fertilizer—increase plant growth, so those nutrients washing into the sea fuel the growth of algae, which are basically single-celled plants. Algae are the base of the marine food chain, so abundant algae create abundant food webs.*

Even without its spuds, PEI would be a powerhouse of algae production. Washed by the nutrient-rich St. Lawrence River and sheltered by the protective bulwark of Newfoundland and Nova Scotia, PEI's coastal waters stay warmer than they have any right to be in this outpost of the Great White North. Note that *warmer* does not mean *warm*; during a September visit I took the plunge and was instantly disavowed of any such notion. But I was swimming on an incoming tide; if I'd waited and caught the outgoing tide, it might have been a different story, because the real secret to PEI's productivity is that the island is etched by long embayments. These shallow, dark-bottomed inlets act like solar collectors, catching heat and passing it to the water, cooking up a warm, rich algae bisque.

And waiting to dine on that bisque is a veritable wall of hanging mussel ropes that limn the island like a giant bead curtain. Mus-

---

* Of course, too much algae can be a problem. When supercharged algae grows at a rate beyond what the system can absorb, you get algae blooms that expand, die, and decay. As they decay, they use up oxygen, choking the life out of a bay. This is what's behind the "dead zones" now expanding on both coasts of North America. PEI's mussels help to contain the algae population and actually pull millions of pounds of nitrogen and carbon back out of the sea. Several countries are now considering using mussels to mitigate nutrient loads.

sels are filter feeders. They open their shells and pull water across
their gills, straining out the algae to eat. The more food in the water,
the fatter the mussels can grow. In PEI, they grow about as fat and
sweet as mussels can get.

Mussels are native to PEI. Normally they attach to rocks,
shells, or similar surfaces. Long ago, however, islanders came up
with an alternate plan. In June, when mussels spawn, ejecting sperm
and eggs to create billions of larvae, fishermen hang eight-foot
ropes from the surfaces of PEI's bays and lagoons. When mussel
larvae encounter the ropes, they attach to them, usually to the tune
of five hundred to a thousand larvae per foot. From there, the mussels are transferred to twenty-foot mesh socks (for protection from
predators and storms) and hung in bays throughout PEI. Look out
over almost any bay on the island and you'll see the telltale black
buoys that mark mussel floats. In summer, boats maneuver huge
trays under the socks, then cut them from their surface connection
so they fall into the trays. In winter, however, when three feet of ice
can cover PEI's bays, holes must be cut in the ice and the lumpy
socks hauled to the surface.

PEI grows nearly forty million pounds of mussels per year.
In many places, such intense farming of the sea would be greeted
with suspicion. Some people simply wouldn't want any human
activity to mar the views from their coastal houses; others would
resist the idea of commerce on the pristine sea, despite the fact
that shellfish farming is the most benign and healthy form of
food production on the planet. Resistance to shellfish aquacul-
ture is disappointingly common on both coasts of North America. But PEI has such a strong and deep-set agricultural tradition
that the extension to raising food offshore has raised hardly an
eyebrow. Besides, is it really farming? The mussels, after all, are
wild creatures that choose to set on the ropes. PEI's mussel farmers are simply capturing wild critters and allowing them to live in

more hospitable and protected conditions than they'd find in the wild.*

What I love about the PEI mussel industry is that it is the exact kind of enhancement of wild resources that sustained human populations for many millennia before agriculture. And I also love that it has helped to create a perfectly terroir-driven local dish: fries and mussels. Ah, yes, the famed *moules frites* of Belgium, but I wonder how many places in Belgium you can stand in one spot and see your spuds and mussels being harvested simultaneously, simply by turning your head. To truly savor this apotheosis of island food I head to Flex Mussels, right on Charlottetown's charming waterfront. Flex does mussels sixteen ways, fries one, and not much else, save for the equally delectable local oysters. It's the best place to sit and smell the sea and marvel at the divergent ways carbon, nitrogen, and salt can delight on one rusty chunk of St. Lawrence sandstone.

---

* One could argue that lobsters, the other big fishery on PEI, are less wild than the mussels. In July and August, the only two months of lobster season, if it weren't for the water, you could hop across the Northumberland Strait from PEI to New Brunswick on lobster traps without ever touching bottom. The lobsters down there are free-range, for sure, but they are mostly ranging on the many tons of herring placed in those traps. You say bait; I say lobster chow.

RECIPES

THAI STEAMED MUSSELS

Steamed mussels are so easy, affordable, fast, and delicious that I don't understand why more people don't make them at home. (In fact, if you really want to keep things simple, replace everything but the mussels and coconut milk in the following recipe with a tablespoon or two of jarred red curry paste, and away you go.) Avoid buying wild mussels, which are invariably filled with grit. Of the many versions of steamed mussels, I find the one with Thai flavors to be the best, though I wouldn't kick the Indian (curry and ginger), the Italian (white wine, garlic, tomato, and parsley), or the French (white wine, cream, and tarragon) varieties out of bed, either. If you're not serving this with fries, a hot loaf of crusty bread is essential for mopping up the sauce.

Serves 4 to 6

4 pounds mussels
4 cloves garlic, minced
1 14-ounce can coconut milk
½ teaspoon red pepper flakes (optional)
juice of ½ lime
1 tablespoon fish sauce*
1 cup chopped fresh basil
1 cup chopped fresh cilantro

1. Rinse and scrub the mussels under cold running water. Discard any with broken or open shells; these are already dead. Remove any "beards"—the byssal thread, which sticks out of the middle

---

* Bottles of fish sauce (often with a freaky-looking baby on the front) are available in most supermarkets these days. Three dollars gets you a lifetime supply. Used like soy sauce, it will improve the taste of half the things you cook.

of the mussel and which it uses for web-slinging itself around, Spider-Man-style. It's an impressive piece of hardware, and unbelievably tough. To remove it, use a paring knife for leverage and yank it out with your thumb. You can also snip it off with scissors, but then you leave a little beard inside.

2. Combine everything but the fresh herbs in a large pot, cover, and cook over high heat, stirring occasionally, until the mussel shells have opened and the mussels have plumped up, about 12 to 15 minutes. Turn off the heat, dump the mussels into a large serving bowl, toss the herbs on top, and let everybody have at it. Or, if decorum is of the essence, serve them in individual bowls. Either way, you'll need a bowl for the discarded shells.

FINE FRENCH FRIES

There is wide agreement on the proper way to cook French fries, and there is wide agreement that it's a pain in the ass. You have to presoak the fries in ice water to bring down their temperature and add a little moisture to the interior; this keeps the inside from drying out later. But the real pain is that you have to fry the fries twice: first at a fairly low temperature, to cook the center; and second, after the fries have cooled, at a higher temperature to crisp the crust. I'm sorry, there's really no way around this. But it's worth it; you get killer, puffed-up fries that are snappy and savory on the outside and tender and fluffy inside. Try it. The potato to use is russet, the classic, starchy baking potato, and the recommended oil is peanut, with its high smoking point, although lard will give you the tastiest potato of all.* Serve them with aioli on the side. And a crisp, hoppy beer, of course.

---

* Canola, on the other hand, produces lightly flavored fries. The real dirty secret, as spilled by Russ Parsons in *How to Read a French Fry*, is that dirty oil—oil that's been used already—makes the most perfectly golden fries of all.

Serves 6

4 large russet potatoes, peeled and cut into ⅜-inch-wide sticks
1 quart peanut oil or lard
salt

1. Put the potatoes in a large bowl, cover them with cold water, add a tray of ice cubes, and place in the refrigerator for at least 1 hour, or up to 2 days. When they're ready to be cooked, drain the potatoes and pat them dry with a kitchen towel.

2. Pour the oil or lard in a large, heavy pan or pot (with sides high enough to catch splatters) and heat it to 325 degrees (or medium hot, if, like me, you're eyeballing it).

3. Place the potatoes in the oil and, stirring occasionally, cook them for about 6 minutes. The potatoes should be limp but still light in color. Turn off the heat and remove them from the oil with a slotted spoon. Let the fries cool to room temperature, at least 20 minutes. (They can sit for an hour at this point.)

4. Reheat the oil to 375 degrees (smokin' hot). Add the fries. They are ready when they puff a little and turn golden brown, about 5 minutes. Remove the fries from the pan, drain them on paper towels, toss with salt, and serve.

RESOURCES

Mussels are at their best in early spring, when they are at their peak of buttery, brothy richness before spawning—both sweet and succulent. After spawning in summer, they go downhill.

AMERICAN MUSSEL HARVESTERS
www.americanmussel.com
401-294-8999
This is a superb U.S. source for reliably fresh and tasty PEI mussels.

FLEX MUSSELS
www.flexmussels.com
In addition to Flex's waterfront location in Charlottetown, it has an outpost on Eighty-second Street in Manhattan. Same mussels, same fries.

GREEN GABLES MUSSELS
www.greengablesmussels.com
902-886-2770
Anne of Green Gables is the patron saint of PEI, the lure for most tourists who visit the island. Calvin Jollimore, with his massive shoulders, bear paw hands, and rough fisherman talk, seems an unlikely person to have hitched his business to Anne's star, but then again, with his close-cropped red hair and generous personality, he could be her rustic uncle. Calvin harvests his Green Gables mussels from three closely situated bays on the northern, wilder side of PEI, near Anne's home of Cavendish, and by tasting a mussel he can easily tell which of the bays it called home. If you don't taste mussels every day, like Calvin does, you might not detect the differences, although he insists that the mussels from one bay are so distinctly sweet that anybody could tell. In any case, he doesn't keep mussels from his three "vineyards" separate, but any Green Gables mussel will be a primo mussel.

Little Truths

FOREST GASTRONOMY, QUEBEC

CRINKLEROOT TASTES LIKE peanut and wasabi. Dried redfoot boletes smell of cocoa and cherries; sweetgrass of almond paste and fresh-cut hay. Milkweed-blossom syrup is like perfume on a fox. Cattail hearts are the love child of cucumber and asparagus. Sea spinach, the robust and meaty green that garden spinach has always wanted to be, is undoubtedly the stuff that fortified Popeye. Dried beebalm petals smell . . . irreducible. I could say they're like oregano, orange peel, and saffron, but I'd be missing the mark. They smell like the first time you walk into your lover's apartment.

I knew none of these things until François des Bois and Nancy Hinton opened my eyes in the summer of 2009. I was spending the weekend with three friends at a fishing camp on Lake Champlain, and we'd popped up to Montreal for the day. We were looking for the same thing four middle-age guys away from their wives in a strange and exotic city are always looking for: weird food. We were finding it, too. At the expansive Jean-Talon Market we'd worked our way through caribou sausages and spruce beer, bacteria-smeared orange cheeses and tubs of duck fat, when we hit a booth that stopped us cold. It was called À la Table des Jardins Sauvages, and a sign identified its business as GASTRONOMIE FORESTIÈRE AUX AROMES DES BOIS. We'd stumbled into the world of forest gastronomy.

Forest gastronomy is a trend you've surely noticed. What self-respecting bistro doesn't have fiddleheads and wild leeks on its spring menu? And what self-respecting eater doesn't long to tango with these wild things? But this was more like a full-scale rave. Verdant piles of salsify leaves and sea spinach filled a display counter. Roots of fresh crinkleroot lined the top. Bags of dried mushrooms hung from the walls: boletes, morels, black trumpets. There were jars of wild-ginger mustard, sweet-and-sour boletus sauce, and pickled daisy buds. A ramekin of wild-herb oil was out front for sampling. Needless to say, they had us from *bonjour*.

We ate a mess of sautéed salsify with the perch that we fished out of Lake Champlain that night. The salsify was sweet and peppery and hinted at the cucumbery flavor of Pacific oysters. I had a new touchstone for all future visits to Montreal. More important, I was eyeing the roadside weeds that whipped past our car on the trip home in a whole new way. For I'd learned that the booth was the outlet for a legendary forager named François Brouillard and that what had been available that day was but a tiny taste of the bounty that appeared over the course of the year, and even that was just a hint of the true possibilities of forest gastronomy, which takes terroir to a new level. We can start to understand a place by paying attention to the ways it influences an agricultural product, like apples or coffee, but we really grasp its essence when we work with the unique suite of wild edibles that call it home—when we truly eat the landscape. It sounded like that's what François was up to. To get the full François experience, though, I'd have to venture to his stronghold, a funky little restaurant in the Quebec countryside.

FRANÇOIS DES BOIS

François Brouillard picked fiddleheads before fiddleheads were cool. He picked ramps and chanterelles and cattails. It was what his grandmother did, and his aunts and uncles and cousins, so it was what he did, too. It wasn't called foraging back then. It was called survival. François' family has made or supplemented their living off the woods since 1895.

ttles of maple syrup in the
agonfly Sugarworks sugarhouse.
OTO BY ROWAN JACOBSEN

ul Limberty in his high-
ountain sugarbush.
OTO BY ROWAN JACOBSEN

rading maple syrup by color. PHOTO BY ROWAN JACOBSEN

Craig Line manning the arch i[n] his sugarhouse.

PHOTO BY ROWAN JACOBSEN

Boiling in the sugarhouse by night—a spring necessity.

PHOTO BY ROWAN JACOBSEN

Harvesting ripe
coffee cherries,
Hacienda La Minita,
Costa Rica.

PHOTO BY GEORGE HOWELL

Typically vertical terrain
of a small coffee farm,
Huila, Colombia.

PHOTO BY GEORGE HOWELL

runed shade trees above
e coffee trees at Haci-
nda La Minita, Costa
ica. In the background
one of several forest
serves on the estate.

OTO BY GEORGE HOWELL

Child labor—the dirty secret of the Vermont cider industry. PHOTO BY CHRISTINE OLIVER

Ambrosia apples at Harmony Orchards. PHOTO COURTESY SHARON CAMPBELL

Marina Marchese.

Harvesting Brazilian
pepper honey near
Okeechobee, Florida.

Florida bee swarm.
Contrary to popular
belief, swarms are
not aggressive.

Typical PEI scene: potato fields and a country church. PHOTO BY CARLA BUCHANAN

Potato Harvesting on PEI. PHOTO BY BRIAN SIMPSON, COURTESY GOVERNMENT OF PEI

e red cliffs of PEI. PHOTO BY BRIAN KINGZETT

I fishing community. PHOTO BY ROWAN JACOBSEN

Nancy Hinton and François Brouillard gathering daylilies in Quebec. PHOTO BY ROWAN JACOBSEN

The day's foraging harvest. PHOTO BY ROWAN JACOBSEN

. chanterelle forest! PHOTO BY ROWAN JACOBSEN

athering chanterelles. PHOTO BY FRANÇOIS BROUILLARD

The only Totten Virginica bed in the world, Totten Inlet, Puget Sound.

Plump Totten Virginicas up close and personal.

A stately avocado tree in a Michoacán orchard. PHOTO BY ROWAN JACOBSEN

Cooking avocado-fed pig in its own fat (*carnitas*), Michoacán, Mexico. PHOTO BY ROWAN JACOBSEN

Emmonak, Alaska, on
finger of the Yukon Rive

PHOTO BY JON ROWL

Simon Harpak at his Yukon River
fish camp. PHOTO BY ROWAN JACOBSEN

Yupik Kids in
Emmonak, Alaska.

PHOTO BY ROWAN JACOBSEN

lmon strips at Ray Waska's Yukon River fish camp. PHOTO BY ROWAN JACOBSEN

mon for "dryfish," Emmonak, Alaska. PHOTO BY ROWAN JACOBSEN

Future site of Bonn
Doon's San Juan
Bautista vineyard.

PHOTO COURTESY BONN
DOON VINEYARD

Goats clearing the
brush at Bonny Doon's
new biodynamic San
Juan Bautista estate.

PHOTO COURTESY BONNY
DOON VINEYARD

Red Willow Vineyard and its chapel, with Mount Adams in the background, Yakima Vall
Washington. PHOTO COURTESY RED WILLOW VINEYARD

Ayrshires doing their thing at Jasper Hill Farm, Greensboro, Vermont.

PHOTO BY ROWAN JACOBSEN

The cheddar vault at the Cellars at Jasper Hill.

PHOTO BY ROWAN JACOBSEN

cks of Winnimere in the washed-rind vault. PHOTO BY ROWAN JACOBSEN

Cacao gatherers in
the Bolivian Amazon.

PHOTO BY ROWAN JACOBSEN

An opened cacao pod.

PHOTO BY ROWAN JACOBSEN

Cacao pods
growing straight fro
the trunk.

PHOTO BY ROWAN JACOBS

But somehow with François it was always different. "He was just this little bugger whose pockets were constantly full of critters and leaves," his chef de cuisine, Nancy Hinton, told me. When he was five, he'd dehydrate grasshoppers on the woodstove, steal his mother's rolling pin, and crush them to make a crust for the fish he'd caught in the river. And somehow, as the older generation passed away and his generation grew up and moved to the city, François kept right on living that way. Eventually he became known as François des Bois—François of the Woods.

"He's just a guy that's spent so much time in nature, and these are his family traditions," Nancy said. Nancy is one of the few Anglophones from Quebec City. Five-foot-nothing and finely featured, she comes across as the kitchen elf. "To me, because I'm from the city, it's super interesting. It's fresh, and it's terroir. But to him it's just normal. It's just the way that his grandmother lived. It's not a philosophy or anything. Everybody's embracing Slow Food, but François doesn't know what Slow Food is."

We were sitting on the porch of Les Jardins Sauvages restaurant on a misty July night, sharing a bottle of hard cider, the roar of the Saint-Esprit River coming through the screens. The restaurant occupies the converted camp where François' family has summered since 1923. I'd come there to track down François, which was not an easy thing to do. Like any good hunter-gatherer, he does not like to sit still for more than five minutes. He'd barely managed to sip some cider with us before he leaped up, grabbed a flashlight, and pulled me outside. "Have you tried plantain?" he asked.

Plantain? The scourge of my lawn? I hadn't.

"After a rain, the new leaves smell like mushrooms," he said. With his longish gray hair and potbelly, he looked like an ex-member of Pink Floyd. He knelt in the wet grass and crawled his fingers through it until he'd isolated and picked a baby plantain leaf. I bruised it and held it up to my nose. "Like a porcini!" I cried.

"Only after the rain," he said.

The next morning François and Nancy took me foraging. It was Thursday, and they had just two more days to pull together their weekend menu. Les Jardins Sauvages offers a five-course prix fixe every Friday and Saturday night that consists almost entirely of wild edibles. I'd seen that weekend's menu and couldn't quite believe it was possible:

Daylily bud and petal salad, house-smoked duck,
lamb's quarters and live-forever, wild ginger vinaigrette

*   *   *

Stinging nettle and sea spinach soup,
crinkleroot yogurt foam, smoked arctic char, lady's sorrel

*   *   *

Cattail-flour crepe stuffed with braised piglet, boletes,
and 1608 cheese, creamed corn, sea parsley, cattail spear

*   *   *

Venison from the farm, elderberry and juniper sauce,
wild rice with chanterelles, milkweed broccoli tempura

*   *   *

Dark chocolate and sweet clover tartlet,
field strawberries and dwarf raspberries, white chocolate
and sweetgrass semifreddo, milkweed-flower syrup

Les Jardins Sauvages' meats are farmed (the venison, in fact, right on the property) because, by law, commercial establishments can't serve wild game, but virtually everything else is foraged. The entire menu channels the place and season. Forest gastronomy in California or Florida, in winter or spring, would have had a completely different look.

François gathers many of the ingredients himself. "He's been tracking the same woods and areas for so many years," Nancy said. "Always checking for the signs, waiting for things to show up. It's not a question of what he's gonna find. It's more a question of when." He's also trained foragers throughout the province. As we walked through the fields around the restaurant, his cell phone jangled with calls: Did he need any lady's sorrel? Boletes? How was he doing on pigweed?

They call François for the same reason that he decided to open the restaurant: Because it is very difficult to make forest gastronomy work at a traditional restaurant. For years François had tried to make his living by supplying wild edibles to the top restaurants in Montreal. He was always the first person with fiddleheads, battling swollen spring rivers in his canoe to get them. He was the rock star of provisioners, hanging out for hours at each restaurant, showing off his braided-sweetgrass key chain and telling stories. Normand Laprise of Toqué, Montreal's most renowned restaurant, once said, "He brings things from the woods that no one knows about." But that was the problem. Even when chefs were willing to try something totally new, François had to train them to work with the ingredient, and even if they learned and put that dish on their menu, they would then need the same amount of that ingredient every week. The forest doesn't work that way.

Eventually François decided the only proper way to promote forest gastronomy was to have as many people as possible dine at his own woodland table. Les Jardins Sauvages was born. At first he did much of the cooking himself in what was decidedly a seat-of-the-pants operation. "Before I got here," Nancy said, "there was not a lot of order. François made the tisane about five minutes before it was served, walking around the restaurant, smelling dried things, and pulling it together by intuition. The waitresses were drinking wine with the customers." I refrained from saying that this sounded like the restaurant of my dreams.

Nancy was the chef at the Laurentians resort L'Eau à la Bouche when she met François, who was supplying the restaurant with wild greens and other edibles. She already had an affinity for wild plants. "When I went to visit my farmers who supplied the restaurant, I noticed they were just weeding out the purslane. Purslane has a nice texture and a lemony taste. It's great in salads. I asked if I could have it all." Nancy had concocted a wild-ginger mustard to accompany a sesame-crusted tuna. She invited François to try it. He liked it. And he liked her, too. They began dating immediately, and she began pitching in at Les Jardins Sauvages. In 2005 she left L'Eau à la Bouche to devote herself to Les Jardins Sauvages.

THIRTY-EIGHT PLANTS

I had expected to plunge straight into the deep woods with François, but he began our morning of foraging in the overgrown fields around the restaurant, grazing on daylilies and daisies on the way there. "I love daisy leaves," Nancy said idly. "So sweet." Indeed they were, with a medicinal parsley zing. François pulled on rubber gloves to strip the leaves from some tall, vivacious green spikes. "Stinging nettles," he said. "Don't touch them with your skin. But if you do, the antidote is usually nearby." He whacked the back of my hand with a nettle and, once the burn had started, ripped up some jewelweed that was mixed in with the nettles, crushed the stems, and the mucilaginous juice took the pain away.

We harvested daylilies for the first-course salad—the petals, the tiny buds, and even the yellowy-orange pistils, which, dried, are the saffron of the Northeast. We nibbled on pigweed, which, like milkweed and purslane, is one of those much-reviled "weeds" that actually tastes better than the crops it is culled from. We passed a fence festooned with wild grapes, which Nancy would make into a balsamic-vinegar-like reduction in the fall. We picked the tender tips of mugwort, a feathery weed in the same family as absinthe. "I call it my pizza plant," said Nancy. "It tastes like fennel and rosemary and oregano all mixed up. It really punches up the wild-herb oil."

"The flavor changes over the course of the day," François added. "It's best to pick it around midday."

A wispy white flower filled an abandoned garden and the roadside near the restaurant. This was melilot, which goes by the name sweet clover in English, but the French have got it right, because melilot, a common cover plant for crop rotation in the Midwest, is one of our most important honey (*miel*) plants. Though you wouldn't look twice as your car zips past it, the plant has an extraordinary aroma of marzipan, vanilla, and fresh peas. "The first time I smelled it," Nancy said, "I thought it smelled just like cookies coming out of the oven." So she made cookies with it, and they were a huge hit. She has made vinegar with it, and a sauce for foie gras, but primarily she likes to bake with it. Today it would go into the pastry dough for the chocolate tartlets.

After plucking clusters of young milkweed buds for tempura, we crossed a road and plunged into a swamp in search of cattails. One of the great wild foods, cattails were a mainstay of eastern Native Americans. The naturalist John Eastman writes that "the food value of cattail is said to almost equal that of corn or rice." He adds, "With cattails present, one need not starve, freeze, remain untreated for injury, or want for playthings." The shoots in spring can be used like asparagus, and the immature female flower heads (the corn dog part) can be boiled and eaten like corn on the cob. In summer, the yellow pollen from the male flower heads makes a protein-rich flour. Cattail broth, made by boiling the mature flower heads, is a staple in Nancy's kitchen.

François grabbed a shoot by the base and yanked it up, then peeled away the outer layers to reveal the white, dripping core. It had the look and crunch of Belgian endive, and a clean flavor of cucumber and fiddlehead, but it finished with an astringency like an unripe banana's; these were too mature.

While in the swamp we picked spearmint and marsh pepper, a tiny nibble of which tears through your mouth like a fistful of black pepper. As we were leaving, François stopped, pointed to a low-lying shrub lurking in the undergrowth, and said, "I can't remember the name of this plant, but it smells like pineapple. It's not common."

We retreated to the restaurant for lunch—a green "lettuce soup" Nancy had made a few days earlier. "I use sea lettuce," she said, "and I add pigweed for richness." It was an offhand comment, but it made me realize that, operating in isolation at Les Jardins Sauvages, taking her cues from whatever François turned up with, Nancy had developed a culinary lexicon all her own. There wasn't another chef in North America nonchalantly uttering the phrase "I add pigweed for richness." While Hervé This and other molecular gastronomists were winning fame and fortune by taking paint sprayers to innocent pieces of goat cheese, Nancy was quietly creating menus wholly outside the matrix of contemporary cuisine. She posts them on the restaurant's Web site, where the collection stands as the *Canterbury Tales* of gastronomy, poetry in some haunting, half-archaic tongue. Muscovy duck with cloudberry sauce? Maple-wintergreen ice cream? Goose-egg frittata with sea spinach, crinkleroot cream, caviar, and pickled fiddleheads?

François barely ate before grabbing his wicker mushroom basket and tromping off for the woods on the other side of the Saint-Esprit River. Nancy and I scrambled to catch up. A handmade bridge—a forty-foot, undulating affair of wood planks and steel cables—crossed from the restaurant to the woods, disappearing into a wall of cedar trees. Swaying and bouncing over the crashing river, it had a distinct *Indiana Jones* feel to it, and I held tight to both hand cables as I crossed.

When I reached the far side, François was already picking some chanterelles he'd noticed on a hillside. A moment later he spotted a glabrescent boletus beneath an oak tree. Nancy likes to use this variety, dried, in her shortbread cookies. Soon after that we hit a tiny patch of hygrophores, bright orange, fairy-size mushrooms. "One of the few mushrooms you can eat raw," François said. And I did. They were mild, the chief thrill being popping a raw, neon-colored mushroom in your mouth.

François moved much faster than we did. We soon lost him, though we'd catch a quick glimpse as he cut across the trail like a coyote. Above all else, François is a mushroom man. "François goes buggy when mushroom season hits," Nancy said. "Forget about the nettles." Mushrooms are the most elusive game. They deliver the most complex flavors and draw the highest prices. At one point he came back to show me a red-foot bolete, one of his very favorite mushrooms. When he cut it open, it instantly stained blue. When I'm on my own, I follow the foolproof bolete rule: Reject any that have red pores or that stain blue. You end up rejecting more boletes than you keep, but you're guaranteed to get rid of the few nasty ones. With François, however, I got to savor the sautéed red-foot bolete later in the kitchen. It was delightfully tangy.

The woods were full of other treats, too. Sarsaparilla and wood sorrel, wintergreen and chickweed. The boletes were making their first appearance of the season. We found a bay bolete and a black and scaly pine bolete that I ordinarily would have given a wide berth. We even found a porcini, a.k.a. king bolete or cèpe, the most prized mushroom in Europe.

I asked François what made this patch so special. "Nothing," he said. "I just know it." But it was more than that. Civilization is closing in on François des Bois. "When I came here as a kid," he said, "this was the middle of nowhere. Now it's all been developed. This is the last patch of forest." The issue isn't houses so much as agriculture. Ranks of corn advance right up to Les Jardins Sauvages' property line. Other good hunting grounds have been lost to logging. "The government replants, but they plant spruce trees. That's good for chanterelles, but the old, mixed hardwood forests, with the oak and maple and cherry, are where you find tons of crinkle-root and wild ginger and violets and trout lily. There's just so much more in those forests."

To get certain ingredients, he finds himself traveling farther. He will disappear without warning and be gone for days. He goes to his family's fishing camp in western Quebec to access the rich forests there, or to the Gaspe Peninsula for sea greens and sweet-grass. He has considered going farther. At a friend's hunting and fishing lodge on Ungava Bay, not far from the Arctic Circle, he discovered the most beautiful mushrooms he'd ever seen. "They were pristine," Nancy said. "There are no worms that far north. And the Inuit don't eat mushrooms. They won't even try them." He experimented with shipping freezers to the lodge, loading them with mushrooms, and chartering a plane to fly them back, but the costs were prohibitive. "Now I think drying them up there would be the only way to do it," Nancy said.

After the woods, we hit one of those government-planted spruce farms to look for chanterelles, which made flying to the Arctic for mushrooms seem quite unnecessary. Creamsicle-colored chanterelles dotted the spruce-needle floor. We divided the plantation into three rows, took out our knives, and picked. I was thrilled, but François' roving eye compelled him onward. Soon he whistled me over and pointed. A hundred fat, handsome chanterelles radiated out along the roots of a single spruce. I'd never seen such rich mushrooming grounds. In an hour we filled our baskets.

The chanterelle is God's gift to the novice mushroom picker. It's difficult to mistake for anything poisonous. It is the color of treasure, and its discovery provides similarly heartening little bursts of dopamine. It is about as hard to spot as neon golf balls on a green. It flouts nature's general rule that tasty things must be hard to find or hard to catch. Bright, showy mushrooms usually taste terrible or poison you, yet somehow the chanterelle thrives despite making no effort to discourage pickers or slugs.

None of this would matter if it weren't so enchanting. It is the Audrey Hepburn of mushrooms. It may be common, but its scent is beguiling and elusive, slipping away just as you begin to grasp it. We tend to describe aromas in terms of other aromas, as language falls short and we grasp at other nouns to try to compensate. People like to say that chanterelles smell like apricots, which is mnemonically convenient because of their color. But the smelling circuitry goes straight for the limbic system; memory and emotion are often the best way to capture the essence of a scent. To me, chanterelles smell insistently wistful; they are the wet and mossy trout stream you fished as a kid.

What they really smell like, of course, is chanterelles. I thought about this as I also came to the observation that the woods itched. They bugged me. They nettled me. Things, activities, and even words were reverting to their simplest forms. The forest was full of little truths.

François, who was wearing a white T-shirt, watched me claw at my arms and told me that bright white and yellow keep mosquitoes away. Too late—I was a sitting duck in navy. After an hour or two, I was happy to head back to the restaurant to meet Nancy's crew of cooks and begin the evening's prep work. We carried with us twenty-five pounds of chanterelles. The next day, many would be for sale at Jean-Talon Market for forty dollars a pound.

Back at Les Jardins Sauvage, we unloaded our bounty, and Nancy set her cooks to work. François went out prospecting, cell phone glued to his ear. "He has ADD," Nancy said. "Not that he knows it. He can't sit around and talk. But he's supernaturally plugged into nature. He notices everything. Sometimes we'll be driving, and I'll be telling him some long story, pouring my heart out, and suddenly he'll slam on the brakes and run into the woods to get something he's seen."

I slipped out to the garden by the river and ate my cut of the chanterelles. In a single day of foraging, I had sampled thirty-eight wild (or wildish) plants. Here's the list: daylily, Johnny jump-up, spearmint, daisy, bee balm, raspberry, black raspberry, plantain, yarrow, Labrador tea, mugwort, purslane, pigweed, marsh pepper, nettle, milkweed, cattail, wood sorrel, lady sorrel, purple vetch, melilot, wild ginger, crinkleroot, wintergreen, sarsaparilla, chickweed, sweetgrass, sea spinach, sea parsley, sea lettuce, oyster plant, chanterelle, red hygrophore, porcini, bay bolete, glabrescent bolete, red-foot bolete, pine bolete.

I felt great—sharp, alert, calm, utterly satisfied. My cells felt like they were grooving on some long-denied micronutrients. Nibbling on such a variety of things, I'd lost the interest to gorge on any one. This phenomenon, called "sensory-specific satiety," is common in humans and other omnivores—after a few bites of something, it becomes less desirable. We actually perceive it as having diminished flavor, while other foods suddenly seem more desirable. We are built to forage.

It made me wonder whether François and his ADD were on to something. Because it wasn't just my mouth that was satisfied; it was my brain, too. Foraging is the antithesis of running. Instead of moving fast through a landscape, oblivious to your surroundings as you obsess on your own internal psychodramas (the state of your body, the state of your finances, the mean thing your eighth-grade English teacher said to you), you move slowly, your mind a pellucid extension of your senses as you try to score a little chow.

In his book *Against the Grain: How Agriculture Has Hijacked Civilization*, Richard Manning argues that the idea that agriculture saved humanity from a brutish and tenuous existence "had to have sprung from the imagination of someone who never hoed a row of corn or rose with the sun for a lifetime of milking cows. Gamboling about plain and forest, hunting and living off the land is fun. Farming is not. That's all one needs to know to begin a rethinking of the issue." Indeed, contrary to popular belief, the archaeological record shows that the conversion to an agrarian lifestyle is generally accompanied by the "diseases of civilization"—cardiovascular disease, diabetes, tooth decay—as well as stunted stature and shortened life span, which may explain why most contemporary hunter-gatherer societies resist every nonprofit's efforts to foist agriculture on them.

And so, full of pigweed soup and daisy leaves, I sat contentedly in the garden and rethought the issue, watching a well-fed woodchuck emerge from under the porch and make green things disappear at an impressive rate, working tip to base in the woodchuck manner. I raised my glass to him. He stood up on his back legs. We held each other's eyes for a moment and tipped our heads. Then we went back to our respective passions.

A FOREST OF SIGNIFIERS

Plants, of course, are the original molecular gastronomists. For hundreds of millions of years they've been creating novel flavor molecules. The bitter bite and heady rush of a coffee bean, the burn of a chili, the intoxicating scent of a rose—all exist because some plant had the Next Big Idea (usually as a way to manipulate animal behavior). A few of those big ideas we've incorporated into our agriculture and cuisines, and most of us have the general sense that all the best inventions are in common use. But after a couple of days at Les Jardins Sauvages, I began to realize how narrow the modern palate has become. The handful of plants that comprise most American diets have not been chosen because they are particularly compelling, but because they are convenient and efficient. Many of the Top Chefs of the plant kingdom have not had their day.

Yet that evening and night, as I watched Nancy and her cooks process the summertime harvest, I saw why forest gastronomy will never become a mass movement. In addition to requiring constant creativity and flexibility, it is labor-intensive. One cook was blanching a hundred pounds of stinging nettles. This wasn't even for the weekend dinner. To be a year-round restaurant, Les Jardins Sauvages must do things the way they were done before the availability of airlifted Chilean produce. The summer and fall harvests must be prepped for the rest of the year. Those nettles would be blanched, squeezed to remove as much water as possible, vacuum-packed, and frozen. Cattails, too, present a massive processing challenge: Cattail broth is a staple in many of Nancy's recipes, and the year's supply must be made during the one to two weeks when the cattails are ready. "We missed them this year," Nancy sighed. "I don't know how it happened."

The first thing that greets a visitor to Les Jardins Sauvages is the dehydrator, which runs 24/7 in the foyer. When I was there, it was stocked with racks of bee balm, melilot, daylily pistils, and mushrooms. The shelves in the kitchen, as well as the stairs in the dining room, resemble a mushroom apothecary, with at least thirty one-gallon jars filled with dried or powdered mushrooms and hand-labeled: *Bolet orange*, *Pied de mouton*, *Trompette de la mort*. I spent a heady hour opening jars and sniffing, on a magical mystery tour of lands far off the usual gastro-tourist routes. Aspen boletes had the pure umami scent of Vegemite; glabrescent boletes smelled like skate in black butter sauce.

Boletes are the family of mushrooms that have spongy, porous undersides instead of gills. They can be fairly mild fresh but take on crazy flavors as they dry. "I barely bother panfrying them anymore," Nancy said. "They're the only mushroom I systematically dry. They're such naturals for dessert."

Dessert? Certainly. Many of our traditional dessert ingredients—cocoa, cinnamon, lemon—have nothing inherently sweet about them. They were paired with sugar somewhat arbitrarily. Certain boletes excel in the role. Nancy likes the yellowfoot. "It smells like vanilla and coconut. It's more subtle. Kind of a honey, floral, fruity, apple flavor. That one I use in pre-desserts. I made rice pudding with it once. I make milkshakes, shortbread cookies. Porcini is another that's great in desserts. I make little caramels with it." Dried red-foot boletes give a flavor like Black Forest cake. Nancy once made cookies with them, sandwiched around a crème filling flavored with almond-scented sweetgrass: "It was just a small black cookie with a white center, but all the customers said, 'Oh! Oreo cookies!'"

The mushroom desserts turn up at Les Jardins Sauvages' fall mushroom festival, a seven-course orgy of wild-mushroom veneration featuring about twenty different varieties. The restaurant uses more than a ton of mushrooms during the festival. "It started out as one weekend," Nancy said, "then went up to two to accommodate the crowds. Now it's three. It could go up, but we can't possibly process any more mushrooms. Almost every mushroom needs to be cleaned by hand. We call everyone we know and ask them to help."

Even the typical five-course dinner I was attending required late nights of prep work. Miraculously, when guests started trickling in for dinner on Friday evening, everything was ready. Groups walked up the garden path carrying bottles of wine (the restaurant has no liquor license), which gave the evening the feel of a big dinner party. People settled in the garden near a stone inukshuk and a laminated picture of François' grandmother and drank a glass of wine. Everyone took pictures. A few tried out the bridge, which was lit with red Christmas lights. Two old women in pink dresses sat at the far end of the garden and chatted and laughed like they hadn't seen each other in years.

As the mosquitoes descended, we slipped inside, past the dehydrator and the open kitchen door, and took our tables. The restaurant seats forty-five in winter and sixty-five when it's warm enough to use the porch. The decor is unapologetically funky. On this night, a duct-taped tarp covered the porch, yet every table had a fresh bouquet of wildflowers. Two huge spikes of Canada lilies were crossed in the foyer.

A thousand mementos cover every available surface in the dining room: old magazines featuring François, dried clusters of sweetgrass and cattail, pamphlets with information on edible sea plants of the

Gaspe Peninsula, a shelf of condiments and teas for sale, and framed photos of François' beloved wild plants. Stacks of photo albums contain shots of spectacular finds—Nancy juggling giant puffballs, François crouched amid carpets of chanterelles or forests of fiddleheads.

Ramekins of bolete butter and bee balm butter waited on each table. The bolete butter was deep and fruity; the bee balm butter was minty and floral and gorgeous, pink flecks swirled in yellow cream. I was spooning it straight into my mouth when the salad arrived, crisp and sweet daylily petals playing off crunchy daylily buds and toothsome duck, smoked so lightly that it was still full of juice. Daisy buds played a caperlike role, and the woodsy tingle of wild ginger filled the background. It was like Quebecois *kaiseki*, texture and color evoking summer on the Saint-Esprit River. The nettle and sea spinach soup countered the salad with a deeply green and soothing monochrome, a puddle of white crinkleroot foam supporting three heart-shaped and tangy lady's sorrel leaves. I dipped my spoon and fished up a piece of smoky arctic char.

The golden cattail-flour crepe had the warmth of sweet corn. It was thick with creamy pork and cheese and mushrooms—comfort food gone wild—and crossed by a single pencil-thick cattail spear. I picked up the spear and ate it like miniature corn on the cob until I was left holding the central quill.

By the time the tender planks of venison arrived, bathed in a gamy, ginlike sauce of elderberry and juniper and accompanied by the chanterelles and popcorn-scented wild rice, I was lost in a forest of unfamiliar signifiers. Taste is deeply contextual. Even the wine I'd brought, a Pinot Noir I knew well, tasted new and exciting, more cedary than I'd remembered. It became impossible to compare the meal to others I'd had; it was what it was. All I will say is that when the desserts arrived—the tart dwarf raspberries, the pink milkweed-flower syrup, the vanilla affinities of the melilot pastry crust and the sweetgrass semifreddo—I was in full accord with the birds and the bees. Summer is a fine thing.

François turned up late in the dinner, canvassing the dining room and fielding people's questions. He grabbed photo albums to show exactly what they were eating and where it had come from. Buzzing with energy and conversation, the groups drifted off into the night until just a few of us remained. Nancy came out of the kitchen and sat down. We opened more wine. A heavyset man with sad eyes approached. He looked a little overwhelmed. "I travel for a living," he said. "I've eaten in thirty-nine different countries." It appeared that he might cry. "Why doesn't anybody else do things like this?" He trailed off and looked forlornly at the door, as if he didn't want to have to return to the other thirty-eight countries. Then he smiled weakly at us and trundled away.

Nancy looked tired. She had to prep for a full house the next night. And she was preoccupied with finding some cold locale where the cattails might not have gone by, where she might still find the main ingredient for her broth for the year. I asked her what dream ingredient she'd like to put on a menu.

"I'm not sure." She sighed and flagged down François. "What's the best thing you've ever found?" she asked.

He looked straight at her and crinkled his eyes. "You," he said.

RECIPES

NANCY HINTON'S WILD MUSHROOM SABLÉS

These shortbread cookies take on an amazing woodsy-chocolate character, thanks to the dried mushrooms. Mushroom powders are sometimes found in gourmet food stores. Dried mushrooms are more widely available and can be ground into a fine powder with a food processor blade or a coffee grinder. For a fine powder, pass it through a fine mesh strainer (keeping any remaining bits for sauces or soups). The variety of mushroom matters. Nancy prefers boletes such as red-mouth bolete, larch bolete, and king bolete (porcini). A mix is nice, including such sweetly fragrant types as chanterelle, hedgehog, yellow-foot chanterelle, fairy ring, matsutake, and black trumpet. The dough can be frozen in logs, then half-thawed in the refrigerator before it's sliced and baked. It can also be rolled out between two sheets of plastic wrap or parchment and chilled before it's cut into shapes and baked.

Makes 30 cookies

1 cup butter, softened
1 cup plus 2 tablespoons powdered sugar
1 large egg
1½ cups all-purpose flour
½ cup almond powder
¼ cup dried mushroom powder

1. Cream the butter and sugar (by hand or in a mixer with a paddle). Add the egg and mix.
2. Sift the dry ingredients together and gently fold them in with the wet ones (or use a mixer on low speed). Avoid overmixing.
3. Roll the dough into logs (using a small amount of flour if needed). If the dough is too soft, refrigerate it until it is workable but

not too stiff. Rolling it in parchment or cling rap is easiest.
Refrigerate until ready to bake.

4.   Preheat the oven to 350 degrees.

5.   Cut the logs into thin (1/10-inch) slices and place them on
     a baking sheet lined with parchment paper. Cook in the
     middle of the oven for 20 to 25 minutes, until they're slightly
     golden. Remove the baking sheet from the oven and allow
     the cookies to cool before moving them with a spatula (they
     are delicate). They will keep in an airtight container for a
     week.

PRISMATIC SALAD

Once you get used to adding flowers to your salads, the flowerless
ones begin to look seriously diminished. In addition to color and
geometry, flowers contribute lively flavors. My favorite eye-popping
trio is orange daylily petals, magenta bee balm, and purple violets,
but the only rule is to use whatever is freshly opened. I've never seen
a color combo that made an ugly prismatic salad! Keep the dressing
light here (in both flavor and weight), so as not to overwhelm the
floral qualities. Some choice edible flowers: bee balm, borage, ca-
lendula, carnation, chamomile, daisy, daylily, impatiens, jasmine,
Johnny jump-up, lilac, mallow, nasturtium, pansy, rose, violet, zuc-
chini blossom.

Serves 4

½ cup extra-virgin olive oil
zest and juice of ¼ lemon or Meyer lemon
a big pinch of flaky sea salt
a grind of fresh black pepper
½ pound mixed greens, washed and dried
1 handful chives or green onions

optional ingredients: toasted walnuts or sunflower seeds, cucumbers,
    shaved carrots, avocado
several handfuls mixed flower petals

1.   Whisk together the oil, lemon, salt, and pepper.
2.   Add the greens, chives or onions, and any optional ingredients
     to a large salad bowl and toss with the dressing. Sprinkle the
     flowers over the top and serve.

RESOURCES

FAT OF THE LAND
http://fat-of-the-land.blogspot.com/
Fantastic foraging blog with a Pacific Northwest flavor by Amazon
.com refugee Langdon Cook.

LES JARDINS SAUVAGES
www.jardinssauvages.com
450-588-5125
Open for dinner, with one seven P.M. seating only, Friday and Saturday nights year-round. The many foraged products are also available
at Jean-Talon Market and other locations throughout Montreal.

"WILDMAN" STEVE BRILL
www.wildmanstevebrill.com
New York's very own foraging legend leads tours of Central Park,
Prospect Park, and the greater New York environs.

HUNTER ANGLER GARDENER COOK
www.honest-food.net/blog1/
Northern California's Hank Shaw seems to be able to turn virtually
any organism into something delicious. As he writes, "I am the om-
nivore who has solved his dilemma. This is my story." And this is
his blog.

That Totten Smell

TOTTEN INLET OYSTERS, PUGET SOUND

APRIL 7, 2008, was a sad day for the Atlantic Ocean. That was the evening I sat at a banquet table in a hotel in Providence, Rhode Island, with nine of the most discerning oyster palates in America, including Peter Hoffman of Savoy, Bruce Sherman of North Pond, and the Bishop of Bivalves himself, Sandy Ingber of Grand Central Oyster Bar. We were there to crown a king of the Atlantic. Which Eastern oyster was the best?

A hotly contested issue.

In 2007, I published *A Geography of Oysters*, a guide to the oysters of North America. I'd been an oyster fanatic since I was a kid, but I'd written the book after becoming fascinated by the fact that oysters are one of the only foods that, like European wines, are named for the place they come from. Whether from coastal towns like Bluepoint and Wellfleet, or bays like Apalachicola and Malpeque, oysters have always been identified by their home waters, because they taste like those waters. Oysters live in estuaries—brackish bays and inlets where rivers meet the sea—because that is where their food is. They eat algae, which are basically single-celled plants, and algae proliferate in estuaries because that's where *their* food is: the fertile nutrients washed into the sea by rain and rivers. All day long, oysters sit with their shells cracked open and suck water across their gills, filtering and eating the algae and any similar-size particles. Each bay has a unique blend of salts, minerals, and algae species circulating in it, all of which have a profound impact on an oyster's flavor. I think of an oyster as a bouillon cube condensed from a bay's broth. Yes, it tastes like the sea—or, in the immortal words of the French poet Léon-Paul Fargue, "like kissing the sea on the lips"— but the sea changes all along the coast.

Which is why I find oysters such a fascinating subject for exploring terroir. If you want to quickly grasp the essence of a bay, to understand what makes it different from another, you would do well to spend some time getting to know its oysters. And so I had.

After my book came out, I heard from oyster growers across the country. Though there are still a few healthy populations of wild oysters in North America, most of our oysters are farmed. Oyster farmers buy "seed" oysters the size of a grain of sand from hatcheries, then grow them out on the tide flats. They know that the spot makes the oyster, and they are usually pretty enamored of their spots, which makes them downright zealous about their oysters. Most oyster farmers I spoke with claimed, with utter conviction, to have the best oysters in the world. The possibility that there were approximately 132 best-tasting oysters seemed mathematically unlikely, so I was eager for a more rigorous test, and the East Coast Shellfish Growers Association gave me just the chance, arranging the most extensive blind tasting of oysters ever undertaken.

Any grower of *Crassostrea virginica*, the species native to America's Atlantic and Gulf coasts, could enter, yet only twenty dared represent. But what a twenty. These were the legendary oyster "appellations," names that turned up on any oyster bar's most-wanted list, like Moonstone, Mystic, Pemaquid, Watch Hill, Island Creek, and Apalachicola.

To say that the score sheet was thorough would be like calling the SAT a quiz. It was burdensome. Categories included External Visual Appearance, Shuckability, and Internal Visual Appearance. There were five aroma categories (Briney, Seaweedy, Earthy, Fruity, and Metallic) and five taste categories (Salty, Earthy, Sweet, Seaweed, and Umami). Meat texture and meat-to-shell ratio had to be considered, and the aftertaste had to be rated for metallicness and astringency. Penalty points would be assessed for the presence of the off-flavors of boiled potato, wet burlap, raw cabbage, bitter, garlic oil, agar, ammonia, wet dog, sour, fishy, petroleum, and the dreaded fecal. All this came together in a rating for "overall experience." And if that wasn't enough, room was left at the bottom for "descriptive adjectives."

The event began. A phalanx of volunteer shuckers brought out the first entries, each labeled with only a number. We wrote the same number on our score sheets, took a swig of water to clear our palates, and got to work. And it *was* work—tasting three of each entry to be certain we'd taken its measure, weighing whether an internal visual appearance was pretty (8 points), nice (6 points), or out-and-out flawed (2 points).

Being the one writer on the panel, I felt the need to hold up the literary end of the bargain, so I peppered my score sheets with adjectives. I described one as "meaty but mild," one as "thin and salty," and another as "one-dimensional." I was not kind. For one oyster I wrote "really peppery!"—something I've never encountered before or since in an oyster. That one turned out to be from New Jersey. Another oyster I docked for the impressive combo of "boiled potato," "wet dog," "fishy," *and* "garlic oil."

Then there was the oyster that didn't quite look right, the way disturbed dogs don't quite look right, even from a distance. I sniffed it suspiciously. It sure as hell didn't smell right. Repulsed, I eyed the thing and thought about my options. The weight of responsibility bore down on me. Against my better judgment, I popped the oyster in my mouth, chewed, and concentrated. Let me just say that the fact that oysters strongly exhibit their terroir is not automatically a good thing. This particular mollusk seemed to be representing a little patch of terroir somewhere downstream of a pig farm. My description of that one simply read, "The Worst!"

It amazed me that certain growers knew their oysters were going to be judged in the equivalent of a movie close-up, with nowhere to hide, and this was what they managed to scrounge up. Had their nasal cavities been hopelessly seared by a withering assault of horseradish and Tabasco? One had to wonder.

Thankfully, other entries were superb. I awarded Ninigret Cups (from Ninigret Pond, Rhode Island) a perfect score for sweetness and saltiness, though they were light on flavor and came in third overall. Moonstones (Point Judith Pond, Rhode Island) I called "classic" for their savory mix of salt, minerals, and tannin. And Island Creeks (Duxbury Bay, Massachusetts) were at their briny bar-snack best—"Great with beer" in my blind opinion.

But only one oyster received a perfect 10 from me for overall experience. It had a fruity umami depth unheard of in Eastern oysters. Picture the difference between a homemade fish stock and canned broth. That extra zest was the difference between this oyster and everything else I tasted. And it wasn't from the Atlantic at all. Like the other nineteen entries, it was a *Crassostrea virginica*, the Eastern species of oyster, but this one was a transplant. Which is why I say that April 7, 2008, was a sad day for the Atlantic. Because this was the showcase for its very own oyster, held on its home court. These were the best of the best. And, to my taste, they were blown away by an exile from three thousand miles away.

That is why six months later I found myself in the depths of a still and starlit October night, slogging across a Puget Sound tide flat with a crystal wineglass in one hand, an oyster knife in the other, a giant battery strapped to my waist, and a rickety homemade headlamp on my brow. I was in the company of Joth Davis, research director for Taylor Shellfish Farms, the largest shellfish company in North America, and Brian Allen, a well-known Puget Sound ecologist and shellfish grower, and we were there to grasp the gestalt of Totten Inlet, Washington, the home of the oyster that had awed me in Providence. What was going on in that inlet, I'd asked Joth a few months earlier. Why did its oysters taste so great?

Joth had smiled. "Ah, Totten Inlet's a special place," he'd said.

"But to really get a sense of it, you've got to be there at low tide, to walk around the oyster and clam beds and experience that Totten smell."

And here we were. And because we needed to be there at the lowest of low tides, when the oysters wouldn't be underwater, and because in autumn low tide falls in the wee hours, it was now somewhere beyond two A.M. And because the black waters and evergreen banks of Totten Inlet can suck the light on a moonless night, we didn't mess with puny LED headlamps. Thus the six-volt batteries on our waists and the wires running from them to the floodlamps on our heads.

The wineglass needs a little more explanation. Joth and Brian had cut directly out of a shellfish growers' conference to meet me on the tide flats. A man named Jon Rowley had also been at the conference. In addition to being an oyster marketing guru, Jon is the founder of the Pacific Oyster Wine Competition, a rigorous, three-city, blind tasting held each year to determine the greatest West Coast wines to serve with oysters. As they left the shellfish conference, Joth and Brian told Jon where they were headed, and Jon, because he's sensible about such things, said, "Well, you'll need some wine," and handed over a bottle of one of the winners—a Willamette Valley Vineyards 2007 Pinot Gris. The original plan called for plastic cups on the beach, but Brian, because he's also sensible about such things, had detoured to his house in Olympia for the crystal.

We parked our trucks at the edge of the inlet. Before we'd even opened our doors, the Totten smell was well in evidence, a low-tide bouillabaisse of fennel, pine nuts, dried fruit, and fish oil. It was like a bay of Sicilian sauce.

Perhaps a hundred feet of black beach were exposed. Beyond it I could just make out the gently undulating waters, which quickly disappeared into blackness. I stepped onto the beach and was surprised by the firmness. Bags of Manila clams, harvested earlier and awaiting pickup, were piled in front of us. Joth gave one bag a friendly whack, and it squeaked as the clams clamped down a little tighter. "They talk to you," he said. "I love that." I whacked a few bags and listened to them peep back at me—more of an interaction than I generally expect from shellfish.

We left the clam petting zoo and headed in the general direction Joth thought our quarry might lay. Oyster shells crunched under my boots. The entire tide flat was making small sucking and spitting sounds. I panned my light over the ground. Little jets of water shot out of the mud and arced all over the beach—horse clams spitting at each other. The ground was alive.

My light fell on what looked like the end of a mini elephant trunk, sticking out of the beach and winking at me. "What's this?" I called.

Joth and Brian came over. "Nice," said Joth. "Good find," said Brian. He tapped the thing with his finger, and it retreated into the ground. "That's a slippery-neck. A big, burrowing clam. Put your finger down there. There's a hard object that it burrows under, probably a piece of clay or a log under the surface. The lower half of its shell has this wicked serration, like something that Batman would use to drive through a mountain. It moves it back and forth with its foot and just saws through structures. It can go through rock. One of the cooler bivalves out there."

"Let's keep going," said Joth. "I want to find a certain oyster bed."

Joth Davis has an impressive oyster pedigree. He grew up in Osterville, the Cape Cod town named for its most famous bivalve, on the shore of a salt pond thick with *virginicas*. He apprenticed as an oyster farmer on Fishers Island, in Long Island Sound, before coming to Washington state for graduate school. He's raised shellfish ever since. Preternaturally enthusiastic about both shellfish and quixotic adventures, Joth was the perfect Virgil for my quest.

We picked our way over bags and bags of oysters staked to the beach with rebar. Most oysters in Totten Inlet are grown in mesh bags, which protect against predators and make for easier maintenance. The bags are no hardship for the oysters, which, like plants, stay rooted to a single spot their whole lives. There are no free-range oysters. Quality of life for an oyster is a simple combination of lack of predation and good food supply—a given in Totten Inlet. As Joth explained to me, "The sheer amount of food is a consequence of the richness of the water. Totten is extremely rich in its variety of plankton. I think it's the way the water circulates. There's lots and lots of turbulence because of the tidal action. As a result, the water turns over and you get lots of primary production. We have long summer days—plenty of light during the growing season." Nutrients in water tend to sink, but algae do best near the light-filled surface, where they can photosynthesize to their heart's content. A bay that turns over keeps bringing new fertilizer to the surface to feed the algae. And the algae in turn feed the rest of the food chain, including the strong runs of chum salmon that pass through Totten on their way to their spawning creeks.

I was astounded at Totten's abundance. The oyster bags stretched along the shore into the night. You can fit thousands of bags of oysters on an acre of Totten tide flat, and each bag holds a hundred oysters, so an acre of Totten can produce hundreds of thousands of oysters per year. That means it generates ultra-healthy protein and omega-3 fatty acids at a rate that is the envy of any terrestrial farm in America.[*]

This is not news. Native Americans located their settlements along the shores of Totten Inlet and other bays in southern Puget Sound millennia ago to take advantage of the rich shellfish grounds. Some are still there. Settlers have been farming oysters in the area since the late 1800s, and a century ago oysters from Totten Inlet netted an extra two dollars per sack because of their superior quality.

---

[*] Shellfish farms can produce ten times as much protein per acre as cattle farms, with zero inputs of any kind. They are one of the greenest forms of food production on the planet.

As for the distinct Totten smell, that's a matter of geography and geology. If you were sailing on the Pacific Ocean and wanted to get to Totten Inlet, you would have to enter the Strait of Juan de Fuca at Cape Flattery and sail a hundred miles east before curling around Port Townsend, navigating the twenty miles of Admiralty Inlet, and pushing another twenty miles south on Puget Sound just to reach Seattle. Then you'd have to continue onward through another sixty miles of increasingly slender bays and inlets before finally reaching Totten, a good two hundred miles from the open ocean. The tide surges all the way, and Totten's water is still mouthwateringly salty (unlike that of, say, Baltimore Harbor, at the top end of the Chesapeake, which is almost fresh), but its character is dominated by the surrounding land, which provides the inlet with a steady supply of rain-washed nutrients. Nitrogen, one of the building blocks of life, comes in different isotopes, depending on whether its source is the ocean or the land, and an analysis of the plankton in Totten Inlet found that its nitrogen is from the uplands. These are oysters built out of land recently made sea.

In contrast, Willapa Bay, another famous Washington state oyster appellation, which opens directly to the Pacific, has nitrogen that is marine in origin. Its oysters have a wholly different flavor, light lettuce and sea breeze, as opposed to the low-tide Totten funk.

Sometimes that funk can be too much. The oysters we were stepping over were Pacific oysters, a species imported from Japan in the 1920s that quickly came to dominate the West Coast industry because of its prolific growth, replacing the slow-growing and overharvested Olympias, which are the only oyster species native to the West Coast. But Pacifics also have an indelicate flavor, made all the more indelicate by Totten. Like a ripe cheese, they dance a dangerous line between "crazy good" and "don't put this in your mouth." They were not the *virginicas* that had won the blind tasting. Those still lay somewhere out there in the night.

"We need to go a little deeper," said Joth. "The oysters I'm looking for are grown low on the beach. They like being covered with water all the time." We stepped over bags of Kumamoto oysters, smaller relatives of Pacifics that have a sweet taste and a melon-like aroma. Kumos go for three dollars a piece in oyster bars; this beach was paved in gold.

Then we hit an area the size of a volleyball court that was covered in a rectangular mat of luminous green seaweed. Crabs and small fish picked their way through the vegetation. Beneath the green, PVC pipes poked an inch out of the mud. We were standing on a geoduck* farm.

A geoduck looks like something that might owe a lot of money to Jabba the Hutt. A giant clam that burrows so deep that armor becomes superfluous, it maintains a vestigial shell that sticks to its backside like a G-string on a sumo wrestler. From three feet down in the dirt, it sends an inch-thick siphon to the surface for food and oxygen. Inarguably phallic, the geoduck commands big bucks in Asia, where its siphon is eaten raw as an aphrodisiac. I've seen geoducks at Tokyo's Tsukiji fish market going for more than a hundred dollars a piece. They are the most profitable shellfish in the Pacific Northwest. They are also the most controversial.

It takes a geoduck several years to burrow to its deepest point and to reach market size. The PVC tubes, which penetrate about ten inches into the ground, are inserted by the growers to protect the baby geoducks. Moon snails, with their inflatable sinus the size of a throw pillow, which they use to blow dirt out of the way, and their chain-saw-like tongue† for devouring flesh, will latch onto any geoduck they can find. The PVC tubes prevent the moon snails from eating the geoduck crop.

To an environmentalist, a beach of PVC tubes looks terrible.

---

* Pronounced "gooey-duck," it's from a native Nisqually word meaning "dig deep."

† Technically, a radula.

The tubes do get removed once the clams have burrowed deeply enough, but it's the harvesting of the geoducks—done using water cannons to blow away the sediment and expose the clams—that many people object to. What type of impact do the cannons have on the tidelands? Massive, say the activists; minor, argue the shellfish farmers.

Joth and Brian, ecologists by temperament, believe that geoduck farming is less destructive than most types of farming. Joth pointed to the mat of seaweed. "This green algae comes in to cover geoduck beds," he said. "Then you get this incredibly diverse assemblage of critters that come in to feed on this artificial reef. It's a little reef that will be removed, but when it's here, it provides habitat that's being utilized by a lot of different critters. It's ephemeral, but it lasts for several generations of these animals."

Glowing pairs of tiny red eyes flicked across the reef. I asked Joth what they were. "One of the magic things about being out here at night is the shrimp," he said. "Those are little coonstripe shrimp. They're the best. And there's a kelp crab over there. I like being on the tide flats more at night than in daylight. Once you're out here, you embrace it."

We left the geoduck bed and kept splashing through the shallows. Something snored wetly offshore like a linebacker with a head cold. "Sea lion," said Brian.

It was somewhere beyond three A.M. Where the hell were we going? Why wasn't I in bed?

Suddenly my light fell upon an oyster that looked different from the rest. Loose on the beach, a good four inches long, it had a gray, teardrop-shaped shell without the ridges of Pacifics or Kumamotos. It looked familiar. "I got a *virginica* here!" I shouted.

"We're in it!" Joth said.

"I'll grab the wine," Brian said.

Brian uncorked the Pinot Gris while Joth and I scrounged through the water, pulling up oysters. Big, fat *virginicas* stippled the tide flats. Joth produced an oyster knife and whisked off the top shell. Plump, ivory-colored flesh glistened in our spotlights. "Look at that freaking oyster," Joth said. "That is just gorgeous." He slurped it and shivered with delight. "Oooh, they give me chills."

Doubled over, my light sweeping the beach in front of my toes, I waddled along until I found a handsome and deep-cupped *virginica*. I scooped it up, pulled my own oyster knife from my back pocket, shucked, and tipped the oyster into my mouth. Saltspray, rust, and a picklelike crunch. Then sweetness, nori, and the lingering grassy richness of raw milk. I felt an inner surge of Paleolithic zeal. This was the oyster that had beckoned me across the continent.

It is called the Totten Virginica, and it has a colorful story. The West Coast oyster industry took off with the California gold rush of 1849. Olympias were the only game in town at the time, and San Francisco eliminated its own supply in a few short years. Washington state, with the best oyster grounds on the coast, was only too happy to keep the pricey bivalves flowing to the Bay Area. The Transcontinental Railroad of 1869, however, brought with it the first load of East Coast *virginicas* to San Francisco, and the diminutive Olympias soon became a distant second choice for West Coast gourmands. San Francisco Bay oyster farmers began farming *virginicas*, and by the 1890s Washington state oyster farmers followed suit. Taylor Shellfish staked out an area of Totten Inlet for its "Eastern Bed." But *virginicas*, which like to spawn when the water temperature reaches seventy degrees Fahrenheit, would never reproduce in the cold shower of the Pacific Northwest. New seed had to be brought in every year by train, so in the 1920s they were abandoned for the Pacific oyster, which was unfazed by the cold. The Pacific oyster (along with its little cousin, the Kumamoto) now makes up virtually the entire West Coast oyster industry.

But a few years ago the people at Taylor Shellfish decided to revive the Eastern Bed, to see what would happen. What happened is they discovered a creature that captures what people love about oysters from both coasts. The *virginica* is a firmer beast all-around than the Pacific oyster, which has a yolky center. The *virginica* is clean in flavor and fun to crunch. Yet it doesn't have a lot going on. Oysters grown in Totten Inlet, however, get sweet and a little smutty. Totten Virginicas take a stiff and salty New England reserve, then ladle on just enough West Coast funk, and they have become one of the most coveted oysters in the world. The oysters hail from one acre and nowhere else on Earth, and we were standing in the middle of it.

I asked Joth why the oysters weren't in bags, and he told me they do a lot better if they are in touch with the beach. They start out in bags, but once big enough to fend for themselves, they get scattered across the mudflats. This hardens up their shells, but it may do more. "I have this theory," Joth said. "This mud is a sticky conglomeration of sand, but it's also got the glacial till—post-glaciation sediment that has that clayey consistency. And I believe that contributes to the flavor of the oysters here. These bays get stirred up periodically by winter storms. What's in the sediment gets taken up in minute quantity by the phytoplankton. The oysters also feed on detritus; they can't discriminate perfectly between the living plankton and the detrital particles. I'm convinced that there's flavor imparted by the particular stuff that's in the sediment here. It's not just the water and the plankton; it's what's in the substrate of these intertidal bays."

So I had glaciers to thank for these oysters. And storms barreling out of the North Pacific. And spring sunlight incubating the upland algae flats. And the particles of phytoplankton and krill and whatever else made up the broth of Totten Inlet. These oysters were truly a group effort.

We ate another round of oysters. The wine, the oysters, and the night air were all the same crisp temperature. Four A.M. came and went. I marveled that I had ever worried about washing my oysters before shucking them. Here, in the dark, whatever couldn't get out of the way in time went down the hatch, and it all tasted good. I leaned my head down to within inches of the water and squinted. Squadrons of sea monkeys swirled through the light. "What are all these little things racing around?" I asked.

Joth scooped a cupful of sea in his wineglass and held it up to his headlamp. Translucent flecks whirled through the light. "Cool. They're not copepods. Amphipods, maybe?"

"Weird," said Brian. "They've got these long trailing appendages coming out of both sides. They almost look like larval fish."

"Are they little crustaceans?" Joth wondered. "Euphausiids? Krill?" They didn't like the light; they quickly curled up and dropped from the water column, clumping in the bottom like residue in an old Burgundy.

"Whatever we've got here," Brian said, "we're pretty close to the frickin' bottom of the food chain."

Which felt like a fine place to be. Joth swirled his glass and the tiny creatures spun up in a disk, whirling in the light of the headlamps like a distant galaxy. The blackness of a quiet October night settled around us as we watched this glowing microcosm, worlds within worlds, and us caught somewhere in the middle, making our lives in the endless flow.

RECIPES

LEMON MIGNONETTE GRANITA

The classic French sauce for raw oysters is mignonette, a piquant mix of shallots, red wine vinegar, and pepper. The acid cuts the salt in the oyster, which is a fine idea, and brings out a certain fruitiness. But it doesn't ride on the oyster very well, and you often end up tipping a shellful of vinegar into your mouth, which obliterates the oyster. By turning the mignonette into a granita, however—a slushy, by any other name—you can titrate your dosage much better, and at the same time keep your oyster cool with nice little iced flavor capsules that burst in your mouth. I'm not a big fan of acetic acid (vinegar)—no matter how you dress it up, it still smells like dyed Easter eggs—and prefer citric acid and tart white wine in almost all cases.

Makes enough sauce for dozens of oysters

1 shallot, peeled and finely minced
½ cup bone-dry white wine
1 teaspoon black pepper
1 lemon

1. Combine the shallot, wine, and pepper in a bowl.
2. Using a fine grater, grate the zest of the entire lemon into the bowl, being careful to avoid the bitter white pith. Then halve the lemon and juice it into the bowl. Stir.
3. Pour the mixture into a small bowl or pan, so that it is only 1 inch deep, cover it in plastic wrap, and place it in the freezer. Also place a small serving dish in the freezer to get it really cold. Every half hour, until the mixture is completely frozen, scrape the tines of a fork through it to break up the ice crystals. This is how you avoid getting a pan of solid ice. The final product should look like shaved ice. Keep it covered until serving. To

serve, scrape the granita into the cold serving dish, then spoon ¼ teaspoon of it onto each oyster.

FRIED OYSTERS IN LOW-TIDE SAUCE

Seaweed and oysters—the shore at its savory best. Add the smoky note of bonito flakes and you have an umami-fest of the first order, a sort of dream version of what tidelands might taste like. Dried seaweed, panko, and bonito flakes can be found at any good natural-foods store. Resist the urge to use tins of pre-shucked oysters here; unless they are very fresh, they'll ruin any dish they touch.

Serves 4 as an appetizer

1 ounce dried wakame or hijiki, or a mix of the two
⅓ cup rice wine vinegar
¼ cup bonito flakes (katsuobushi)
2 tablespoons honey
1 teaspoon soy sauce
¼ cup peanut or canola oil
24 oysters, shucked, drained, and patted dry
1 cup panko (Japanese bread crumbs)

1. Soak the dried seaweed in a large pot of water for 10 minutes. (It will expand greatly.) Then simmer it until softened, about 15 minutes. Remove it from the water and drain. If you're using wakame, note that the central rib can be tough, so taste one and decide whether you want to remove it. Cut the seaweed into bite-size pieces (scissors work best) and put them in a mixing bowl.

2. Pour the vinegar into a small saucepan and bring it to a simmer. Turn off the heat, then scatter the bonito flakes over the top and let it sit for 5 minutes so the flavor of the bonito flakes is absorbed by the vinegar. Remove the bonito flakes with a strainer, pressing the strainer with the back of a wooden spoon

to squeeze the vinegar back into the saucepan. Discard the bonito flakes.

3. Add the honey and soy sauce to the vinegar and stir. Taste and adjust the sweet/sour/salty ratio as you like. Pour half this sauce over the seaweed and toss.

4. Heat the oil in a large skillet over medium heat. Dredge the oysters in the panko, then fry them until they're golden on the bottom, 1½ to 2 minutes. Turn them and fry on the other side until they're golden, another minute or so.

5. Divide the seaweed onto four individual salad plates, top each with six oysters, and drizzle the remaining sauce over the top. Serve immediately.

RESOURCES

BAYWATER SWEETS

Joth Davis's own Pacific oysters, from upper Hood Canal, have an elegant balance of sweet and salty. Joth doesn't sell to retail consumers, but Baywater Sweets are mainstays at many Seattle oyster bars, including Elliott's, F.X. McRory's, and the Brooklyn Seafood, Steak, and Oyster House.

HAMA HAMA COMPANY

www.hamahamaoysters.com
888-877-5844
Here you'll find very special oysters from the Hamma Hamma* River delta in Washington state. The wide, flat, pristine delta is one of the more perfect spots on Earth for an oyster, which is why millions of wild baby oysters still choose to settle there. The growers simply manage the beds, moving the oysters to prevent overcrowding and so on. With the icy meltwater of the Olympic Mountains thundering out of the uplands, it's a beautiful spot with a palpable terroir. The oysters are big, meaty, and cucumbery, with a mild brine, thanks to that river water. A family operation since 1922, Hama Hama also sells its own pickled oysters and smoked oysters.

ISLAND CREEKS

www.islandcreekoysters.com
781-934-2028
For the record, Totten Virginicas did not win the overall competition in Providence (though they did on my score sheet). They received the highest marks for flavor, but when appearance and shuckability were factored in, they came in second to Island Creeks, classy oysters

---

* Yes, the oyster name has two m's and the river four, due to some ancient spelling schism.

grown in Duxbury Bay, Massachusetts, near where the Pilgrims landed. The bay stays unusually cold, owing to wind currents that blow the warm surface water out to sea and pull in cold ocean water from the depths to replace it. Cold, salty water makes for firm, savory oysters. Mouth-tinglingly briny, always good, and widely available, Island Creeks have become standard-bearers for *virginicas*.

TAYLOR SHELLFISH FARMS
www.taylorshellfish.com
360-426-6178
In addition to the Totten Virginicas,[*] Taylor grows another favorite of mine: Shigokus, brightly briny oysters from Willapa Bay, tumbled throughout their lives so that they stay small, deep-cupped, firm, and full of meat. Also available are Olympias, Kumamotos, Totten Inlets, Hawks Bay (Shigokus sans tumbling), and others.

---

[*] Due to two successive years of high mortality, Totten Virginicas are in short supply until 2011, when the next bumper crop should reach market size.

Fat of the Land

SLOW-RIPENED AVOCADOS, MICHOACÁN, MEXICO

*T*HERE ARE FRUITS that act like vegetables (the tomato), vegetables that act like fruits (rhubarb), and then there are fruits that act like space aliens. There you have the avocado. Cut in half, it could be a flying visitor from *The Jetsons*. This little oddball is perhaps the only fruit that has no sugar, and it doesn't even have the refreshing acidity so important to the appeal of citrus, apples, grapes, and most other fruits. What it does have, in abundance, is fat. Loads of heart-healthy, monounsaturated fat, which is what's responsible for the avocado's famously rich and creamy taste. A fully ripened avocado can have an off-the-charts oil content of 30 percent. But it can achieve such heights only in its native land.

Avocados are not actually from another planet. They are from Mexico. There they evolved untold millennia ago, and there their wild ancestors remain, populating the central Mexican highlands' forests. Occasionally their fruit makes it into markets in Mexico City. Rick Bayless, America's premier authority on Mexican cuisine, used to live in Mexico City, where he became a fan of wild avocados. "They're very small," he told me during a recent visit to Michoacán, Mexico's avocado capital. "They have a thin, edible skin, not much pulp, and lots of pit. But they have a much more concentrated flavor. It's quite nutty and herbal. The flavor just fills your mouth. That's why I sometimes introduce a nut element to guacamole, to try and re-create that."

We didn't see any wild avocados in Michoacán, nor did we expect to. With scant edible flesh, the elusive wild avocado is little more than a curiosity. Its descendants, however, are another matter. The crowning glory of avocados is the Hass variety, which is what surrounded us and what we'd come to experience in its ideal environment. Hass avocados have the richest, creamiest flavor, along with thick skins that hold up well in transport. They are one of those rare exceptions where the best-tasting variety of a fruit also happens to be the easiest to produce, which is why they are virtually the only avocado grown commercially in Mexico and the United States.*

It took people in Mexico a good eight thousand years to selectively breed the wild avocado into something with a little more meat on its bones. The archaeological record shows avocado seeds slowly transforming from the small, round, wild shape to the large egg shape of the domesticated fruit, which was prized in Mesoamerica. As Sophie Coe explains in *America's First Cuisines*: "There is good reason for the popularity of the avocado. The diet of pre-Columbian America was what we would consider low fat. The avocado is one of three fruits that contain large amounts of oil in their flesh . . . In addition to fat, avocados also contain two or three times as much protein as other fruits, and many vitamins as well."

None of this was lost on the Spanish explorers who first encountered the leathery, wrinkled, big-seeded fruit the Aztecs called *ahuacatl*, or "testicle."† In a land where calories were at a premium, the avocado was gold. "Like butter" was the typical description.

Mexicans don't dip. The idea of sweeping a tortilla chip through a bowl of either guacamole or salsa is largely an American invention, as is chunky, thick salsa that can stick to a chip. In Mexico, salsa and guacamole garnish your food. Mexicans use avocados the way Tuscans

---

* The exception is Florida, which still grows the Booth and Lula varieties. Both are distinguished by their huge size, smooth skin, and watery flavor.

† This is how it always gets translated, anyway. I suspect that "scrotum" might be more accurate.

use extra-virgin olive oil, lavishing a little over-the-top goodness onto so many dishes. That gets to the heart of the avocado's role in Mexican cuisine; think of it as the olive tree of the Americas, a long-lived, stately oil factory. The numbers are staggering. An acre of avocado trees can produce eight tons of fruit per year—twice as many as an acre of olive trees. With an average oil content of, say, 25 percent, that's four thousand pounds of fat coaxed out of an acre of land.

It's a funny strategy for a fruit tree. Plants produce fruit to entice animals to eat the fruit and inadvertently spread the seeds around, helping the plants to colonize a much wider area than could be done by gravity alone. For this plan to work, they have to make their fruit tasty. Almost every fruit plant uses sugar to do this, because sugar is cheap and effective. The simplest carbohydrate, sugar is very easy for plants to make, and it drives most animals wild. It's the standard giveaway, whether you're an apple tree or a bank teller with a basket of lollipops.

Fat, on the other hand, is costly. It's a much more complex molecule, harder to make and harder to store, but it's also a dense and valuable form of energy. So what was the avocado tree thinking, giving away such a nutritional bonanza wrapped around a gigantic seed? Well, it must have been catering to some big spenders. Gomphotheres (New World elephants), toxodons (New World rhino-hippo things), and giant ground sloths were its likely clientele. All were massive enough to benefit from the quality and quantity of calories on offer. They could have swallowed the seeds whole—and expelled them whole, too, which is essential to the avocado's plan. All went extinct about the time we showed up,* but fortunately for the avocado, we stepped into the partnership.

Like Google or Walmart, the avocado can afford to give away such generous loss leaders because it has such massive resources at

---

* Did we do it? Probably.

its disposal. It is a tree born to wealth. Riches shower it from above and nurture it from below. The highlands of Michoacán, west of Mexico City, are rimmed by towering, flat-topped, dead* volcanoes—1,350 in all. Millions of years of eruptions filled the valley with incredibly productive, high-mineral soil, and the avocado tree pumps all those nutrients into its fruit.

Such production also takes tremendous quantities of water—not a problem in this semitropical paradise. Most Americans' vision of Mexico is set by the ungodly strip that borders the States—an arid zone of vice, cacti, and desperation. But Mexico has one of the most diverse collections of climates and peoples of any country in the world. Michoacán looks more like Hawaii than like Juárez. From May to October, the mountains are drenched in storms that barrel in from the Pacific. What doesn't get sucked up by the trees trickles into the porous aquifer, resurfacing in the sparkling rivers that lace Michoacán. The fertility of the region is easily grasped in Barranca del Cupatitzio National Park, right in the heart of avocado country. Here the blue Cupatitzio ("Singing") River rises from a spring and tumbles through a jungle of banana trees and trumpet flowers. More water gushes out of hundreds of fissures in the rock cliffs lining the gorge, giving the sense of a gigantic dam about to give way. *Michoacán* means "the land of abundant fish,"† a description I couldn't argue with as I sat in an open-air restaurant atop one of those cliffs and ate a trout pulled that day from the Cupatitzio's waters.

---

* Or dead-*ish*. In 1943, a farmer in Michoacán was plowing his cornfield when he felt some tremors beneath his feet. He realized the ground was hot to the touch. He put his ear to the ground; the earth was moaning. Then, as steam began to boil out of the field, he did the sensible thing and ran like hell. Shortly after he made his escape, Paricutín, the newest volcano on Earth, blew its stack and continued erupting for nine years, burying an entire town in lava. Today, only the town's church steeple can be seen rising from the rock.

† *Michigan*, an Ojibwe word, means basically the same thing. The Ojibwe and Purépecha languages are distantly related.

All that water was, in fact, the attraction for the early inhabitants of the area. Some three thousand years ago, a mysterious people known as the Purépecha arrived by sea on the coast of Michoacán and followed the rivers into the volcanic highlands. There they found a scintillating landscape of lakes nestled between the mountains. The soil was rich, the summers gentle, the rains plentiful, the lakes full of fish, and the forests dangling with fat, green superfoods. You can see why they decided to hunker down here, and why they fought like hell to keep the Aztecs from overrunning the place. Thanks to their skill in working copper weapons and shields, they managed to repulse three Aztec invasions—the only Mesoamericans to do so. They remained unconquered when the Aztecs fell to the Spanish in 1521, though smallpox quickly accomplished what no invaders had ever managed, wiping out 90 percent of them. Today their descendants still live in a cluster of towns around Lake Pátzcuaro, their ancient rounded temples rising on the hills above the lake. They still fish from the lake and, on November 1, celebrate the Day of the Dead with an all-night candlelit vigil around their family graves and with "The Dance of the Little Old Men," in which they put on decrepit masks meant to mock the Spanish—white faces, long noses, missing teeth, scraggly hair—and limp around, seemingly on death's door, then suddenly burst into a frenzied jig meant to indicate that the indigenous spirit is still strong in the blood of the people.

Michoacán's avocado production is centered on the town of Uruapan, whose name means "the land where fruit and flowers occur at the same time"—an ideal description of the never-resting avocado. Unlike any other avocado region in the world, Michoacán has four different avocado blooms per year, with individual trees blooming twice, and it's not unusual to see fruit and flowers on the same tree. This is the kind of relaxed schedule that trees, not to mention people, can get away with in southern latitudes. With a temperature softly oscillating between eighty and fifty degrees

Fahrenheit, there is no killer frost hanging over the day planner. If they don't bloom today, they'll bloom mañana.

Ripening schedules vary tremendously in Michoacán's orchards, which range in altitude from three thousand to eight thousand feet. The multitude of microclimates means that in any given week of the year, some orchard in Michoacán is at the peak of ripeness. On a warm October day, Emiliano Escobedo, point man for Michoacán's avocado cooperative, led me up a green hillside of sixty-foot avocado trees to explain why. Like magnolias, the trees have smooth, waxy leaves and a stately Southern feel. Emiliano grabbed a low-hanging fruit, cut it open horizontally with a pocketknife, and held it out. "This is an avocado from the second bloom—what we call the *aventajada*, or 'advantaged,' bloom," he said. "Last September, it was a blossom. Now it's ready to be picked." At the end of the summer rainy season, avocados have a lot of water and not much flavor. But as the rains end and the sun shines, the trees transform all that solar energy into fat energy. Water content falls. "If there's no rain," Emiliano said, "you can go from eighteen percent oil to twenty percent in a week." Tall, thin Emiliano has a Vince Vaughn vibe and a connoisseur's taste for avocados; he can recognize certain orchards by the piney taste of their fruit, imparted by local pines that mingle in the groves and flavor the soil with their needles.

It takes an avocado about twelve months to mature, at which point it will have about 21 percent fat—the minimum standard for Mexican growers. An unripe avocado has a wet-pumpkin smell, but as it matures, flavors of pine nut and fennel emerge, along with that inimitable avocado scent, the product of rare fatty acids made by the tree. But an avocado doesn't ripen until it's picked; if left on the tree, it will continue to put on fat for an additional six months, getting richer and creamier all the time. The one in Emiliano's hand was at 24 percent fat and climbing. "This avocado can stay on the tree until May. We can pick whenever it's right, depending on the market. This is what makes Mexico unique. Because of the flexibility of our multiple blooms, we can ship fruit year-round that has high oil content," he explained.

The same cannot be said of Southern California, the other avocado powerhouse. California's avocado trees are on a temperate schedule. They bloom once per year, and peak during spring and summer. Massive irrigation from the Colorado and Sacramento Rivers is the only thing that makes California agriculture possible, and with more and more interests fighting over less and less water, California is in a state of crisis. "The question of sustainability of irrigated agriculture is perhaps exemplified in no better place than California, where different users—urban, industry, agriculture—compete for a dwindling resource," Mutlu Ozdogan, an irrigation specialist with the Center for Sustainability and the Global Environment at the University of Wisconsin-Madison, told me. "In particular, avocado farming, with its intensive water requirements, raises new concerns about the sustainability of irrigation. Each acre of avocado trees requires in excess of 1.3 million gallons of water every year. At sixty thousand acres, California's avocado industry uses the equivalent of two hundred and fifty thousand households. Are Californians ready to exchange 217 gallons of irrigation water per pound of avocado they consume?"

With water allotments slashed in recent years, California has not been able to meet the demands of the U.S. avocado market. Michoacán has picked up the slack. For years, however, Mexican avocados were barred from the U.S. market due to fears of fruit flies, despite protests from Mexican growers that they had no fruit flies. To find out, from 1997 to 2007, USDA inspectors in Michoacán sampled avocados from every crate of fruit, millions in all. No fruit flies were found. Other procedures were put in place to ensure the safety of all avocados sent to the States. The fruit must be picked while still in the tree by pickers wielding long metal poles with open sacks on one end; any avocado that hits the ground stays there.

Having jumped through every hoop, Michoacán's growers finally earned admittance and today supply most of the U.S. market. In fact, Michoacán supplies nearly half the *world's* avocados. More than 100,000 acres of avocado orchards blanket every hill in the region in verdant trees dangling hundreds of half-pound cojones.

And Michoacán's restaurants ooze cool, green creativity. In addition to the ubiquitous guacamole, there's avocado yogurt, avocado soup, and avocado salad. There's avocado-grapefruit soda and avocado margaritas to wash it all down. There's avocado Popsicles and avocado ice cream for dessert. "I have avocado in my veins!" one grower told me. My hotel stocked bottles of avocado shampoo, body lotion, and conditioner.

And as if that wasn't enough, during one intense day of creation, inspired by the bounty in the local markets,* Rick Bayless pushed the avocado to new heights, starting with a quadruple-guacamole smackdown. It's hard to improve on the Aztecs' original *ahuaca-mulli*, or "avocado sauce," made of mashed avocados, chilies, and tomatoes, but Rick gave it a run for its money. Which did I prefer? The basic guac with roasted garlic, serrano chilies, onion, and lime? The one with roasted pumpkin seeds and cilantro added? With bacon and tomato? Or with watermelon, pomegranate, and mint? Honestly, I preferred having them all, though the fruit and mint version opened up a brand-new avocado path in my brain.

Rick also used the avocado, nature's emulsifier par excellence, to thicken salsa verde and green mole. He doesn't skimp on his sauces, with good reason. "What's the first thing you learn in European cooking school?" he asked. "To make stock. Because the whole point of the cuisine is to get the flavor of meat into as many places

---

* Rick explained his excitement this way: "There's such a sense of vitality in a Mexican market. Everything is much more immediate than you find in any grocery store in the United States. In the U.S., we're always looking for shelf life in everything; here, they're looking for ripeness and flavor."

as you possibly can. In the Mexican kitchen, it's all about vegetables. The sauces and stocks are all vegetable-based. People coming from a European tradition are used to thinking of the sauce as an indulgence, but in the Mexican kitchen, that's where all the nutrition is. There's no reason not to do the standard Mexican thing, which is to cover the whole plate in sauce and provide a stack of tortillas on the side."

Sign me up. And then finish me off with a little avocado ice cream. Once you start using avocado in place of butter and cream, you realize why the Mesoamerican cultures had no need for dairy. In everything from creamy soups to decadent desserts,* avocados work like butter and can be grown using a fraction of the resources needed for dairying.

That's the perspective of Agustín Audiffred Ayala, a third-generation organic avocado grower I met. Agustín sees organic avocados as a way to create sustainable agriculture in Mexico. "The conventional farmers think they are in a two-hundred-meter race," he told me. "They don't understand that agriculture is a marathon." Some of his trees are seventy years old and still good producers, creating a canopy and root system to protect the soil. Agustín also preserves a natural forest around his orchard to help maintain the humidity of the soil and to nurture predators that feed on avocado pests. But he also respects the pests that he does have. Like many organic farmers I've spoken with, Agustín told me that the fruit with pest damage actually has more flavor than the perfect fruit. Many flavor compounds are chemicals produced by plants to ward off pests.

To make use of the avocados that fall to the ground, Agustín raises pigs. With a diet of 60 percent avocados, these pigs produce meat that's even richer than the famed Ibérico hams of Spain. The

---

* The avocado brownie, combining two Mesoamerican staples, is a beautiful thing.

pigs' manure, in turn, becomes organic compost that is returned to the trees. "It's a closed system," Agustín said proudly.

My last night in Michoacán, I got to sample the fruits of Agustín's labor. In a restored mill on the banks of the Cupatitzio River, Agustín transformed one of his prized pigs into *carnitas*. In a giant copper cauldron over an open fire, the pig was boiled in its own fat—Mexican confit—and, as is sometimes the case, a bottle of Coca-Cola, for four hours, stirred with a long wooden paddle, then fished out of the pot and heaped on a platter. I took some crackly outer bits and succulent inner strips, piled them on a fresh corn tortilla, then garnished it with salt, lime, chilies, and, of course, guacamole.

After filling a few tortillas beyond capacity, I poured a tequila and grabbed a table on the covered deck over the river. The Cupatitzio sang its sweet, laughing songs in the soft Mexican night. I regarded my plate. Most of it had been avocado at one time. The guac, the pig, the cooking fat. I clinked glasses with Agustín. A lot of him had once been avocado, too. A thirteen-piece mariachi band in tasseled uniforms ripped into an old classic, straining to be heard over a downpour thundering on the mill's tin roof. Some day in the future, maybe a thousand years, maybe a million, the volcanic gods would stir, and this land would be atomized. For now, the rain god was appeased, and the valley brimmed with riches.

RECIPES

GUACAMOLE BAR

I keep making my guac simpler and simpler. Onions, tomatoes, cilantro, chili powder? None of them actually improve the dish. Tomatoes make it watery, and what you really want from guac is a creamy density of flavor. I pared my guacamole to the basics—avocados, chilies, garlic, lime, salt—and people went crazy for it. But after living with it for a while, I decided the raw garlic was also getting in the way. You can roast your garlic on a skillet, as Rick Bayless suggests, or you can skip it. Lately I've dispensed with the chilies, too, and I'm down to a guacamole of the ultimate purity: avos, salt, lime. (Too many people really soak their guac in acid; go easy on the lime.) Of course, all this depends on having avocados of the highest quality and ripeness, because they have to carry the flavor. Once you have that, you probably won't want much else. On the other hand, variety is the spice of life, so feel free to mix it up. Make a large bowl of basic guacamole, then use that to make three or four variations and serve them all. Pitcher of margaritas on the side, of course.

Serves 6 to 8 as an appetizer

BASIC GUACAMOLE:

6 ripe avocados, peeled and pitted
juice of ½ lime
flaky sea salt, to taste

1. Mix all ingredients in a large bowl, but don't overmix. The guacamole should be mashed but still a little chunky. Serve, or add any of the following:

- ° garlic and minced chilies (or chili powder)

- ° garlic, minced chilies, and chopped orange

- ° caviar or salmon roe

- ° pine nuts and roasted garlic

- ° crumbled bacon and minced green onions

- ° minced onions and cilantro

- ° crumbled blue cheese with a sprinkle of pomegranate seeds

BERRY TARTLETS WITH AVOCADO CREAM

We could probably put half the cardiologists in America out of work if we all started using avocados instead of cream in our pastry cream. They are easier to work with, incredibly healthy, and, to me, even a little more scrumptious. They provide a nutty, herbal edge, as well as that indefinable avocado coolness. Any fruit can be used here, but I like the color contrast provided by red and black berries. I prefer my desserts only lightly sweet, which is what this is; if you have a real sweet tooth, add more honey. Make your own pastry if you're hard-core, but if you use the frozen shells, this becomes a simple yet striking dessert.

Serves 6

3 ripe avocados, peeled and pitted
12 mint leaves, 6 for the cream (optional) and 6 to garnish
3 tablespoons honey (I like clover, blueberry, or raspberry here)
1 teaspoon cider vinegar (or juice from ¼ lemon or lime)

6 small pastry shells, baked and cooled
2 cups fresh berries

1. Puree the avocados, 6 mint leaves (if using), honey, and vinegar in a food processor. The final product should have the consistency of pastry cream.
2. Remove the tops from the pastry shells (if they have them) and hollow out the interiors. Fill the shells with the avocado cream. (Do whatever you want with the tops.)
3. Top the shells with a colorful assortment of berries, garnish with a mint leaf, and serve.

RESOURCES

Slow-ripened Michoacán avocados are available in most of North America. Any avocado with an "Avocados from Mexico" sticker is likely to be from Michoacán. A few tips for picking a good one:

o   A perfectly ripe Hass avocado will have black skin, but avocados don't begin to soften until they are picked. You can ripen a hard avocado by leaving it at room temperature until its skin turns from green to black and it yields to gentle pressure.

o   Don't buy a green avocado unless its "button"—the tip of the stem—is still attached. Sometimes the button falls off an avocado when it turns black, but the remaining indentation should still be green. If the indentation is black, don't buy the avocado; it's beginning to rot.

o   Once cut open, a Hass avocado should have yellow flesh near the pit, graduating to pale green flesh near the skin. Green flesh is a sign of incomplete ripeness.

o   Avocados picked in fall, during the rainy season, are sometimes watery, while those picked in spring tend to be the richest.

The Taste of Vigor

YUKON RIVER SALMON

A FLASH OF SILVER in the leaden waters. A riffle as a back breaks the surface. Then another, and another. Soon they are everywhere, submarine streaks surging against the current, as if the river has come to life and is reversing course, heading upstream. Which it is. It's June in Alaska's Yukon Delta, a few misty miles from the Bering Sea, and, under a never-ending sun, the kings are running.

ENDURANCE

Creatures will go to great lengths to pass on their genes. They'll ram their horns against those of other suitors. They'll grow bright blue tail feathers. They'll sneak off with their friends' mates. But few animals brave the endurance test of the salmon.

Salmon begin life in redds, gravelly depressions the females make with their tails in clear-running mountain streams. The fry spend their first months in their home river before moving to a brackish estuary at the mouth and undergoing an extraordinary change, transforming their body chemistry so they can handle the salt of a marine environment. Then they head to the oceans for a feeding frenzy, feasting on small fish and krill-like crustaceans and gaining weight rapidly. After one to six years at sea, depending on the species, they mature and, again adjusting their body chemistry, return to their natal streams to spawn and die. It is this instinct and their diet of crustaceans rich in orange-red carotenoids—lots of fish eat the same crustaceans that salmon do and store the carotenoids in their skin; only salmon and trout store it in their muscle—that give salmon its unique color and flavor, the best of minerally mountain and savory sea.

Much of the fabled productivity of Alaska's forests and streams owes its fecundity to the salmon. By surging upriver each year, salmon act like conveyor belts returning millions of pounds of marine protein to the mountains, fattening bears and birds alike. The decaying carcasses, eggs, and fry feed eagles, trout, and a host of fish and forest creatures, sustaining a bounty unmatched by non-salmon waters.

In many ways, the fabulous forests of the Pacific Northwest were created by salmon. When the Ice Age relinquished its grip on the area ten thousand years ago, and its glacial fingers retreated, it unveiled a barren landscape. The millions of salmon wriggling upstream helped engender new life, as if the ocean were impregnating the land. Up to a third of the nitrogen on the valley floors of the Pacific Northwest was once salmon, and Sitka spruce along salmon streams grow three times as fast as spruce along non-salmon streams. When those spruce eventually fall across the streams, they help create the deep pools that salmon need to rest in during their spawning run. The salmon make the river, and the river makes the salmon.

There are salmon, and then there are king salmon, also known as chinook. The other four species of Pacific salmon, as well as the Atlantic salmon, a different genus, average 3 to 8 pounds. Kings average 20. The record is 126 pounds. Kings have more fat and bigger muscle fibers than other salmon. A king fillet is two inches thick, with huge, glistening flakes that slide apart gracefully. When you bite into it, your teeth sink deep, meeting just enough resistance to feel satisfyingly toothy, and your salivary glands fire as juice explodes in your mouth. It is not an experience normally associated with eating fish.

Once they begin their spawning run, salmon do not eat again.

They must swim upstream all the way to their birthplace, navigating by smell, carrying all their fuel with them in the form of fat. This means that a salmon born on a short river will have less fat and muscle than a salmon from a long river. It also means that every stream's salmon are genetically distinct, having conformed to their terroir. In *King of Fish*, David R. Montgomery explains how "river conditions can literally shape salmon . . . Deep, fast rivers have large, powerful fish, whereas small rivers have smaller, stockier fish." Montgomery quotes a fly-fisherman comparing the salmon of Norway's Laerdal River, which are "'long, taught, and compact,' with huge fins and a large tail well-suited for running up the turbulent rapids that characterize the river," with the salmon of New Brunswick's Restigouche River, which are "'full-bodied, broad, and chunky,' well-suited for life in the 'big, wide, deep, relatively slow-moving river.'"

The Yukon River is the third-longest in North America, cutting two thousand miles west from its headwaters in Canada's Yukon Territory, straight through the heart of Alaska, and out into the Bering Sea. Yukon kings and chum reverse this marathon course, swimming against the current from the Bering Sea across Alaska to Canada. To achieve this epic spawning run, they need an insane amount of fat and muscle.

Few places on Earth could provide the salmon with feeding grounds rich enough to provision them for such a journey, but the Bering Sea is one of them. Because of our terrestrial bias, we tend to think of warmer southern areas as being more productive, but those beautiful turquoise tropical seas are a desert, the color indicative of water bankrupt of plankton. Warm seas are stratified—the surface water is always the warmest, and the deepest water is the coldest. Phytoplankton, being single-celled plants, need sunlight and nutrients to thrive, but nutrients sink, so in a tropical sea most of the sunlight is at the surface while most of the nutrients are stuck on the bottom. Plankton struggle, and the water remains crystal clear.

In colder areas, however, winter chills the surface water, making it colder than the deep water. But heat rises, so in cold seas there is a seasonal "upwelling" as the colder, nutrient-poor surface waters sink and the warmer, nutrient-laden deep waters—the marine equivalent of rich soil—rise to the sunlight, triggering tremendous plankton growth. Each spring the melting ice pack retreats like a tablecloth whipped off a feast. The plankton nourishes krill-like crustaceans, which in turn feed pollock (the world's single-largest fishery), salmon, halibut, king crab, and other species, including whales and seabirds (the Bering Sea supports 80 percent of the U.S. population). These ultraproductive waters have drawn whalers and fishermen since the 1700s. And they make incomparable salmon.

Pull a Yukon king out of a net in the Yukon Delta, just as it is beginning its spawning run, and it is unbearably succulent.* It looks like a shimmering torpedo, thirty pounds of speckled black back and pearlescent sides of pink, purple, and green. Like all torpedoes, this one is built for a one-way mission. The nose cone holds the homing equipment—high-tech nostrils that can sniff out the waters of birth from a thousand others—and the sides bulge with propellant. The payload is held underneath. As it powers upriver, it deflates, incinerating fat and muscle in the fires of its mitochondria like a marathoner, the fuel gauge hitting empty just as it arrives home, the skin no longer silver but enflamed bright red, nothing left to do but blow out sperm or eggs over the gravel, give it all to the river, and die a bag of skin and bones.

---

* We can put some numbers to this. Tests done by the Oregon laboratory Bodycote in 2008 found that Yukon chum have 4.15 grams of omega-3s per 100-gram serving and Yukon kings have 4.38. That's twice the level of any other fish. Sardines (2.29), Atlantic salmon (2), coho salmon (1.96), and herring (1.71) are some of the also-rans. Nothing else is even close. Since omega-3s are the key to brain, eye, immune system, and cardiovascular health, it's safe to call Yukon salmon the healthiest food on the planet.

If you think of a river as a living thing, then the salmon are its way of renewing itself, its trick for overcoming gravity, going back to Start, and beginning again. When you taste a firm-fleshed salmon that is just oozing omega-3 fatty acids, that screams of teak and roses and macadamia nuts, it's the taste of the drive to continue. It's the taste of a river's vigor.

FISH CAMP ON THE YUKON

No river on Earth is more vigorous than the mighty Yukon. It surges thousands of miles through the roughest territory in North America, untamed and unbroken. Upstream, as it cuts through Alaska's mountain ranges, the Yukon is tightly woven, but in the delta flats it unbraids. Like some creature from mythology, the lower Yukon has hundreds of tendrils and six mouths.

I visited Emmonak, a Yupik Eskimo village that sits smack on the best salmon fishing grounds in the whole river, to get a sense of the place that had shaped this fish. To the Yupik, the salmon is everything—their food, their economy, their entertainment, their religion. Their ancestors, crossing the Bering land bridge millennia ago, chose to settle wherever the salmon fishing was good, and have not budged since. No one understands the fish like they do.

To see the Yukon, I hitched a ride upriver with Joey Kameroff and Leonard Westlock, two employees of Kwik'pak, the only fishery in Emmonak, or "Emo," as the locals call it. Up close the Yukon is brown with silt, but skipping over it at forty miles per hour in our thirty-two-foot steel Raider, the *Emo-10*, in the weird light of an Alaskan summer, it looked like a mile-wide, endless plain of beaten zinc. We passed hour after hour of unbroken alder swamp edged in driftwood from the spring floods. Bald eagles loitered on the banks. Hundreds of swans and the occasional moose scattered ahead of us, but humans had left no mark on the landscape.

Uncountable sloughs snake between the main channels, and I

was lost within minutes. But Joey, our captain, knew every slough, detouring down the ones most likely to hold moose, and every one had a Yupik name that stretched back beyond memory. Leonard didn't know the river as intimately and was there to learn the hazards from Joey.

The Yukon constantly shifts its banks, fanning the delta like a man watering his lawn. Each slough chews into one bank, caving it in, while laying down sediment on the other side. Alders are ripped into the current on one side, but new ones soon colonize the quiet side, interlocking their roots like they're playing Red Rover, waiting for someone to send the Yukon right over. They manage to capture a few feet of land before, years or decades later, the water comes back. I'd never been anywhere so formless. The spongy land was mostly water, the turgid river was thick with earth. The whole delta seemed to belong to some earlier, inchoate form of matter.

Night and day were equally boundless. The subarctic light never disappeared. The midsummer sun doesn't rise and set so much as boomerang away from a point, spinning high and far, and then come back. Around two A.M. it acquiesces to slide below the horizon for four hours. The light becomes the color of cocktail hour. And then the sun is back.

It was June, and the village was practically deserted. The pink, fleshy backbones of salmon carcasses hung in the open air all over town, drying for winter dog food. The entire town smelled like smoked salmon. But most families were at fish camp. Although there are no deeds, each family has a spot on the river that has always been theirs. A typical camp comprises a main cabin for sleeping, a smokehouse, an outhouse, a covered pavilion for filleting and air-drying salmon, and a tiny log cabin for sauna-like steam baths—until recently the only bathing in the delta.

Multiple generations and both genders attend fish camp. The men spend the days fishing, while the women clean, cut, and smoke the fish that have already been caught. The children help some but are otherwise turned loose to play along the river and listen to the elders' stories. Fish camp is the heart of Yupik culture. It's where the old ways are taught to the next generation, but it's no artifact. Salmon are the Yupik's main food. They eat it almost every day, and a family would starve in winter if they didn't preserve several hundred fish.

As we approached seventy-three-year-old Simon Harpak's camp, Joey said to me in awe, "This old man is really tough. He's not scared of bears at all. My father calls him hundred-pound-heart man, because he's so small and so tough." An instant later Joey leaned close to me and added, "Don't tell him I told you that." With his round, bald head and permanent twinkle, Harpak looked like an Eskimo Mickey Rooney. The toughness wasn't evident, but it turned out he'd killed his sixteenth grizzly bear—an Emo record— just the day before. The bear had turned up in camp, drawn by the hanging salmon, and Harpak dispatched it with his rifle before it eliminated any of the grandchildren wandering about. The first anyone in town knew about it was when they heard the call over the radio asking for help butchering it.

Harpak is one of the last surviving Yupik who managed to dodge the Jesuits and never learn English. (Up until the 1950s, the Emo missionary schools had signs that said IT IS FORBIDDEN TO SPEAK ESKIMO. Now the schools teach Yupik.) His wife translated our conversation, but some of the concepts were hard to translate. "This month was fast for elders," he said, "but us, we think it's slow. Kings Month was already passing before the ice moved. Now the new moon is here again, and when it ends, the people will be catching chum already." He was predicting a lousy season for kings but a good one for chum, a smaller species of salmon with less fat. The Yupik value chum as a subsistence food, but they look down on it the way a Burgundy *vigneron* turns up his nose at Beaujolais.

Ray Waska, the patriarch of another fish camp I visited, explained the value of fat king salmon: "When you have two or three pieces, you don't get hungry or cold for a long time. In winter, when we're going out hunting all day, we'll have some dryfish and strips with bread and tea, and that's good enough to keep you going all day."

"Dryfish" is like salmon jerky, chewy and concentrated. Its flavor approaches anchovy, but sweeter. "Strips" are long strips of salmon, skin left on one side, that are dipped in brine,* hung for a day to air-dry, and then cold-smoked over alderwood for two weeks or more. Hanging en masse in the smokehouse, they look like twisted silver-pink tinsel, and they are the most succulent, flavorful smoked salmon I've ever had. Thinking of the sushi potential of such fish, I asked Ray and Joey if they ever ate it raw, but Joey screwed up his face. "Man, I'm not *that* native!"

Ray has the biggest fish camp in the delta, and he's been as responsible as anyone in maintaining the Yupik's traditional smoked-salmon culture. "It's been our main food for generations. Some families may run out in May, but my family, we don't run out. We make sure there's enough for everybody. I have a big family, seven sons—six with wives—plus two daughters and thirty grandchildren. When we get fish, they all come over and help. We all work together, and we all share. If we know of some poor family that doesn't have anything, we'll share with them. And elders who can't fish—we share with them, too. Sometimes we'll trade with other families who have extra caribou or reindeer, or maybe fresh berries."

The Yupik have a word, *slungak*, that they translate as "coming to." It describes when awareness first blossoms in a child, when the child stops living purely in the moment and becomes aware of time and place and self and starts to lay down memories. For many Yupik, *slungak* kicks in when the kings run. Everyone in Emo has vivid

---

* The favored recipe for making the brine is to place a potato with a nail in it into a bucket of water and then to pour salt into the water until the potato floats.

memories of their first fish camp. So much is on the line, and it happens in such a short period, under a midnight sun. That gives those few weeks in June—"Kings Month"—an almost unbearable poignancy.

One night I went fishing with Billy Charles, chairman of the Yukon Delta Fisheries Development Association, and his wife, Grace. We motored to Big Eddy, a bend in the river famous for its swirling currents, which round up the salmon. "You see that riffle of dark water," Billy said, pointing. "That's where they'll be." He threw the hundred-foot net over the side in bunches while Grace inched the boat backward to keep the net taut. Rain lashed our faces, and we could see storms pounding the flat distance. The top edge of the gill net floated on white bobs while the rest dropped to form a curtain five feet deep. Whenever a bob began to bounce and disappear under the surface, Grace made a trill of deep contentment and said, to no one in particular, "Mmmm, caught a king."

Rather than a steady migration, kings move upriver in "pulses." The arrival of flocks of blue swallows in the delta presages the first pulse of salmon, known as the black-head kings for their distinctive facial markings. After a hiatus of a few days, the second pulse, the white-nose kings, moves through. Later pulses of kings are hoped for, but not guaranteed. The Yupik agree that a south wind brings the kings, though reasons differ. One man told me that a west wind (the other prevailing direction) holds the freshwater back in the channel and the salmon have more difficulty smelling it. More convincingly, Grace suggested that the south wind brings the tide in high and allows the big fish to pass over sandbars and other obstacles rather than queuing up in the few deep channels.

After a half hour of drifting and Grace's murmuring, Billy hauled in the net, calling for Grace's assistance. "Used to be able to do this alone," he said laughing. They pulled hand over hand, and a dozen shining, silvery black-head kings flopped into the bottom of the boat. "Mmmm," said Grace, "caught a king."

THE SALMON ECONOMY

Salmon is more than food for the Yupik. It is also the only economy in the isolated, roadless Yukon Delta. "There's no timber in this region," seventy-one-year-old Martin Moore told me. Moore has a classic round Emo face, an avuncular manner, a few missing teeth, and a permanent smile. "There's no gold mining. There's no other potential for earning money. Salmon is the reason for our survival from day to day. The commercial fishery has been here for over a hundred years." For decades, foreign processing barges would show up at the beginning of the season, hire the Yupik to fish and can, then disappear once the season ended. "It started out with the Japanese salting king salmon. They put it in eight-hundred-pound totes and shipped them. Then, starting in the early 1900s, we supplied the Jewish market in New York with lox. We had five canneries here. But that industry died because somebody got poisoned by botulism."

By the mid-twentieth century, most salmon fishing in the area was being done on the Bering Sea, bypassing the Yupik. The Japanese were the big players. "I remember flying over the Delta and looking down," Jack Schulteis, Kwik'pak's general manager, told me one afternoon back at the fishery headquarters. "You'd have thought there was a little city out on the water. A Japanese mothership is four hundred feet long and has a dozen hundred-foot gillnetters serving it. It's a floating factory. It cans fish, freezes fish, smokes fish, salts fish. It does everything. It can stay out for years without returning to Japan."

That style of high-seas salmon fishing was banned by the United States in 1974 when it asserted sovereignty over waters within two hundred miles of its coasts. The fishing moved upriver, where the Yupik suddenly found they had a monopoly. The only commercial fishing permits in the delta are issued to the Yupik. About seven hundred permits exist, generally handed down from father to son. By the 1990s, Emo, sitting on the biggest runs of the very best salmon on Earth, was again the center of a thriving fishery. As many as eight companies moved their processor barges into the area for the season, dwarfing the little village. Big boats can't ply the wide, shallow Yukon River and its shifting sandbars, so all the fishing was done by individual Yupik drift-netting in their flat, twenty-foot open skiffs.

"It was a circus," said Schulteis. "The competition was unbelievable. They had everything from fish-ticket bingo* to trucks being given as prizes to the fisherman who delivers the most fish in a season." Japan, where Yukon king sushi went for top dollar, drove the market, keeping the price for Yukon kings extraordinarily high. Fishermen could get five dollars a pound, meaning a single big Yukon king could bring two hundred dollars. And they could catch a hundred fish in one hour of drift-netting. "You could walk across the river there were so many fish," Schulteis said. "Right out here on this little channel, you couldn't even make a whole drift; you'd have to pull your net up because it was full. It was that good. Such a huge river, such a big watershed, such good spawning streams, wilderness, all the natural things that salmon need. This was a huge, huge run. We'd take one hundred and twenty thousand fish and they'd still get three hundred thousand fish on the spawning grounds."

Flush with cash for the first time in their people's history, Yupik fishermen invested in shiny new aluminum skiffs that could hold more fish, powerful outboards that could get them to more fishing grounds in less time, and state-of-the-art nets. Emo sprouted satellite dishes and fleets of red Honda ATVs. A lot of small changes occurred, but not many big ones. In fact, the influx of cash allowed the Yupik to keep their community intact. Young men had no reason to leave for Anchorage or the Prudhoe Bay oil fields when they could live well hunting and fishing, as their ancestors did.

---

* A game where, after every fishing period, all fishermen who have delivered fish put their names in a hat and the winner gets a thousand dollars.

Helped in part by their supreme isolation, the Yupik have done a better job than most indigenous groups of holding on to their traditional lifestyle, depending on how you define it. The props have changed—now it's outboards and snowmobiles instead of kayaks and dogsleds—but they still follow the seasonal rhythms of nomadic hunters: fish camp in late spring, berry picking in the summer, moose hunting in fall, impromptu seal and beluga hunts anytime the call goes out over the radio. Their lives are still salmon-powered, though instead of it all fueling the people and dogs directly, much now gets converted to cash and oil first.

THE DISASTER YEARS

In 1998, the king season opened on schedule. But the fish didn't show. "That was a spooky time here," Jack Schulteis said. "I remember the opening of the season. A lady pulled up with eight fish, and they looked like they'd grown up in Auschwitz." The few fish that made it back to the river were emaciated. For whatever reason, they'd been starving in the Bering Sea. Scientists still debate why.

Whatever the cause, the results were unequivocal: disappearing salmon, followed by disappearing fish buyers. The next two years, 1999 and 2000, had marginal fish runs; 2001 had virtually nothing, and the commercial season was canceled. The time became known as "the Disaster Years." A town that had briefly raised its head above the poverty level fell hard back into it. Then, in 2002, the fish came back—not at the levels of the 1990s, but enough that thirty thousand or forty thousand kings could be taken for the commercial fishery.*

---

* Numbers are tightly regulated by the Alaska Department of Fish and Game, which monitors the river with sonar and test nets. Only after enough fish have passed upriver toward the spawning grounds is the season opened. The Yukon is rated one of the best-managed fisheries in the world. Problems with the salmon runs are believed to be connected to warming trends in the Bering Sea.

By then, only one fish processor, Bering Sea Fisheries, remained near Emo, and it looked anything but stable. Bering Sea Fisheries would pay only fifty cents per pound for salmon. So, just days before the season was set to open, the Yukon Delta Fisheries Development Association—charged with fostering economic development in the region—took a radical step. It formed Kwik'pak Fisheries and cobbled together processing equipment left in the exodus during the Disaster Years. A native-owned, for-profit corporation, Kwik'pak guaranteed its fishermen a living wage for their fish ($4.45 per pound in 2007), becoming the first fair-trade fishery in the world. Not many locals took their salmon to Bering Sea Fisheries, which closed its doors in 2007.

"Kwik'pak" sounds like a cheesy marketing name for a company that guarantees to ship its fish to Anchorage the day it's caught, but the village elders who chose it were unaware of the English echo. Some of them didn't even speak English. To them, *Kwik'pak* means something like "great river" or "river of life." It is the Yukon, their universe.

Kwik'pak has the same problem that other fair-trade businesses have. If you're going to pay your workers a premium wage, you need to get a premium for your product. The fish is great in Emo, but a thousand miles by barge or bush plane can take the premium out of any product, and a Yukon king fillet, because of that oil content, is terribly delicate. If not handled properly, its flesh will turn too soft. "Soon as you catch 'em, you gotta bleed 'em and ice 'em," Ray Waska told me. "All you gotta do is take your finger and pull two or three gills and they'll bleed out. That keeps the meat firm. In the old days, they'd just throw 'em in their tote whole."

Still, no level of handling could meet Waska's high standards. "I don't understand how all these restaurants can say they've got fresh king salmon. I say no—it's been dead how many days? That's not fresh fish. Where I'm from, it's called fresh when it's still kicking when the wife is cutting it up."

On the other hand, I've found that most fish is too soft when first caught. Ice it for a day or two to let rigor mortis develop and it gets much more satisfying. A Japanese seafood buyer who stayed in my bunkhouse at Kwik'pak goes further. He insists on letting salmon fillets age for four or five days until the protein starts to dismantle and savory umami compounds form.

At the Kwik'pak bunkhouse, we grilled a thirty-pound king salmon every night. In the aisles of Whole Foods, it would have been a six-hundred-dollar fish. In this dry community at the end of one of the world's longest transport routes, it was served with plain rice, canned green beans, and powdered lemonade. After being polite at the first dinner, I ignored the sides and just ate king salmon and drank bottled water. For breakfast, it was a plate-size slab of cold king salmon and coffee. For lunch, I kept working through the leftover salmon while everyone else ate sloppy joes. They thought I was nuts. By day four I'd eaten the most expensive salmon on the planet for twelve straight meals and had foregone carbohydrates and vegetables. Dr. Atkins would have embraced me as a prodigal son. I felt immortal. I needed no sleep. My neuroreceptors lit up like a pachinko parlor. Sometimes the Yupik are referred to as the People of the Salmon, but truly, that week, if there was anyone on Earth who was the Person of the Salmon, it was me.

But what about the rest of the country? Few people in the Lower 48 had ever heard of Yukon king salmon. And that's where Jon Rowley came in.

Rowley is the marketing guru who put Copper River king salmon on the map.* Because they come from the relatively warm southeastern part of the state, Copper Rivers are the first kings to begin their spawning run in Alaska. They are a cause for celebration because they kick off the fresh salmon season. Rowley managed to

---

* And created the Pacific Oyster Wine Competition (see page 142). The guy gets around.

convince U.S. chefs to create menus around Copper River kings, and he convinced consumers to pay jaw-dropping prices to be a part of the action. The first Copper River kings of the year are now flown by Alaska Airlines to Seattle hours after they are caught. They are delicious fish, but they have nothing on Yukon Rivers. Rowley helped to let the rest of the country in on the secret.

Rowley let Seattle DJs taste Yukon and Copper River kings side by side on the air. Yukon 1, Copper River 0. Then he overnighted a prime fish to Rick Moonen, America's premier seafood chef. Moonen made his name as the chef at Oceana, in Manhattan, before starting his own restaurant. Moonen is passionate about both seafood and sustainability; it was he who turned the tide on Chilean sea bass, convincing chefs to stop serving the endangered antipodal fish. He serves only top-quality, sustainable fish at his RM Seafood in Las Vegas. Moonen fell in love with the Yukon king's unmatched richness. "It's the foie gras of the sea," he told me. "The best fish I ever ate. It's silk. Melts in your mouth."

Rowley also improved Kwik'pak's trade show presence. The Boston Seafood Show is the heavyweight event for the seafood industry. Almost every major seafood buyer in the world attends. At first, the Yupik did what made sense to them. They filled little plastic cups with pools of salmon oil, floated slabs of salmon on top, and handed them out. Somehow American buyers were not seduced. By 2007, Rowley had Jeremy Anderson, one of Seattle's best seafood chefs, cooking the kings on the trade show floor.

That was where I first encountered Yukon king salmon, lured by the aromas wafting from Jeremy's pans, and it stopped me dead. There were hundreds of booths at the trade show, seemingly half of them handing out the characterless, farmed smoked salmon that fills every supermarket in America. The center of the floor was dominated by a giant, circular booth three stories high run by Aqua Star, the Chinese farmed-shrimp behemoth, with leggy Chinese women in skimpy black dresses and killer heels handing out breaded shrimp. Authenticity was scarce. Yet at one far end of the trade show floor, there were these Yupik women in traditional flower-print dresses quietly handing out what was easily the best fish I'd ever put in my mouth, rich with nutty and flowery macadamia notes and an oystery sea flavor.

Sharing the booth with the Yupik was Jim Friedman, who has been called the Mozart of caviar. Friedman travels the Yukon, buying salmon eggs and making caviar by hand, gently pressing the egg sacs through a mesh so they'll separate without breaking. Most roe today is made by an industrial process using enzymes from crab stomachs to separate the eggs. Friedman had set up a pile of plastic spoons next to a giant vat of salmon eggs. Passersby struggled to maintain their dignity. I tried to play it cool, sneaking the occasional spoonful while chatting with Friedman, who explained that egg quality is inversely proportional to meat quality. As the female salmon travel upstream, their meat deteriorates, but their eggs fatten in preparation for deployment. The midrange of the Yukon has the best eggs.

I scooped in another mouthful and let nature's omega-3 capsules burst in my mouth while Friedman regaled me with stories of caviar barons he knew who were in jail for consumer fraud, and of wildcat caviar operations in Uruguay. "Want to know about the best caviar I ever ate?" he asked me. Yes, I did. "It was in Germany, of all places, in 1988. An old woman there told me she liked them with strawberries. I'd never heard of that. So I bought three flats of strawberries and hulled them and hollowed them out. Then I took an eight-hundred-dollar container of king salmon roe and filled all the strawberries and ate them all. It was the best thing I have ever eaten. The flavor contrast! After that, I got more strawberries and just sliced them and threw them in the tub with the eggs and ate it all with a spoon. I ate the whole eight-hundred-dollar container."

By show's end, a scrum had formed around Friedman, the Yupik, and their salmon.

GRATITUDE

The past few years have been weak runs for the Yukon salmon. Enough fish have made it to the spawning grounds to ensure the salmon's future, but very few have been available for commercial harvest. Let's hope 2011 is better, for everyone's sake. If you see a Yukon salmon in a store, pay whatever it costs. That's the price for keeping the fishery—both fish and fishermen—sustainable. When I eat a Yukon salmon, I do it with reverence and gratitude. Reverence for the muscular brown river that spawned and nurtured it, and reverence for the cold, primordial soup of the Bering Sea that fattened it with years of oceanic essence. Maybe this fish was caught by Joey Kameroff, or Ray Waska, or Billy and Grace Charles, or maybe it was caught by a fisherman I don't know. Either way, I'm full of gratitude to the strong-shouldered Yupik who hauled it out of the net by hand, to Kwik'pak for making sure my money gets back into those hands, to the Alaska Department of Fish and Game for making sure the fish make it to their spawning streams year after year, and, most of all, to the fish itself, for having the drive to continue.

RECIPES

SLOW-ROASTED SALMON

When you have a really rich salmon, like Yukon or Copper River, grilling can be a mistake, unless you get a thrill from grease fires. Slow roasting at a moderate temperature, however, as Rick Moonen taught me when we were up in Alaska, gives you a meltingly soft salmon with the most concentrated flavor. It basically bastes itself. The bright volatility of coriander and mint, and a splash of acid at the end, help cut the fattiness. Serve simply, with fresh bread, green leaves in any form, and a rich and minerally white wine such as Riesling. Despite much hype, I've never found Pinot Noir to be a good match for salmon.

Serves 4 to 6

2 pounds salmon fillets
salt
1 tablespoon ground coriander
2 tablespoons chopped fresh mint
wedges of lime or balsamic vinegar

1. Preheat the oven to 300 degrees.
2. Place the fillets on an aluminum-foil-covered baking pan (for easy cleanup). Dust with the salt and coriander. Let them sit while the oven warms.
3. Roast the salmon for 30 to 40 minutes, depending on how rare you want it.
4. Remove the fillets from the oven, sprinkle them with mint and the lime or vinegar, and serve.

MISO-BROILED SALMON

Once, in the middle of a four-hundred-year-old Japanese garden in Tokyo, I stumbled upon a teppanyaki restaurant hidden amid the carp ponds and bamboo. I plunked myself down at a table with a built-in griddle, and a chef emerged from nowhere and made the most delightful salmon right in front of me, paying special attention to the skin, which he fried separately until crisp. Ever since, I've stopped ignoring salmon skin, which, when crispy, can be the best part of all.

Serves 4 to 6

½ cup red miso
¼ cup maple syrup
2 pounds salmon fillets, cut into 2-inch-thick slabs
1 lime, cut into wedges

1. Combine the miso and maple syrup in a small saucepan and warm over medium heat, stirring, until the sauce is smooth and silky.
2. Paint the sauce over the fillets and marinate them in the refrigerator for at least an hour and ideally overnight.
3. Preheat the broiler.
4. Place the fish slabs on their sides on a broiler pan about 3 inches from the heat. Broil them until they're browned and crispy, about 4 minutes. Flip them and broil until the other side is crispy, about 3 minutes.
5. Serve immediately with the lime wedges.

RESOURCES

FISHEX

www.fishex.com

888-926-3474

Kwik'pak Fisheries doesn't sell retail, but it recommends FishEx, an online source for its fish and other premium Alaska seafood. While ordering your Yukon salmon fillets, you can load up on reindeer sausage, too. (Whole Foods is another excellent outlet for Yukon Delta salmon.)

KWIK'PAK FISHERIES

www.kwikpakfisheries.com

This is a great site for information on Yukon River salmon and the Yupik communities of the Yukon Delta.

The Farm Girl and the Pole Dancer

WINES WITHOUT MAKEUP, CALIFORNIA

IN 2007, THE Teutonic wine importer Terry Theise published a letter in *The Art of Eating* in response to an article by Derrick Schneider titled "What Does It Mean Now That a Winemaker Can Select the Structure of a Wine?" "It means," Theise replied, "that, if we accept any manipulation that materially falsifies the 'structure' and flavor of a wine, we change—ineluctably—our relationship to wine. It becomes yet another thing that we demand must please us, must entertain us, must ensure that we are never bored and never fearful that nature might do something we won't like. Such manipulation insists that wine has no other function than to dance for us like a stripper on a pole."

Well. What Theise is so worked up about is that much of the wine you drink is not the spontaneous creation of grapes and yeast the label might lead you to believe. It may have been altered with spinning cones or reverse-osmosis machines and micro-oxygenation. It may have been enhanced with tannins, acids, enzymes, or wood chips. It may have been doctored with milk, egg, or fish proteins. It may have been souped up with Mega Purple or Ultra Red. It is the market-tested product of a lab.

Hence Theise's rant. I like that it stresses *relationship*. Does wine have a function other than to dance for us? I believe so. We dip into every glass with the hope, rarely fulfilled, that profundity and pleasure await, that some vineyard's soul will be revealed to us. This is why we are willing to pay such foolish sums for 750 milliliters of sour juice.

But let's face it, most wines are simply offering you a lap dance for your twenty bucks. They know what you like, because they've seen your kind before. In fact, they probably know a lot more about what you like than you do. They are pros, after all; they know how to put a smile on men's and women's faces. You may think you're different, special, but once that cork comes out, well, your pleasure centers fire the same as anyone else's.

And what's wrong with that? What's wrong with a nice, straightforward transaction, twenty bucks for a half hour of foggy delight?

Nothing at all. Except . . . maybe you're different. Maybe you're one of the people who found your first exotic performance compelling, but then, after three or four such experiences, you started to recognize the moves. You could almost see them coming. And what had once seemed like a no-holds display of nature's glory suddenly started to feel a little . . . programmed.

Not everyone is like this. Most people want the same experience from a wine, every time. In fact, if any of the standard moves are left out, they feel cheated. To them, that *is* the relationship. I've disappointed a lot of these people by serving them red wines that didn't follow the script. They certainly didn't have the 38DDs so many people have come to believe are natural in red wine.[*] These wines may have been light-bodied, they may even have had a little awkwardness, and they didn't always reveal much on cue. The reaction by my guests was predictable: Man, is that it?

So much of it has to do with expectations. I won't claim I'm immune to the charms of a well-choreographed wine. But there are

---

[*] Initially I intended to keep this metaphor gender-neutral, but that would have been painfully clunky. I could contort these paragraphs into a paragon of politically correct neutrality, I could decry the objectification of strippers, I could even summon the dreaded *s/he*, but you wouldn't want me to do that. The fact that you are reading this means that you are a reader of books and, as such, one of the last human beings still capable of complex thought. So I'm counting on you to apply your great mind to the metaphor and bend it to suit your tastes.

pole dancers, and then there are pole dancers. There are the six-dollar Australians found at every corner store who have just one service to offer and they do it fast, reliably, and without finesse. And if you think that's what the experience is all about—if you've never known anything else—then you'll probably be satisfied.

Then there are the high-priced French ones, infinitely more complex. So captivating, so classy, and seemingly so natural. If you could see where they started, however, you'd realize they've had a lot more work done than you think.* But it was done by the top ma-nipulators in the field, who know how to hide their tracks. Thirty years ago, the predecessors of this new wave of French stars were indeed all-natural, but that kind of body just doesn't cut it anymore.

There, in a nutshell, is the current debate roiling the wine world. Natural wines versus manipulated ones. Wines with the body and structure that God gave them versus wines that have been nipped, tucked, and enhanced. Quite a few wine geeks declare their preference for natural wines—wines that show off their terroir, wines without makeup—while unwittingly choosing wines that are as caked as a Texas socialite. We're all suckers at heart.

Yet the memorable wines, the ones that stay with me, aren't trying to be attractive. More girl-next-door than performer, they are quirky and sometimes even flawed from a conventional perspec-tive. They just are what they are. These are the wines to engage. You won't get a striptease out of them, but you may discover something genuinely lovely. You may even luck into a steady relationship.

MONSTER IN A BOTTLE

When people talk about the structure of wine, they mean the sug-ars, acids, alcohols, and tannins that form its scaffolding and sup-port its more ethereal aromas. The sugar and alcohol are two halves

---

* French winemakers refer to this work as *maquillage*, "makeup."

of the same coin. If left to their own devices, yeast, the single-celled fungi that eat the sugar in grape juice and convert it to alcohol, will eat all the sugar, making dry wine. Winemakers who want to preserve some sweetness in their wine must kill or filter the yeast at the right moment, before the fermentation is complete.

But even wines that have no sugar in them can come across as slightly sweet, thanks to glycerol, a natural by-product of fermentation that tastes about half as sweet as sugar. A thick and slippery liquid, glycerol has a viscosity that enhances a wine's body—its tactile sense of substantialness. Warm, sunny growing regions—like most of California and Australia—tend to make wine with lots of glycerol. It's one reason why so many New World wines feel thicker and less dry than their Old World analogues.

In practice, people's perception of "dry" has as much to do with acid as it does with sugar. For example, an orange and a honeydew melon have similar concentrations of sugar, but the melon seems sweeter because it has only one sixth the acidity of the orange. Acid has a sharp, piercing taste (think lemon or lime), which makes foods and drinks refreshing and "bright." Without acid, lemonade would taste unbearably cloying, and the same is true for many wines. Grapes make more acid in cold climates, which is why wines from northern France and Germany, or from mountain vineyards, tend to have more zing.

A wine's body is also enhanced by tannins—molecules that link proteins together into a mesh. Tannins, which are found in red grape skins, apple skins, tea, coffee, and chocolate, begin attaching to the cells in our mouths as soon as they enter, which is where that astringent, sandpapery feeling comes from. They'll also snare molecules in the drinks themselves, giving a feeling of thickness to the liquid and holding aroma molecules in suspension. Tannins are why red wine seems so much more intense than white wine. They are also bitter, so too many tannins can make a wine unpleasant, like tea that has steeped too long.

Alcohol conveys certain flavors and adds body while helping to buffer the attack of tannins and acids, smoothing out the wine. Too little alcohol can make a wine taste biting. Yet too much alcohol prevents fruity aroma molecules from escaping into the air (and your nose) and tastes hot. Medium levels allow a wine full expression.

There you have the basic structure of wine. Why would a winemaker want to alter it? Originally the surgery was more reconstructive than cosmetic. Most places, in most years, do not naturally produce beautifully balanced wine, so techniques were invented to correct defects.

Most of northern Europe, for example, naturally produces wine that is thin and nasty. This is what happens when you grow grapes in the cool drizzle at the same latitude as Newfoundland. The sunnier the climate, the more sugar grapes will make. The cooler the weather, the more acid they will retain. On the other hand, the achievement of "physiological ripeness"—the seeds mature, desirable tannins and aroma compounds form, and astringent or unripe flavors diminish—always occurs in the fall, fairly independently of weather.* In a typical year, northern Europe experiences a relatively cool and cloudy summer, followed by a notoriously rainy late fall. Under such conditions, grapes struggle to make much sugar. The challenge for winemakers has always been to let the grapes hang on the vine as long as possible, to produce maximum sugar and to achieve physiological ripeness, yet to get them picked before the fall rains (or frosts) come. This is why vintage has always been such an important consideration with European wines. Many years just don't cooperate. Either the grapes have to be picked early, when they are still low in sugar and unripe—meaning low-alcohol, acidic, and astringent wines—or the grapes are diluted by fall rains, meaning low-alcohol *and* low-flavor wines. The exceptions to the

---

* All this is the grape's way of keeping itself inedible until its seeds are mature and ready for distribution.

rule—great years when the weather has broken just right, or great estates that have managed to make good wine even in poor years—have been rightfully celebrated.

The traditional solution to underripe wines has been to add sugar. This method was popularized in an 1803 French government booklet by Jean-Antoine-Claude Chaptal, who later became Napoleon's minister of the interior. Adding sugar to the juice before fermentation doesn't sweeten the wine, because yeasts convert all the extra sugar to alcohol; it simply raises the alcohol level and buffers the sourness. Chaptalization, as the technique is called, is perfectly legal in Europe and is, in fact, standard practice in more wines than you'd think.

Chaptalization isn't allowed in California wines, nor would any California winemaker dream of such a move. Getting enough sugar into their grapes isn't the issue; keeping sugar *out* is. Thank California's warm and sunny climate. True, Mark Twain famously complained that the coldest winter he ever spent was a summer in San Francisco, but if you move just one mountain range inland, the fog is firmly walled off on the Pacific side and the days burn bright and hot. So bright and hot, in fact, that by the time the region's grapes reach physiological ripeness in fall, their sugar levels are off the charts and their acidity is almost nonexistent. If California* winemakers pick early, when sugar levels are lower, the grapes are still full of "green," unripe flavors. If the winemakers wait for physiological ripeness (which almost all of them do), the grapes will produce fat, unrefreshing, and wildly alcoholic wines with a cooked or a tropical fruit flavor. California wines routinely ferment to an unpleasantly hot 17 percent alcohol or even higher, versus the 12 to 13 percent traditional in Europe.

And this is where reverse osmosis comes in. The wine is shipped to a laboratory, where it is passed across fine filters that separate the

---

* This applies to Australia, too.

water and alcohol from the solids. The alcohol is cooked off in a
still, then the water and some of the alcohol is reincorporated with
the solids. The winemakers taste the wine at a variety of alcohol
levels to find its "sweet spot." Alcohol can also be removed by using
centrifuges called spinning cones. About half the wineries in California manipulate their alcohol levels in some way. In Europe, they
use reverse osmosis to fix their age-old problem of thin wine, re-
moving water instead of alcohol.

This is the kind of information that freaks out some wine
drinkers. Even if its flavor has been improved, wine that has been
dismembered in a laboratory, and then, like Frankenstein's monster,
reassembled, is not what most people think they are paying for.

And that's just the tip of the iceberg. To deal with the flabby,
jamlike qualities, winemakers often add a shot of acid to the juice
before it ferments. Other wines that are aggressively acidic receive
bacteria that transform malic acid (the sharp acid in apples) into
lactic acid (the gentle acid in yogurt). Pinot Noir, which tends to
be pale in color, also sometimes gets a dose of Mega Purple, a kind
of grape juice concentrate that gives the wines the plush look that
sells.* Many red wines receive enzymes that help break down grape
skins and pull more of their color and flavor molecules into the
wine.

The milk, egg, and fish proteins I mentioned at the beginning
of this chapter? Traditional fining agents, used for centuries.† When
these are thrown into a wine, other particles stick to them; and once
the clumps are heavy enough, they fall to the bottom of the tank. This
clears the wine of its natural haze and removes some harsh-tasting

---

* And turns your teeth black. Either the enamel on my teeth is getting thinner
  or wines are getting darker—probably both.
† There are worse ones. Ox blood, poured right into the vat, was commonly used
  in Europe until being banned in 1987, which gives a whole new feeling to those
  oh-so-eighties bottles of Sangre de Toro with the little plastic bull hanging
  around the neck.

tannins, but it also removes some exciting ones. Unfined and unfiltered wines are full of unexpected twists.

Another way to deal with those harsh tannins is to micro-oxygenate, which involves percolating microscopic air bubbles through the wine. This softens the tannins in an accelerated version of the oxygen-induced aging that normally happens over years in the bottle.

Then, of course, there are the designer yeasts. The discovery that most of the fruity flavors in wines are by-products made by yeast, and that different yeasts make very different flavors,* led to the isolation of those yeasts in labs. Today yeast companies offer hundreds of strains, and winemakers can order yeasts that produce flavors of flowers, coconut, citrus, passion fruit, cream, spice, and so on. It's not quite like flavoring the wine directly, but it's close. Today a minority of wineries still use the indigenous yeasts on the grapes and in the winery to ferment their wines. Everyone else kills the indigenous yeasts with sulfur to clear the way for the added yeast. My hunch is that the terroirs of European wines owe as much to the unique strains of yeast that have adapted to each particular microclimate as they do to the soil, and that their decline is a tragic loss.

The least controversial additive is oak. Oak barrels first became popular for aging wine during the Roman Empire. Chemical compounds that leach out of the wood give the wine buttery, vanilla flavors that most people love.† And because oak barrels are not entirely airtight, they allow just enough oxygen to get at the wine to soften its tannins. But oak barrels, which come from century-old trees, are very expensive, so most wineries now age their wines in

---

* The ultimate proof of this is sake, which Harold McGee describes in *On Food and Cooking* as "the flavor of fermentation itself." Sake's tremendous variety derives from the different yeasts used.

† The taste of cheap Chardonnay in America has become predominantly the taste of oak, with the wine itself adding mere background flavors.

stainless steel tanks and add oak chips. The chips float on top and impart more vanilla flavor than a barrel can, though they don't provide the oxygenation, which is where micro-oxygenation comes in.

I could go on, but you get the idea. Few wines make it through the chop shop untouched. Yet none of this is revealed by the label. Wine is not, according to the U.S. government, a food, so the Food and Drug Administration has no jurisdiction over it. The Alcohol and Tobacco Tax and Trade Bureau, which has never been big on ingredients lists, does. The only thing a wine label need reveal is the presence of sulfites, which are added to all but organic wines.*

There is a movement to require wineries to come clean on the label. It would look something like this: "Ingredients: Grapes, selected yeasts, tartaric acid, grape juice concentrate, pectinase, lactobacillus bacteria, and sulfur dioxide." It'll never happen, because, for many wine consumers, nature is at least part of the selling point. Labels will continue to extol the glories of sun, slope, and soil.† And wineries

---

* Additional low levels of sulfites are naturally present in all wines. And, contrary to popular belief, more sulfites are added to white wines than to red wines.

† Here's the label I'd *really* like to see: "At Wacky Wallaby Wines, our lifeblood is selling wines in the United States at $5.99 a bottle. A couple of years ago we tried raising our price to $6.99, but we lost market share to Chile, so $5.99 it is. To survive at that price point, we scour Australia for the cheapest grapes we can find, and we buy them in massive quantities, which allows us to really shaft the growers for every nickel. All those grapes come from vineyards that maximize yield, meaning there isn't a whole lot in them other than sugar and water. Unsurprisingly, these grapes tend to make wine that tastes like Hi-C with grain alcohol sprinkled over the top. But here's where we at Wacky Wallaby go the extra mile so that you, the consumer, can have drinkable wine for the price of a Double Whopper meal deal. We start by dusting the juice with powdered acid, the better to approximate the fresh juiciness of Hi-C, plus a quick shot of Ultra Red to give it the inky blackness that usually only comes from low-yielding, expensive vines. Next we order a yeast, developed in Australia's finest lab, that gives the aromas of jam and chocolate to red wines. (Taste tests have shown that you, the consumer, really, really like anything that tastes like chocolate.) We use sulfites to kill any indigenous yeasts in the juice (indigenous

will continue to manipulate their wines to suit the market. Admittedly, all wine is a manipulation at some level. Grapes don't spontaneously transform themselves into wine without human intervention. Somebody has to pick them, crush them, and put them in oak barrels or stainless steel tanks, neither of which occur naturally. So where do you draw the line?

Lots of people have tried, in lots of different places, but this may be one of those examples of mission creep where there is no obvious place to stop. If this German wine would come out too thin and harsh for anyone to drink, why not throw a little sugar in? If four out of five consumers prefer this California Chardonnay with a little extra acid in it, why not? While you're fixing my deviated septum, why not add a little retroussé curl?

Hey, if it makes winemakers and wine drinkers happy, go for it. (Although not coming clean on the label seems awfully cynical.) What it does, though, to bring us back to Terry Theise's complaint,

---

† *cont'd.*

yeasts can be *so* unpredictable), then add the choco-yeast and ferment the juice. The resulting wine is wildly alcoholic because the sugar content of the grapes is so high (hey, that's what happens when you grow vines in a desert!), so we throw it in the ol' reverse-ossy and remove enough alcohol to drop it to a drinkable 14 percent. We could go further, but you, the consumer, have shown that you like to get hammered. Independent studies have also shown that you actually prefer the taste of Hi-C to that of wine, so our next move is to push the flavor profile in that direction. To soften that rough, tannic taste of red wine skins, we micro-oxygenate. The same thing would happen naturally if we stuck the wine in our cellar and let it age for six years, but we at Wacky Wallaby have to service our debt long before then, so micro-oxygenate it is. Next, we shovel mountains of wood chips into the vat to give a vanilla flavor. And you, the consumer, have shown that the only flavor you like even more than chocolate is vanilla. You like it in everything, and, much to even our shock, you like more than we ever could have imagined. So on those rare occasions when we suffer an attack of standards and consider stopping, we remind ourselves that wineries are going under right and left, and we start shoveling wood chips again. Our commitment to you, the consumer, is that we will follow you to the vanilla-candle-scented ends of the earth if it makes you happy!"

is to constrict the definition of beauty in wine. Supermarket shelves groan with bottles of wine that could have been churned out of the same factory (and often were). These wines will not surprise you. They will ask virtually nothing of you. You've paid your money, so just sit back. The show is about to begin.

Those of us who still like a little mystery in our lives, who are captivated when we don't know what the hell to make of a wine at first meeting, should not give up hope. California is still full of weird and wonderful wines that have been allowed to be themselves. The state has some of the most diverse terrain of any place on Earth. Some of those sites can make achingly beautiful wine that has something unique to say. And in one such spot, a man is gambling his fortune that if he lets his wine say any damn thing it pleases, the result might be poetry.

THE QUEST FOR CALIFORNIA COOL

Randall Grahm has made plenty of wines that could bust a move— "wines that were pleasing, harmonious, and gave a certain intellectual frisson," as he puts it. You probably know some of them. Pacific Rim Riesling, for example. Or Cardinal Zin, with Ralph Steadman's unhinged cleric on the label. Or, most famously, Big House Red, with the prison on the front and the "yadda yadda yadda" mock copy on the back. The only thing these wines have in common, other than the fact that they are perfectly tasty, is their loony labels.

Grahm got his start with a postcollege job in a Beverly Hills wine store, which gave him "the opportunity to taste an ungodly number of great French wines." From that he developed a reverence for the classics, with their balance, complexity, and strong sense of place. With some family money, he purchased property in the Santa Cruz mountains, planted vines, and set out to make "the Great American Pinot Noir." Pinot Noir, the source of all red Burgundy,

can make wines of unparalleled aromatic elegance that are the holy grail for many winemakers, but it is also the moodiest of grapes. Anywhere unlike its cool Burgundy home, it tends to disappoint. In California's Santa Cruz mountains, Grahm had a Mediterranean microclimate on his hands. His Pinot was not pretty, so he re-planted the vineyard with grape varieties used in France's hot and dusty southern Rhône region. The wine that put his Bonny Doon Vineyard on the map was Le Cigare Volant, a stand-in for Châteauneuf-du-Pape, the explosive Rhône red. First released in 1986, at a time when most American wine drinkers were unfamiliar with any grapes other than Cabernet Sauvignon and Chardonnay, Le Cigare Volant sports an archetypal French wine label: a château, neat rows of vineyards, poplar trees. Yet what is that thing floating in over the trees and shining a red ray on the estate? It's the epony-mous Flying Cigar, a sort of wooden dirigible, and it pretty much sets the tone for Bonny Doon's position vis-à-vis wine: fascination with the tradition, spiked with irreverence toward the baloney that generally accompanies it.*

Bonny Doon was something new in the bland American wine scene of the 1980s, and critics and consumers noticed. Yet every-thing changed in the early 1990s, when the Bonny Doon Vineyard was permanently ruined by an incurable bacteria infection called Pierce's disease that is carried by the blue-green sharpshooter, which is not Cupid's evil twin, spreading melancholy, but a type of insect. Grahm continued to make Le Cigare Volant by buying good grapes from other vineyards. Yet he was deeply scarred by the loss. The les-son he took was to turn his back on terroir, to protect himself by not

---

* Grahm was having fun with a quirky bit of Châteauneuf-du-Pape history. In 1954 a cigar-shaped UFO was reported by multiple witnesses in the area. The farsighted village council passed an ordinance banning the landing of any such "flying cigars" in the town's vineyards. Though the law has apparently never been violated, the incident continues to be immortalized on the label of Bonny Doon's signature wine.

getting rooted. If you stay unattached, you have nothing to lose. Instead of committing himself to a single vineyard, Grahm played the field, experimenting with a dizzying and ever-changing assortment of sources, grape varieties, and techniques, always ready to bail at the first sign of trouble.

Grahm became a master of blending and of using emerging technology to achieve the flavors he wanted. He used every trick in the book, and invented some more. (Adding ground-up stones to the wine to impart minerality is one of my favorites.) Above all, he became a master marketer, using gonzo labels and publicity stunts to get attention for his wines, but also always managing to stay half a step ahead of the industry and to give the public exactly the wine and overall package it hadn't quite realized it was ready for. He made a lot of money.

Most people don't realize how much Randall Grahm has influenced their wine life. If your wine has a jokey label, you can thank Grahm for taking the starch out of the industry. (At first, distributors balked at his designs.) Big House Red was the first affordable Côtes du Rhône imitator on the market; today shelves are filled with others. Bonny Doon was also the first major winery to embrace the screwcap. Its sacrilegious attitude made it more and more enemies in the wine trade,[*] even as it delighted consumers.

Yet Grahm himself was not delighted. Never has a winemaker been so publicly ambivalent about his own product. In a speech at the 2001 International Pinot Noir Celebration, he said, "When I taste my own wines and compare them to their Old World counterparts, I become slightly nauseous. My wines strike me as simple, puerile. Yes, they have tons of fruit and soft tannins and they're easy

---

[*] Or perhaps it was because Grahm populated Hell with them—by name!—in an epic spoof of Dante titled *The Vinferno*. Robert Parker, for instance, is depicted being devoured by Satan himself, who scribbles in his tasting notes, "Rather fleshy 'round the middle, with a huge and complete nose."

to like, but they are puppy-dog wines. I ask myself every day, 'When will the world wise up, figure out that my wines and I are a total sham and take their business elsewhere?'"*

In 2003, at the age of fifty, Grahm's life was pleasantly jolted. He had a daughter. Shortly after that came an unpleasant jolt. An attack of osteomyelitis, a severe bone infection, put him in a brace for three months. With time and reason to reflect, he realized that making wines that were clever impersonations was leaving him seriously unfulfilled. (A quick glance over the remarkable angst vented in ten years' worth of Bonny Doon newsletters would have confirmed the notion.) While such wines could be stylish, he wrote in a 2009 newsletter, they "carry with them the great limitations of the human intelligence. They often rely upon the most up-to-date winemaking technology and the winemaker's bag-o'-tricks to create their stylistic effects." These are the exact wines that drive Terry Theise nuts. And Randall Grahm did not want them to be his legacy.

What he wanted to make—what he had always wanted to make—were *vins de terroir*. "To my thinking," he writes, "this represents wine's most sublime possibility. If a *vigneron* (wine-grower, not winemaker!) has the wit to identify a wonderful site capable of elegantly solving a vine's environmental imperatives—water, light, heat, fertility, air drainage, etc.—in a Three Bears kind of way— neither too much, too little, but rather just right—said wine-grower may be given the opportunity to participate in the creation of a wine of real originality. A *vin de terroir* is one that has captured the absolute uniqueness of a given grape-growing site and the unique qualities of a vintage year; its singularity and congruity to its place of

---

* This speech, and many of Grahm's other writings, can be found in his magnum opus, *Been Doon So Long* (University of California Press, 2009), a book that confirms his place as the James Joyce of winemakers—verbally gifted, intellectually restless, yet tortured by self-imposed exile from his own soil.

origin is what is treasured above adherence to the agora's stylistic predilections *du jour.*"

Love it or leave it, a *vin de terroir* dances only for itself. But how do you create such a wine?

For starters, you scrub your karma. Like a monk preparing for spiritual purification, Grahm stripped down. He sold the Big House and Cardinal Zin brands, spun off Pacific Rim into a separate company based in Washington state, and pared the number of wines he made from thirty-five to ten.

Next, you put down some roots. Grahm became focused almost exclusively on wines made from a single vineyard. "We are terroir seekers," Bonny Doon's new flyer avows. "The vitality is present in the wine; it is now a matter to polish and to refine and eventually to reveal the wine's inherent terroir."

To do that, Grahm renounced his tricks. No more microoxygenation, no more alcohol adjustment, no more added tannins or acids. In a move that made the industry profoundly nervous, he began listing all ingredients used in the wine and the winemaking process on his labels.

Beginning in 2004, he began converting the one vineyard he actually owned, Ca' del Solo,* in the Salinas Valley east of Monterey Bay, to biodynamic farming: no more pesticides, herbicides, fumigants, or chemical fertilizer. And he asked the other vineyards he continued to work with to do the same.

Biodynamic farming, a holistic approach first articulated by Rudolf Steiner, is often described as "beyond organic," but that doesn't do it justice. Rather than simply eschewing the use of chemical fertilizers, pesticides, and so on, biodynamic farming views the soil as a living entity and seeks to promote its vitality. This means not poisoning it with chemicals, but it also means adding certain micronutrient "vitamins" for the microorganisms that comprise the

---

* "Home alone."

life force of the soil, and doing so in conjunction with the cosmic calendar (sun, moon, stars, planets) and the seasons. It can get downright kooky. Some of the mixtures added to the soil include quartz crystals and stinging nettles. "Preparation 500," the subject of much snickering in certain quarters, involves stuffing manure into a cow horn, burying it on the fall equinox, digging it up six months later, making a "tea" out of the compost, and sprinkling it over one's land.

For whatever reason, it seems to work, or so think a surprising number of top European wineries that have embraced the practice. All they care about are results: Biodynamic wines tend to be more complex, to be more subtle, and to be filled with quiet surprises that could never have been drawn up by a human designer.

Grahm is convinced that biodynamic practices are the key to developing California wines that have the depth and elegance of the best Old World ones. Partly this is because the practices promote the health of the vines' symbiotic mycorrhizae—or "microbial demiurges," as he calls them. Virtually all plant species have symbiotic partnerships with these microscopic fungi, which live on the plants' roots and are much better than the roots at taking up water and minerals from the soil. In exchange, the plants provide sugars to the mycorrhizae. Grapevines with flourishing mycorrhizae will thus absorb more and different minerals than grapevines in vineyards where mycorrhizae have been damaged by chemicals.

A second attraction of biodynamics is that it forces vines to work harder for their food. Just like livestock or teenagers, when plants get all the food and water they need delivered right at their feet via fertilizer and irrigation, they get lazy. They don't send their roots deep into the earth in search of nutrients, and they don't develop relationships with mycorrhizae and other soil life. They become susceptible to disease, and they lack complexity.

It's the factory model of farming: nitrogen, potassium, pesticides, and water go in one end of the machine, and grapes come out the other. It works fine if all you want from your grapes are sugar and fruity flavors—if all you want are "painfully pleasant" wines, as Grahm calls them—but not if you want something deeper. And it's the same mistake we keep making in so many arenas: Once we learn the basics of how a system works, we assume we know everything; anything we can't measure or fit into the equation must not exist. Only much later do we start to discover that we've hopelessly oversimplified things and missed vital pieces of the puzzle.

Instead of this factory model, biodynamics sees farming as managing a kind of dialogue between plants, animals, soil, and people. Each member of the partnership responds to the others. And biodynamic winemaking seeks to capture that dialogue in a bottle. That is terroir—the natural rhythms that emerge from a place, which we can detect with our senses, and which, just for an instant, allow us to perceive some of the underlying principles of existence.

"The experience of a *vin de terroir*," Grahm writes, "floods us with associations, memories, and emotions linked to something beyond our direct experience—to archetypal forms that seem to antedate our individual short-term tenures on this earth. Maybe what we experience is the sense of mirrors within mirrors—the knowledge that the golden ratios that obtain in musical scales, in the figures of regular polygons, and in starfish are the same ones that describe the geometry of our bones and our cathedrals and condition our ability to create order out of the seemingly chaotic universe that comprises our world. A *vin de terroir* carries the strong imprint of Nature's greatest ideas—which are undoubtedly particularly felicitous ratios."

The first biodynamically certified wines from Ca' del Solo were released in 2008. What remarkably different wines they are. Eschewing conventional American beauty standards, they hearken back to something that hasn't been seen too often in California in decades. They might not fit in glossy magazine spreads, but if you find a certain elegance in all nature's truths, they are beautiful indeed. The

Albariño, for example, embodies the cold, clean smell of river stones. Those used to the gawky assembly-list style of New World wines (Vanilla? Check. Fruity esters? Check. Softened acids? Check) might be taken aback by its Zen stillness.

In contrast, there is nothing still about the Nebbiolo. True to form, it tries to drive you away with sharp tannins and acids—an unusual combination in a red wine, which is why the recommendation with Barolo and Barbaresco, the two famed Italian wines made from the Nebbiolo grape, is to leave them alone in the cellar for ten years until they've had a chance to calm down. But I love young Nebbiolo's spirit and the way it makes your cheek and gum squeak together.

I was once arguing with a Mexican friend about hot chilies. A little spice is nice, I said, but mind-blowing spice just prevents you from actually tasting your food. He suggested maybe I hadn't taken things far enough. Once the wave of spice rolls over you, he said, it knocks you out of your comfort zone and reawakens your perception. Like a vision quest, after the discomfort, something sublime emerges. Nebbiolo's tannins work the same way. Waves of deliciousness tend to arrive on their heels. In the case of Bonny Doon's Nebbiolo, that deliciousness includes Darjeeling tea flourishes and lively riffs of atomized blood orange mist, bolstered by base notes of fig and tar. Tasting it, I realized that most red wines become tiresome halfway through the glass. They shimmy their tassels, they do the upside-down thing on the pole. So what? But this one had me riveted. It was dancing, all right, but the dance was no performance. It was a gyre of life force that had come together in a rocky field, and I was lucky enough to catch it still in motion. I was reminded of the film *Manon of the Spring*, of Emmanuelle Béart capering au naturel with her goats. This is what we want from wine. The startling apprehension of golden ratios. The quickening jolt of connection. The callipygian curve of wildness.

Yet, despite the verve of the Ca' del Solo wines, Grahm knew that the vineyard wasn't the place for him to make his dream wine. He had chosen the site for its quirks—cool temperatures and highly mineral soil—but those quirks make the site unprofitable. And ultimately, if American terroir is to take on a life of its own, it must be economically sustainable. Ca' del Solo is cool, all right, which leads to plenty of bright acidity in the grapes, but it's also very windy, which jostles the grape leaves and hinders their photosynthesis. The only way to grow premium grapes with enough ripeness to balance their acidity is to severely limit yield—lots of leaves making sugar for every grape. Bonny Doon can't charge enough to cover its costs (especially for wine styles unfamiliar to the average drinker), and doesn't even try.

A second problem is the soil. High in minerals, yes, but also depleted of certain nutrients. "Until we added a massive dose of potassium to the soil," Grahm told me—something that needs repeating every ten years—"we just could not get anything to properly ripen. While I adore the quality of the Albariño, Loureiro, and Moscato Giallo grapes, and the Grenache and Nebbiolo are better than anything else I've been able to find in California, the whole proposition of growing grapes in the Salinas Valley, especially where we are, is largely untenable. We are obliged to irrigate, and the water that we use to irrigate is slightly saline, thus gradually degrading the soil. Nothing at all sustainable in that proposition."

But Ca' del Solo has helped crystallize Grahm's vision of his ultimate vineyard. It would have to be cool, with enough precipitation to forgo irrigation but not enough to deplete the soil, which would have to be rich in minerals and nutrients. The soil also would have to be what Grahm calls "smart soil"—able to hold on to every precious drop during dry times but resist oversaturation. Limestone and calcareous clay both fit the bill. Most important of all, it would have to have "a distinctive mojo."

After years of searching, and some tortuous negotiations, in 2009 Grahm signed the purchase contract on the site of his dreams—

literally. "I happened to dream about the San Juan Bautista site before I actually saw it," he told me. "I see that as some sort of sign." The 280-acre site features northeast exposures—unthinkable in Europe, where every drop of sunlight is precious, but a savvy move in klieg-light California. "The real opportunity for great wine here in California is in some of the cooler climates where there is also a very long growing season"—an impossible combination in Europe. "These conditions will allow for a wine that has great natural acidity as well as potentially superb varietal character."

As for mojo, the area contains a number of minerals found nowhere else. Grahm plans to farm the area as a biodynamic polyculture, using animals (primarily goats) to improve the soil quality and creating his own power from the site's abundant winds. The area gets twelve to fourteen inches of rain per year. That's marginal for nonirrigated grapes (hydrology consultants told him he was nuts to plant a vineyard on the site; a dowser told him he'd be fine), but Grahm thinks it might work to his advantage. If he plants the vines farther apart, giving each one more soil to work with, he might meet their water needs and deepen their expression of terroir at the same time. Those vines will have to be ones that do well in drought and wind; Grahm plans on planting Grenache, Sagrantino, Ruche, Grenache Blanc, Grenache Gris, and Petit Manseng—not a one of which has any caché with consumers. Against his better judgment, he will even attempt "an acre or two" of Pinot Noir, in one final stab at the Great American Pinot. It probably won't work. In fact, there's more than an idle chance that none of it will work, and the Flying Cigar will splinter on the rocks of San Benito County. But with a little luck and the blessings of the mineral gods, Grahm will soon be producing wines that are new to this world. Wines that are neither European poseurs nor Sam's Club bimbos. Wines that are as vivacious as California itself.

RECIPES

BRAISED LAMB SHANKS WITH RED WINE AND PUY LENTILS

Sometimes when I'm around chefs or other foodie types, I like to say, "I don't think red wine goes with food." Shocked silence ensues as they figure out what to do with this poor rube. Ignore him? Insult him? Try to bring him into the fold of cultured souls? Usually, they just get upset and try to find somebody else to talk to. I admit, I'm exaggerating for effect in my declaration, but I do mean it. Most red wine, particularly the overblown oak and tannin bombs of the New World, doesn't work with food at all. Taste it with food, and pay attention to the writhings in your mouth. The wines that do work, the happy exceptions to the rule, have light or medium body and alcohol and not a hint of American oak. And they work with only a handful of dishes. Of those, one stands head and shoulders (or should that be leg and shoulders?) above the rest. Lamb is the great friend of red wine, and you find them mated for life in the Rhône region of France. Lamb's aggressive flavor and funky fat make a perfect foil for the sweaty reds of the Rhône and their California cousins. And there's no better way to appreciate their affinities than in a good braise.

The secrets to a good braise are long, slow cooking (the oven works better than the stove top for this); a cut of meat with enough collagen to keep itself tender through the process; a delicious braising liquid; and something worthy of soaking up the juice. Lamb shanks (from the upper forelegs) are tough enough to make classic braising candidates, staying moist and flavorful even as they melt into tenderness. The wine must be lively and rustic, but not fat. Côtes du Rhône is the sensible choice; Châteauneuf-du-Pape the extravagant one. Bonny Doon's Le Cigare Volant would be unforgettable— one for the dish, one for the cook, as Julia Child might say. Save a splash of wine to throw into the sauce at the end to get some of that vibrant, uncooked wine energy into the dish.

To absorb that numinous gravy, and in keeping with the rustic France theme, I like Puy lentils, the first (and, you gotta think, last) lentil to be given *Appellation d'origine contrôlée* status. Grown only in the thin soils of Le Puy-en-Velay, a town in south-central France, the tiny, speckled, greenish-black lentils hold their shape better than others, because of their higher protein and lower carbohydrate content, and have an earthy, peppery flavor. If you can't find them, other lentils will work fine; they'll just turn into more of a mash.

Serves 4

1 tablespoon olive oil
4 lamb shanks
salt and pepper
2 onions, peeled and chopped
6 garlic cloves, peeled
3 large carrots, peeled and chopped
2 cups chicken broth
1 bottle red wine
1 14-ounce can diced tomatoes and their juice
1 teaspoon dried thyme
1 teaspoon fresh rosemary, minced
1 pound dried lentils

1. Preheat the oven to 350 degrees.
2. Pour the olive oil into a Dutch oven or other ovenproof pot and cook over medium heat until it's shimmering. Sprinkle the lamb shanks with salt and pepper and brown them in the oil, turning as necessary, for about 5 minutes. Remove the shanks to a plate.
3. Add the onions, garlic, and carrots to the pot and sauté for 3 minutes. Add the chicken broth, 2 cups of the wine, the tomatoes, and the thyme and rosemary. Stir. Return the shanks to the pot.

4. Cover the pot and place it in the oven. Cook for 1 hour. Pour the remaining wine into a glass and start drinking—but save some in case you run out of braising liquid.

5. Open the pot, turn the shanks, and add the lentils. Make sure they are fully submerged in liquid, then cover the pot and return it to the oven. Cook for an additional 1 hour, adding wine if needed to keep things wet.

6. Uncover the pot and cook until the shanks brown a little on top. The lamb is done when it's falling off the bone. Let it sit for a few minutes, then serve each shank atop a mound of lentils.

SHALLOT-MUSHROOM PAN SAUCE

One place where I find that typical New World red wines do fare well is in a pan sauce, where their body and quasi-sweetness are desirable. I like pan sauces because they recoup all the yummy brown bits otherwise left in the bottom of the pan, and (quite important to those of us who do our own dishes) because they leave behind a much cleaner pan. The dream match for this sauce is a pan-seared steak, but it's good with any sautéed hunk o' protein (even fish!).

Makes enough for 2 steaks

¼ cup red wine
¼ cup peeled and minced shallots
¼ cup minced mushrooms
½ teaspoon freshly ground black pepper
1 tablespoon butter

1. Cook your hunk o' protein in a heavy skillet to desired doneness. Remove it from the pan and place it in a warm oven.

2. Add the wine to the skillet. The pan should begin to hiss and bubble almost instantly. Push a spatula (wooden is ideal) across the bottom to loosen all the brown bits.

3. Add the shallots and mushrooms and cook, stirring constantly, until the veggies are soft and the sauce is reduced to a gravy-like consistency, about 2 minutes. Turn off the heat.

4. Add the pepper and butter, stir, top your protein, and serve.

RESOURCES

BIEN NACIDO VINEYARD

www.biennacidovineyards.com

805-937-2506

Bien Nacido is a vineyard, not a winery. Its grapes have developed such a reputation that most of California's top wineries compete to get their hands on a few, and proudly trumpet the vineyard name on the label when they do. This makes Bien Nacido almost unique in California, and the closest thing in America to a real appellation in the European sense: The quality is associated with the place, not the winery. In fact, to maintain Bien Nacido's standing, the vineyard owners taste all wines made with their fruit and *won't allow* the wineries to use the vineyard name on the label unless it meets their own quality standards. If you do see it on a label, it's a guarantee of a good time to come.

Bien Nacido Vineyard is nestled in the Santa Maria Valley, a California aberration. While all of California's other ridges and valleys run north-south, the Santa Maria Valley runs east-west, funneling the cool Pacific fog into the region every morning. This significantly cooler climate, combined with marine soils (also rare in volcanic California) and extreme care in tending the vineyard, allows Bien Nacido wines a vast departure from the typical hot, jammy, flabby California style. Bien Nacido has become particularly famous for grapes that like it cool, such as Chardonnay, Pinot Noir, and Syrah. Au Bon Climat's Chardonnay, made with Bien Nacido fruit, has been famous for decades for its depth and zing. Bonny Doon makes a dazzling Bien Nacido Vineyard Syrah that fills your mouth with dark cherry richness and then leaves chocolate, mint, and coriander fumes rippling through your sinuses.

BONNY DOON VINEYARD

www.bonnydoonvineyard.com

888-819-6789

An amazingly creative variety of wines, many biodynamic, as well as a thoroughly entertaining Web site. Members of Bonny Doon's wine club receive a steady trickle of Randall Grahm's occasionally bizarre and always provocative fringe wines throughout the year. Look for the Vol des Anges, a dessert wine that is botrytised: A friendly fungus attacks the grapes, breaking their skins and dehydrating them. Sugar levels soar, and the wine becomes dessert. Intense sweetness is balanced with coy chanterelle aromas. The whole thing smells like the inside of a beehive—wood, smoke, wax, honey, flowers, and baby bees—and it finishes like pears browned in butter.

CAYUSE VINEYARDS

www.cayusevineyards.com

When I pressed Randall Grahm to list what he felt were some authentic American *vins de terroir*, he would name but one: Cayuse Vineyards. This tiny, cult winery in Washington state's Walla Walla appellation is famed for its Syrah, which is likely the best in the country. Christophe Baron, a scion of the Baron Albert Champagne house, founded his winery in 1996 after seeing soil in the eastern Walla Walla Valley that was little more than grapefruit-sized stones—the deposits of ancient flooding of the Walla Walla River. Baron knew that some of the finest Rhône wines came from similar terroir, which drains so well that it stresses the vines and forces them to dig deep for nourishment. Walla Walla summers also resemble those of the Rhône Valley. Baron farms the vineyards biodynamically and keeps his yields very low, using only the most super-concentrated fruit. The wines, I'm told, have intense berry, leather, and spice notes. Good luck scoring a bottle.

CHRYSALIS VINEYARDS' NORTON

www.chrysaliswine.com

540-687-8222

Every variety of wine grape you can name—Cabernet, Chardonnay,

Merlot, Syrah, Riesling, and so on—is a member of the same species, *Vitis vinifera*, the European grapevine. Though that species
has been carried around the world to make wine, it isn't the only
game in town. America has its native grapes, too—and no discussion of American terroir would be complete without considering
them. There is *Vitis labrusca*, New England's grape, of which Con-
cord is the most famous. Known for making "foxy" wines, it has
never fared well with connoisseurs. But there is another species that
once beat the European grape at its own game and, though it somehow slipped through the fingers of history, it may be poised to make
a big comeback. *Vitis aestivalis*, known as Norton, was already wildly
popular with Virginia and Missouri winemakers* when, in 1873, it
mixed it up with the big boys at a Vienna competition and was
named "Best Red of All Nations." Convinced, the Europeans tried
to adopt it, but Norton hated their limestone soils. It was truly an
American. Europe has ignored it ever since, and the Europeans
who pioneered winemaking in California kept right on ignoring it.
In the Midwest and Mid-Atlantic, however, it has labored on in
anonymity, making great wines for a few diehards.

Now Norton is hot again—as it should be. The grapevine scoffs
at all the diseases that regularly smite the maladapted European vines,
and it makes wines with all the power of a Cabernet or Zinfandel,
plus a little herbal American intrigue thrown in. The best Nortons are
made by Chrysalis Vineyards in Virginia and Stone Hill Winery in
Missouri. They benefit from some time in the bottle. Chrysalis's 2008
Barrel Select Norton is a dark and inviting burst of blackberry and
chokecherry, with a hint of grilled summer squash, but its 2005 Estate
Norton balances the fruit with earthy notes of raw cacao, black Keemun tea, and smoky barbecue. Rich and deep, it has a singularly
American optimism, enthusiastic and strong. This is a farm girl who
could bench-press you—an American archetype for sure.

---

* It's sometimes called "the Cabernet of the Ozarks."

LONG ISLAND'S NORTH FORK

www.liwines.com

Long Island's North Fork—a slender spit of glacial debris lashed by the Atlantic—has a climate more like France's than California's, and wines to match. Without the "endless summer," their wines are clouded by doubt and mortality—yum. To me, great wines, like great flower arrangements, have an element of sadness to them—beauty will fade, winter will come, this moment will not last. Wines from this lonely strand of Long Island can capture this sadness—when the winemakers don't Botox the hell out of them in an effort to turn them into California clichés. Pinot Blanc and Cabernet Franc are the varietals to look for, from classy, restrained growers like Lieb Family Cellars and Bedell Cellars.

RED WILLOW VINEYARD

www.redwillowvineyard.com

A unique 120-acre site in Washington state, Red Willow Vineyard sits on a stony promontory jutting above the Yakima Valley—not far from Harmony Orchards, in fact (see page 74). It's one of the best places in the country to grow Syrah, which needs a long ripening period to soften its impressive tannins, rocky soil to stress the vines and concentrate the fruit, and cool nights to maintain its acidity so it doesn't become candy. Red Willow Vineyard sells its grapes to a number of wineries. Look for Columbia Winery's Red Willow Vineyard South Chapel Block Syrah, made from a block of vines that are 93 percent Syrah and 7 percent Viognier, the same mix used in Côte-Rôtie, the famed Rhône wine. It's a powerful Christmas spice cookie of a wine, like blueberry or cherry pie with a chocolate graham cracker crust, layered with hints of floral, citrus peel aromatics from the Viognier.

The Whisperer in Darkness

WASHED-RIND CHEESE, NORTHEAST KINGDOM, VERMONT

*T*HE HACK HORROR writer H. P. Lovecraft set only one of his feverish stories in Vermont, but it was a doozy. "The Whisper in Darkness," published in 1931 in *Weird Tales*, tells of mysterious things lurking in the state's gloomy hills. A flood in November 1927 (which actually occurred) flushes some of these things out of hiding and into the swollen rivers. "What people thought they saw were organic shapes not quite like any they had ever seen before." This jibes with legends in the area, going back to Native American days, of strange creatures occupying "certain caves of problematical depth in the sides of the hills."

Lovecraft's narrator, a folklorist at Miskatonic University in Arkham, Massachusetts, goes to investigate after receiving some cryptic letters from a Vermont resident who lives in an old country farmhouse. He is immediately creeped out by the place. "I could tell that I was at the gateway of a region half-bewitched through the pilings up of unbroken time-accumulations; a region where old, strange things have had a chance to grow and linger because they have never been stirred up."

If you happen to be a character in an H. P. Lovecraft story, you can bet your life that unspeakable horror awaits in any region where old, strange things grow and linger. Any card-carrying terroirist, however, experiences a certain watering of the mouth at the very mention of such a region, for one man's horror is another man's lunch.

Lovecraft's narrator, it turns out, is referring to the sentient "fungi from Yuggoth." Yuggoth is what you call Pluto if you're from

Pluto, which these particular fungi are, though for some time they've been hunkering down in Vermont's "hill-crowded country-side with its towering, threatening, close-pressing green and granite slopes," which "hinted at obscure secrets and immemorial survivals which might or might not be hostile to mankind."

The fungi from Yuggoth aren't especially hostile to mankind; they just want to remove our brains from our bodies and implant them in metal cylinders, the better to take us on a tour of the galaxy. This is one of those twitchy Lovecraftian details that could be generated only by a mind too long unemployed in Rhode Island, yet I believe Lovecraft was onto something—a "general impression of weirdness in the Vermont landscape," as he later wrote to a friend, that you certainly don't see mentioned on state brochures. In any case, it's impressive how many details of Vermont's cheese revolution Lovecraft managed to anticipate. There are indeed, in certain caves in the sides of certain hills of the Green Mountain State, old and strange things. These otherworldly creations indeed owe their existence to certain mycological visitors. I speak not of the fungi from Yuggoth, but of the fungi from Greensboro.

FARMING THE HILLS

It's hard to imagine a place less hostile to mankind than Jasper Hill Farm on a sunny summer day. Snuggled into the side of a slope in Vermont's Northeast Kingdom, a quilted region of farms and forest that has been preserved by poverty, Jasper Hill is a study in blues and greens: the youthful green of the pastures framed by the black-green spruce woods, and the robin's-egg sky curling behind the slate-blue hills. All are players in the Jasper Hill symphony, as are the brown-and-white Ayrshire cows picking their way across the rocky meadows. To understand the nature of Jasper Hill cheeses, you need to understand that orchestra.

Jasper Hill is a classic Vermont hill farm. Its sloping pastures and rocky soils might not be as productive as those on the flats of the Mid-Atlantic or Midwest, but the variety of microclimates they encompass result in a dazzling display of herbs, grasses, and flowers. Studies in Europe have shown that alpine farms have significantly more diverse forage than plains farms, which results in greater flavor in the milk and cheese.

Of course, to get the benefits of all this flavorful forage, you need to access it, and that's where the Ayrshires come in. Ben and Jerry's has managed to imprint in America's collective mind an image of black-and-white Holsteins gamboling across Vermont's hills, but the Holstein is a problematic cow. If you bioengineered the cow genome to create a freestanding udder, you'd have something resembling a Holstein. Holsteins make uninteresting milk low in butterfat and flavor. Originally bred in the flat pastures of the Netherlands, they have weak legs and don't navigate terrain well; they prefer to have food brought to them. They have calving issues. The one thing they do well is produce prodigious quantities of milk, which is all that matters if they live their lives in a barn on a giant industrial farm.

Ayrshires, on the other hand, a Scottish breed that arrived with the unruly clans that settled northern Vermont two centuries ago, are perfectly adapted to grazing rough hills. Their tasty milk also has tiny fat globules—it's almost naturally homogenized— which makes it uniquely suited to certain cheeses. The aromas of aged blue cheeses, for example, are formed by the complete breakdown of fats in the milk into their constituent molecules. But the path of breakdown leads through a middle stage of bitter compounds, and sometimes larger fat globules will get stuck in this stage. That's why a Jersey cow, with its huge and plentiful fat globules, makes unparalleled butter, but poor aged cheeses.

Ayrshires are the only breed that the brothers Mateo and Andy Kehler have worked with since they and their wives bought Jasper Hill Farm in 1998. At the time, Jasper Hill was just one more defunct farm in the Vermont landscape. Vermont has lost 1,300 dairy farms since 1992 and now has only a thousand, most of which teeter on the brink of insolvency. The culprit is the massive dairy industry in the Midwest, which has driven the price of milk far below the break-even point for small farms.

The Kehlers bought the 240-acre farm partly out of a desire to save it and partly to maintain their connections to Greensboro. Their family had summered on a nearby section of Caspian Lake known as Winnimere since the early 1900s. "It's a happy place in our collective family childhood," Mateo explained to me. But the booming real estate prices of the 1990s threatened to shut them out of the Winnimere market. Buying the farm over the hill was a much better deal.

But it also forced them to confront the same dilemma faced by generations of locals. "We had to figure out how we were going to make a living on a rocky hillside farm in Vermont," Mateo recalled. Liquid milk was a loser. They had to add value somehow, so they let the land guide them. The farm had uncommonly good pasture, and Ayrshires were the best way to collect that goodness, and cheese was the best way to present it—and receive a premium for it.

After apprenticing with cheesemakers in Europe, the Kehlers took the U.S. cheese world by storm in 2003 with two raw-milk varieties that became instant classics: Bayley Hazen Blue, a rich and crumbly mold-ripened cheese that brought a *New Yorker* writer to her knees; and Constant Bliss, a pillowy ball of whiteness with a chalky center that draws its character from the ambient molds that latch onto it. Two years later, they were emboldened to try their hands at a cheese that pushed well beyond Americans' comfort zone.

MAKING MILK ROT RIGHT

In composition and behavior, a cheese is not unlike a dead body. It starts off fresh and springy and ends up ripe and runny. No surprise,

since cheese, like any animal body, is composed of protein and fat.*
This makes it perfect food for the very same workers that compost
dead bodies. The magic of cheese is really the art of controlled
spoilage, of making milk rot right.

In the great scissors-paper-rock game of life, animals generally
trump plants. We eat them, we make homes out of them, etc. We
think we're at the top of a pyramid, when actually we are only part
of a circle completed by the third kingdom of life, the fungi. Fungi
are the recyclers. They decompose the bodies of animals and plants
(usually, but not always, considerately waiting until we are dead)
and offer the nutrients back to plants in a usable form. More than
90 percent of plant species depend on fungi for their survival. And,
though we rarely notice most fungi, which spend their lives creeping unobtrusively through the soil in tiny filaments, they deserve
our respect: A single fungus can occupy thousands of acres and live
thousands of years. "Immemorial survivals" indeed.

Without fungi, cheeses would never progress in complexity
much beyond the chèvres and mozzarellas of the world. Even fresh
cheeses can have interesting flavor and terroir, due to variations in
what the herds are eating and in the starter culture used to curdle
the milk. But once the whey has been drained and the curds molded
into new cheeses ("green cheeses," as they're called), things get really interesting. Ultimately, all the cheese flavors in the world de-
rive from five ways that animals, microbes, and cheesemakers work
together.

1.   *The Breed and the Feed*
All cheeses begin as fresh milk. Already, differences exist. Goat's
milk is the lowest in fat and has a natural tang. Sheep's milk is the
richest and, well, sheepiest. Cow's milk is by far the most abundant.

---

* It would make a much better "body" for Communion than any silly old wafer—
especially since it goes so well with wine.

Cheesemakers must match their herd to their farm's microclimate. Sheep and goats can adapt to arid areas, but cows like lush pasture. In winter, cows used to get hay. Now, particularly on industrial farms, they often are fed corn year-round. That makes a big difference, not only in taste (corn gives a milder milk) but also in healthiness. Fresh pasture is high in omega-3 fats, which protect against everything from heart disease to Alzheimer's and depression. Corn and other grains, on the other hand, are high in omega-6 fats, which promote inflammation and lead to heart attacks, strokes, arthritis, diabetes, and dementia.* Dairy products' reputation changed from healthy to unhealthy because cows' diets changed. Cheese from pastured animals is very good food.

2.   *Coagulation*

Herds must be milked twice per day, and that milk must be dealt with promptly. The longer it sits, the more flavorful esters dissipate and the greater the risk of spoilage. Industrial cheesemakers will pasteurize their milk, refrigerate it, and let it sit for days before cheesemaking begins. Jasper Hill, on the other hand, makes cheese every day.

Milk, a suspension of solids in sweet liquid, is a device for delivering protein and fat to baby animals. The cheesemaker's first task is to separate these solids (curds) from the liquid (whey). Any acid will cause the solids to come out of suspension and stick together. Mix orange juice and milk and you get the same thing. People tend to think of curdled milk as spoiled, but the two conditions are unrelated.

Most cheesemakers begin the curdling process by adding a starter culture of lactic acid bacteria (LABs) to their milk. LABs are the same healthy microorganisms that make yogurt, and in a

---

* They are no better for cows, which aren't adapted to digesting them. Cows on corn diets usually require antibiotics to survive.

sense every cheese begins life as yogurt. But a cheese made with just LABs will be soft and crumbly—dried yogurt, more or less. Many fresh goat cheeses are made this way, as is Constant Bliss. Cheesemakers who want firmer cheeses must also add rennet, an enzyme found in a calf's stomach whose sole purpose is to curdle milk—a handy way for calves' bodies to quickly get at the fat and protein. About five thousand years ago, people discovered that a touch of rennet added to a vat of milk would cause very quick and firm coagulation.

Cheese at this stage is tart, rubbery, and squeaky. Cottage cheese, more or less, and about as interesting.

3.   *The Whey of All Flesh*

As the cheese curdles, most of the watery whey separates and can be drained off.* But much whey remains trapped inside the curds. Now it's up to the cheesemaker to guide the cheese in its future development. As with a compost pile or a science experiment in the back of the fridge, the rate at which a cheese decomposes depends on oxygen and moisture. Salt can also subdue the microbe party inside a cheese.

For a cheese, size and shape are destiny. You can't make a tiny cheddar or a giant Camembert. If a cheesemaker wants to make a soft-ripened cheese like Camembert, she must preserve as much moisture as possible to encourage the fungi and bacteria that create flavor. She needs to handle the curd gently, ladling it into plastic molds where only a little whey can drip out as the cheese takes shape. She also has to keep the cheeses small so that no part of the cheese is too distant from the molds that colonize the surface and work their way inside.

---

* It makes good pig food. Employees at Jasper Hill get one whey-fed pig per year as part of their compensation. Whey also can be simmered so the remaining solids form ricotta, which is Italian for "recooked."

If a long-lived cheese like cheddar, Gruyère, or Parmigiano-Reggiano is the goal, however, everything must be done to discourage microbes from taking over. So the cheesemaker presses the curds to remove as much moisture as possible and forms the cheese into a giant block or wheel (sometimes weighing more than one hundred pounds) so that as little of the cheese as possible is exposed to the air. Gruyère and Parmigiano-Reggiano curds are also heated to expel even more whey, to kill certain enzymes, and to create new flavor compounds; the result is the nutty flavor these cheeses are famous for.

A last option to prevent any microbe development in the curds is to immerse them in a germ-killing salt-and-acid brine. Feta is the best-known example of these pickled cheeses.

4.   *Send in the Microbes*

Once a green cheese is formed, microbes begin munching on the protein and fat. (They try to do this to you, too, but your immune system keeps them at bay.) They produce enzymes, which are little tools for taking apart molecules. Some break proteins into amino acids and then further into even simpler molecules that have a range of aromas, from fruity, fishy, and mushroomy to rosy and garlicy. Others break fats into fatty acids and then into aroma molecules that smell nutty, fruity, creamy, and peppery.

Every environment has its own suite of microbes. Some will produce lovely aromas in ripening cheese, some not so lovely. Through the ages, certain all-star molds have been singled out for their talent. Most famous is *Penicillium roqueforti*, the mold that gives Roquefort (and most other blue cheeses) its blue veins and piquant flavor. *Penicillium roqueforti* lurks naturally in the limestone caves of Roquefort-sur-Soulzon in the south of France, where Roquefort has been made for at least two thousand years. The characteristically French legend relates that a young shepherd was dining on a relatively dull lunch of bread and fresh sheep cheese when an alluring lass capered by.* The youth abandoned his lunch to pursue her, and when he eventually returned to the cave months later, the cheese had transformed. Today, all Roquefort is still made in those caves, though now the mold is isolated separately and introduced to the milk with the starter culture. Later, the cheese is pierced with steel needles so the oxygen-loving mold will proliferate. This technique has now been adopted around the world, from Danish blue to Jasper Hill's Bayley Hazen Blue.

Another penicillin cousin, *Penicillium camemberti*, is responsible for Camembert, Brie, and many other "bloomy-rind" cheeses. If a cheesemaker wants to create such cheeses, she again must keep the moisture level quite high and somehow encourage the whitish molds to form. Many cheesemakers mist a cultured version of *Penicillium camemberti* onto their cheeses, which produces a standard semisoft-cheese flavor. Other cheesemakers, such as Jasper Hill, are blessed with a tasty suite of native fungi and let the process happen naturally. This, I believe, gives cheeses like Constant Bliss their unique terroir. Unlike blue molds, which create their spicy fruit and cream flavors by eating fat, white molds like *Penicillium camemberti* specialize in metabolizing protein to create their distinct truffle and garlic aromas.

5.   *Ripening*

Cheeses are kept in moist, dark environments (traditionally caves, but now usually refrigerated storage areas) and released once they have reached their peak of development. It's up to specialists known as *affineurs* to decide how long to ripen a cheese. Ideally, flavor and texture are the only considerations, though in the case of most industrial operations, shelf life trumps all. With artisanal cheeses, the *affineur* must keep basting the surface of some cheeses with brine,

---

* Manon's forerunner?

rubbing the rinds of others to discourage cheese mites, and periodically turning the larger wheels of longer-lived cheeses so that their fat and whey don't pool on the bottom. Each cheese has its own arc of flavor development, usually moving from mild to intense to ammonia overload as its microbes and enzymes continue to interact. In this way, it is alive until the moment it is eaten.

WHAT DOES THIS LANDSCAPE DO BEST?

You can see why I think that certain raw-milk, mold-ripened cheeses are the ultimate examples of terroir in action. So many factors of the landscape come into play—the climate, the soil, the vegetation, the animals, and the live enzymes and cultures in their milk. Then there are the yeasts, molds, and bacteria that do the heavy lifting. Slightly different strains exist in every valley, in every cheese cave, though we are only beginning to grasp this. It all makes for an incredibly exciting and complex final product, a way to capture the life of a farm and condense it into a representative wheel.

But Mateo Kehler gets uneasy when food discussions get too romantic. "I can talk terroir," he said to me as we walked his farm together. He stretched his arm toward the cloud-dappled fields. "I can sell grass and sunshine with the best of 'em. But if we're going to be thoughtful about it over a generation or two and actually find what's sustainable here, then it comes down to natural economies that are an outgrowth of a landscape. The sun and soil are factors, but there's a certain inherent economic viability that has to underlie it all. If you look at France, at the Jura, you've got terroir that has been established there. You've got Comte—cow's milk cheese. Why don't you have goat's milk cheese? Because it's more profitable to milk cows there. I would say that, in a generation, there's not going to be any sheep dairying left in Vermont, because cows are a more profitable animal. Look at the places where they do make sheep's milk cheeses, like Spain and Portugal and really dry, mountainous parts of Italy—places where cows can't cut it. That's terroir. There's a landscape with a natural expression of an economy. Vermont, on the other hand, is a great place for cows."

It's an essential point. For terroir to be more than a whim, it has to answer the question, What does this landscape do best? And the market must be knowledgeable enough to support that, to be willing to pay enough for superior foods to keep the producers in business. Say some independently wealthy iconoclast manages to create a tiny supply of superior sheep's cheese in some corner of Vermont, losing money every year. That's terroir, but it's ephemeral.

"I love the idea of terroir," Mateo said, "and I believe in it. What we're doing is trying to define that over the life cycle of our business. At the end of the day, terroir is the combination of so many factors. And the lowest-common denominator is the economic piece. Because nothing else would exist without that. If it's not economically viable, it's not terroir. It's ego gratification. The cult of personality in our culture is so central. When we can start separating the product from the personality, then we're on our way to defining terroir."

Any landscape can express itself through food in numerous ways. The evolution of terroir is the process by which locals try out the options and determine what is special and valuable. Innovation plays a role. For instance, why is Vermont synonymous with cheddar cheese? The state's dairies and hill farms could have made lots of styles of cheese, but they chose one that could go the distance in the days before refrigeration and fast transportation. Cheese's original reason for being was to extend the life of milk, which is highly perishable. Vermont farmsteads needed to make a big, low-moisture cheese that could survive long enough to reach the markets of New York City. Soft cheeses were not an option. Not surprisingly, Vermont dairies kept tinkering until they came up with a cheese that not only survived but also got better with age. (Vermont shares in this terroir-imposed cheese style with most other alpine regions, such as Switzerland, which also specializes in hard, long-lived "mountain" cheeses.)

Now, of course, cheesemakers can get high-moisture, gooey cheeses to market in plenty of time. If anything, the incentives have flipped: Why make a cheddar that must age for a year when you can make cheeses that are ready to eat in a few weeks?

But what kind to make? Mateo and Andy Kehler had already scored big hits with Constant Bliss and Bayley Hazen Blue. So they decided to create a cheese that would be the ultimate expression of their landscape. "The concept of Winnimere was all about cubing terroir," Mateo explained. "You've got raw milk. You've got spontaneously fermented beer. And you've got the local spruce cambium. It's pulling all those things together into a simple cheese."

They had a model. Vacherin and Försterkäse, two of the world's most revered cheeses, are the exceptions to Switzerland's big, hard, mountain-cheese rule. They are small, stinky, seriously gooey cheeses, originally made for local consumption. Instead of cooking the curds and pressing out as much moisture as possible, as they do to prolong the life of their other cheeses, the Swiss let a few cheeses remain raw, wet microbe playgrounds. Then they wash the surfaces of these cheeses with brine to encourage the growth of something known as red mold, even though it is neither red nor a mold. *Brevibacterium linens* is actually an orangish bacteria that lurks everywhere but thrives in moist, salty places and feeds on dead protein.

Can you think of any such environments? Sniff a washed-rind cheese and the answer will come to you right away—your sneakers, where the brevibacteria roam, munching on dead skin cells and producing unforgettable odors. The smell can be off-putting, but many of us, like Pavlov's dogs, quickly learn to associate it with the deliciousness to follow. By digesting protein, the brevibacteria break it down into amino acids, also known as umami, the kind of savory, mouth-filling taste that makes many people howl in crazed joy.[*]

In a normal environment, *B. linens* will be outcompeted by garden-variety yeasts and molds, which is why cheesemakers tilt the playing field by washing their cheeses in brine, which creates a high-salt environment that only *B. linens* can stand. It takes over the surface, turning it orange, and works its way toward the center of the cheese, eating protein and generating riotous aroma and flavor compounds as it goes.

Being so high in moisture and bacteria, these cheeses pass beyond the point of edibility fairly quickly. But just before hitting that point, they achieve a brief and heady peak of luscious beefiness. At the ripeness stage, they are so soft that they will fall apart like a custard, which is why the Swiss farmers, casting about for something to hold their cheese together, hit upon the idea of wrapping it in a thin strip of spruce cambium—the pliant layer of inner bark. Not only did the cambium act like a springform pan; it also imparted a contrapuntal balsam note to the rim of the cheese, balancing the richness. The result is a beautiful cheese so runny that it is often eaten by slicing off the top rind and scooping up the paste with a spoon.

Because they knew they could recruit *B. linens* out of the air, and because they had a plentiful supply of black spruce dotting their farm, the Kehler brothers decided that a Swiss-style washed-rind cheese was the way to go. But then they decided to go one better: Instead of a simple brine, they would wash their cheese in local lambic beer.

All beer is made with yeast, which are single-celled fungi. Yeast eat sugars and excrete alcohol and carbon dioxide. They are the real brewmasters, converting a sugary mash into a dry and alco-

---

[*] Aged cheeses, anchovies, oysters, and soy sauce are some examples of umami-rich foods.

holic drink. Thousands of different yeasts have thousands of slightly different ways of doing this, generating a variety of by-products in the process. Some of these by-products taste better than others, and the yeasts that make the tastiest, most predictable beers were long ago domesticated. Breweries now select their strains of yeast to match their desired flavors or alcohol content. Most go to great lengths to ensure that no wild yeasts contaminate the recipe.

But another style of beermaking leaves the yeast selection up to the gods. Lambic beers are fermented in open barrels, with the brewmasters doing everything short of hanging WELCOME signs around the barrels to exhort passing yeasts to stop in. In addition, many species of bacteria join in the fun. The result is a strange brew of inimitable flavors.

The Kehlers decided to baptize their cheese in a lambic potion of sugars, alcohol, and living yeasts and bacteria recruited from the farm air. They brewed a lambic beer right on the land and basted each rind of Winnimere with it twice per week. The live fungi in the beer kick-start the colonization process, proliferating quickly, breaking down sugar and acid into fruity, spicy flavor compounds and turning the surface a handsome rust. Eventually they pass the baton to *B. linens*, which prefers a low-acid environment, but it remains only one player in the Jasper Hill symphony. Winnimere smells strong but tastes like the richest porterhouse imaginable—salty and beefy and intense. It's a full-contact cheese, finishing with hints of mushroom sauce and filé powder; a touch of bitter, peppery wild mustard; and that kiss of resin from the spruce cambium that wraps each one-pound disk.

This changes with the seasons, as it should. Jasper Hill, to its credit, doesn't fight that. A Winnimere made in winter will be rich but clean in flavor, while a May Winnimere will have all the rutty playfulness of spring. (Full summer is a bit too biological for a washed-rind cheese like Winnimere, so the cheese goes on hiatus from June through September.)

But if Vacherin was a model for Winnimere, it was also a warning. Raw-milk, high-moisture cheeses maximize the growth of flavor-producing microbes, but they also make great homes for the dangerous ones. In the 1980s, an outbreak of listeria killed thirty-one people in Europe, and the source was traced back to Vacherin. Ironically, it had nothing to do with the cheesemaking process itself—the listeria was tracked in by a farmer who was picking up the whey to feed to his pigs—but the Kehlers know they have to be extra careful when playing with high-moisture cheeses. "When we're making that cheese, it's like we're on Code Red," Mateo admitted. "There's the opportunity for all kinds of other things to grow there. We're very conscious of that. In every batch, we test the milk, the cheese, the environment, the brine. But we haven't had any issues. We feel comfortable producing Winnimere because we've developed the monitoring programs that we have."

Indeed, entering the cellars at Jasper Hill feels like the opening credits of *Get Smart*. A series of doors and screens opens and shuts behind you, outdoor shoes are swapped for sterilized Crocs, and hairnets are applied. The U.S. Food and Drug Administration requires raw-milk cheeses to be aged for sixty days before being sold. (The dangerous microbes can't survive that long in the environment of an aging cheese.) "What's possible here is really limited by what the FDA says we can and can't do," Mateo said. "Terroir is affected by these political realities. There's a reason not many people are doing raw-milk, soft-ripened cheeses. A gooey cheese like Winnimere? Raw milk? We're pushing the envelope. It's a challenge to produce a high-moisture cheese that has seventy-five to eighty-five days of life in it, so we can get it out the door while it's still got a couple weeks of shelf life. The FDA rules are intended to prevent the types of cheeses we're making. We've had to become better cheesemakers in order to do it."

That means keeping their environment as clean as possible, so that the rip-roaring microbial wildfire that creates Winnimere, and eventually consumes it, doesn't get out of hand before the cheese hits store shelves. Paul Kindstedt, the director of the Vermont Institute for Artisan Cheese, confirmed this. "Jasper Hill produces incredibly clean milk, with very low bacterial counts. They just do a terrific job in terms of the animals' milk and hygiene," he said. Indeed, festooning the walls of Jasper Hill's creamery are yearly awards for Best Standard Plate Count from the Vermont Dairy Industry Association.

In this case, the FDA rule has been a blessing in disguise, forcing the Kehlers into making a high-wire cheese. In France, where raw-milk cheeses can be sold as young as cheesemakers want, no one goes to the trouble to make a raw-milk cheese whose complexity peaks at three months. When Mateo presented Winnimere to a top French *affineur*, he was told that no such cheese had been made in France for thirty years. And when I presented Winnimere to a consul général of France, a man charged with furthering French culture abroad, he tasted the cheese, looked up, and said, "France is in trouble."

BREAKING THE MOLD

France *is* in trouble. "It's striking to me," Mateo said. "Last time I was in France I spent time with the cheesemaker Herve Mons. I asked him, 'Is there anything new going on in French cheesemaking?' He said, 'No. The terroir of France has been defined.' It's actually in decline. French consumers are going to the supermarket. The eating habits of the upcoming generation are totally different from their parents.' It's the power of Carrefour.* The perverse thing is that the only thing keeping the terroir of France alive is the American consumer."

Almost a decade ago, the food writer Edward Behr wrote,

---

* The largest supermarket chain in the world.

"Cheese in France is becoming increasingly divorced from nature. But nature is the point—its variety from season to season, farm to farm, even one cheese to another ripening side by side. Cheese has always been an expression of nature, and now it risks becoming only an imitation of nature, however highly skilled."

Behr's point is that the industrialization of the process—the pasteurization of the milk, the use of factory-made starter culture and selected molds, the increasingly sterile cellars—has inverted the dynamic of the relationship. Cheese used to be something that nature did spontaneously. We didn't design the cheese so much as guide it, like an equestrian riding a horse. The cheese powered it-self, and the cheesemaker gave it some direction. Some cheeses bucked a lot more than others and provided a wild ride, and usually those cheeses were the ones capable of astonishing performances. They were also the dangerous ones, and occasionally somebody got hurt, as in the case of Vacherin. But the reaction, predictable yet sad, was to get rid of the animal in the equation entirely. Instead of dynamic beasts, we opted for the predictability of mechanical bulls—an imitation of nature, however highly skilled. And something was lost in the process.

That has been the trend all over the world: increasing indus-trialization, automation, and sameness. Which makes the recent outbreak of artisan cheesemaking in the United States—Nature as-serting herself in a dazzling display of terroir-driven delights—all the more astonishing.

Jasper Hill has played no small role in this revolution. From the beginning, part of the Kehlers' mission was to keep an old farm viable, but that mission expanded as they deconstructed their own start-up experience. They had been able to create several world-class cheeses and garner lots of attention for them, but they still strug-gled. In addition to the cows that had to be milked every day and the new cheeses that had to be made every day, they had to tend the aging cheeses. They had to sell their cheeses, promote their cheeses, and deal with all the paperwork that goes with any business. "I spent a lot of time turning greasy cheeses," Mateo said. "The romance disappears fast."

What was holding back an artisan cheese revolution in the United States was not a shortage of talented people eager to put in hard days on the farm; it was a shortage of time and expertise to deal with the other demands of a small business. "The heart of our social mission is to conserve the working landscape of Vermont," said Mateo. "First and foremost, we're interested in sustainability. Our goals go back to being able to maintain our working landscape, and that takes viable businesses on that landscape."

So the Kehlers decided to step in to the aging, marketing, distribution, and fulfillment ends of the business, becoming what you might call an artisan cheese incubator. With investment from a variety of nonprofits, and expert advice from Europe, they built a facility unlike anything in the country: a $3.2-million, twenty-two-thousand-square-foot, state-of-the-art cheese cellar, chiseled into the side of a hill, devoted exclusively to artisan cheeses. "We're investing in infrastructure to support economic viability. Our intent is to create products that develop economies around themselves. We won't know whether we're meeting that mission for a generation."

The Cellars at Jasper Hill got up to speed in 2009. Now, farmstead cheesemakers in the Northeast don't need to worry about anything except making the best cheese they can. They don't need a cave; they just send green cheeses to Jasper Hill and let the expert *affineurs* age them. They get to take advantage of Jasper Hill's well-established distribution network. Best of all, somebody else gets to chase down the invoices. If you have noticed a profusion of diversity at your local cheese counter recently, you may have Jasper Hill to thank.

For a terroirist, touring the Cellars at Jasper Hill is like some sort of fantasy. There are seven temperature-controlled vaults, each separated from the curved main hall by a massive sliding door. Haul open a door and you are socked by a wave of ammonia (a natural by-product of ripening cheese), followed by the aromas peculiar to the style of cheese in that vault. Because of the different molds and bacteria at work, certain cheeses won't play nice with others. One vault was filled with the nutty richness of alpine cheeses, another with mushroomy aromas from small bloomy-rind disks resembling Camembert.

Two vaults were stacked ten feet high with wooden racks of twenty-pound wheels of Cabot clothbound cheddar, a partnership between Jasper Hill and Cabot Creamery. If you think you know what good cheddar tastes like, you'll think again after tasting clothbound. Today cheddars are dipped in wax or bagged in plastic, but they always used to be wrapped in cloth. The cloth was painted with lard, which encouraged a blue-gray mottling of molds to surround the cheese. The molds formed a stable rind, protecting the cheese and changing it from the outside in, but they also allowed the cheese to breathe. Most cheddars are strangled in their cribs and develop the sharp tang of aerobic death. We've come to think that this is what cheddars are supposed to taste like. But clothbound cheddars continue to respire. Like a dry-aged steak, as they lose moisture, they concentrate, developing a caramel richness and a beautifully crumbly texture.

Continuing my magical mystery tour, I left the cheddar vault and slid open the next door. Beside me were wire racks of Winnimeres, quietly bronzing. Beside them was a rack of the same cheeses, washed in wild apple cider from the farm's trees; a custom cheese for the French Laundry. Other washed-rind cheeses stretched into the problematical depths of the vault, beckoning me deeper. The smell was . . . otherworldly. No, that wasn't quite right. It was most definitely of this world. But not the fluorescent world of supermarkets. Here, in the chthonic dark beneath a Vermont hillside, was a whispered reminder of the allure of life's third kingdom.

RECIPES

GRILLED FUNK

In general, the best thing to do with a good washed-rind cheese is to eat it as is, unadorned, uncooked, unaccompanied. But every now and then it becomes necessary to shake things up a bit, to experiment, and that is the time to break out this simple recipe, which is also a good way to get people intimidated by stinky cheese to try it. The sweet and spicy onions and apples play off the savory funk of the cheese, and the crispy bread plays off the meltingly gooey interior. Bread choice is important here; it should be neither soft nor dense. You need something with lightness but also a little structural integrity, like a good sourdough or pain au levain. The optional chutney is delicious but does start to mask the cheese; it all depends on your funk-o-meter. Serve it with pickles and root chips and a dry but fruity hard cider for a hedonistic lunch.

Makes 1 substantial sandwich

1 tablespoon chutney (optional)
2 slices bread
1 to 2 ounces washed-rind cheese, such as Winnimere, Hartwell, Hooligan, Red Hawk, Taleggio, Epoisses, or Munster (Alsatian), cut in ½-inch slices
2 tablespoons butter, divided
¼ apple, peeled, cored, and cut in ¼-inch slices
1 ¼-inch-thick slice red onion

1. Spread the chutney (if using) on one slice of bread, and top with the cheese slices.
2. Melt 1 tablespoon of the butter in a skillet over medium heat until it foams. Add the apple and onion slices and cook, flipping occasionally, until they're soft, about 3 minutes.
3. Top the cheese with the apple and onion slices and the second

piece of bread. Butter the top of the sandwich with half the remaining butter and place it, buttered-side down, in the skillet. Fry about 2 minutes. Press gently on the top of the sandwich to get the softening cheese to glue it all together (without pressing so hard that you squeeze the cheese out the sides).

4. Butter the top of the sandwich with the remaining butter and flip it over. Fry an additional 1 to 2 minutes, again pressing gently. Remove the sandwich from the pan, cut it in half on the diagonal, and serve.

FROMAGE FORT

Every now and then, despite your earnest efforts to eat as much cheese as you possibly can, a few leftover bits get away from you in the back of the fridge and go over to the other side of ripeness. Fear not; they are perfect raw material for fromage fort. "Strong cheese" is what the French called their solution to the problem of remnant cheese odds and ends, and it was strong indeed: They'd fill a stoneware crock with leftover cheese pieces of all varieties, along with some garlic and wine, broth, or even milk, and let it ferment away in the basement on a semipermanent basis, adding to it as new leftovers became available and ladling out scoopfuls of the oozing mass whenever the desire arose, which was apparently often. It must have been great, but I suspect more than one old French farmer went down into his basement for a cup of fromage fort and never came back up again. Nouveau versions like mine can still be wicked strong, depending on the mix of cheeses, but they're less likely to rise out of the vat and start demanding obeisance from you and your pets. Serve on crackers or toast points.

Serves 4 to 6 as an hors d'oeuvre

½ pound leftover cheese, preferably several different kinds
¼ cup white wine, hard cider, or strong ale

1 clove garlic, peeled and pressed

1 teaspoon fresh thyme (or other herbs, or ground cardamom; please experiment)

1 teaspoon freshly ground black pepper

1. Combine all the ingredients in a food processor and blend until smooth. You may need to add more liquid. You may want to add more garlic. You can fill a dip bowl or ramekin and serve it at once, but it gets better the longer it sits. Refrigerate it until ready to use, but warm it to room temperature before serving.

RESOURCES

THE CELLARS AT JASPER HILL

www.cellarsatjasperhill.com

802-533-2566

In addition to Winnimere, Jasper Hill makes several other cheeses, and in its cellars it ages cheeses for numerous other artisan cheese-makers.

CYPRESS GROVE CHÈVRE'S HUMBOLDT FOG

www.cypressgrovechevre.com

707-825-1100

Fresh goat cheeses tend to be tasty but one dimensional—think of the classic white, tangy log of chèvre—but Humboldt Fog, made in California's misty Humboldt County, is a multidimensional experience and a great emissary for Northern California–style cheeses. The Cypress Grove dairy is frequently basted in fog that rolls off the Pacific and through the redwoods, and its herd of goats is well adapted to that environment and its unique forage. Cheesemaker Mary Keehn coats the young cheeses in vegetable ash, with another thin layer of ash running through the middle of the cheese. The ash—and the prevailing fog—promotes a bluish-white mold that covers the cheese and imparts a complex flavor. The bone-white paste and ivory exterior, wrapped in black ash and bisected with a line of ash, makes Humboldt Fog the snappiest dresser in the cheese world. Each zone contributes its own flavor: the bitter ash, the mouth-filling and salty tang of the interior, the melting richness of the outer paste, and the chewy porcini-scented rind all combine like a quartet, plucking chords of flavor on the tongue.

MURRAY'S CHEESE

www.murrayscheese.com

888-692-4339

Simply the best cheese shop in the country, Murray's is a New York City institution, with an unparalleled selection of cheeses from around the world, but also a stellar track record of ferreting out the greatest American cheeses, obscure or otherwise.

UPLANDS CHEESE COMPANY'S PLEASANT RIDGE RESERVE

www.uplandscheese.com

888-935-5558

When people ask me to name my favorite cheese in America, I always mention two, and they couldn't be more different. No-holds-barred Winnimere is one, the Al Pacino of cheeses. The other is Upland Cheese Company's Pleasant Ridge Reserve, from the high pastures of Wisconsin. A well-named cheese, it displays the pleasing reserve of an Ian McKellen. The secrets of Pleasant Ridge Reserve are the mix of summer grasses and wildflowers that the cows eat, the raw milk, and the washing of the rind. Because Pleasant Ridge Reserve is a much larger and drier cheese than Winnimere, it takes on just a hint of those intense washed-rind flavors. Pleasant Ridge Reserve is the only cheese to twice win the Best in Show award from the American Cheese Society. So important are the clovers and wildflowers to the flavor of Pleasant Ridge Reserve that the cheese is made only from spring through fall, when fresh forage is available. The incredibly long finish has the earthy note of chicken livers, lifted by hints of green olive and chive. If you can find it, go for the extra-aged version of the cheese, which has an extraordinary butterscotch color and a beguiling aroma of sweet hay, like the freshest barn in the world—the essence of the Midwest.

The Blood of the Gods

MESOAMERICAN CHOCOLATE,
CHIAPAS, MEXICO

S HE IS NOT the type of woman you associate with human sacrifice. She's clean, sharply dressed, friendly, and successful. She
likes to shop and to go to the movies, but she especially likes to visit
certain temples of chocolate in her city. She's not above going
alone, but she prefers going with friends. Together they sit at a table until the dark offering arrives. Then they intone a few words,
raise their silver forks high, and plunge them into the soft center of
the thing. She takes a little into her mouth, closes her eyes, and
time collapses. For a moment she is not a twenty-first-century
woman in a twenty-first-century city; she is simply a bundle of re-
ceptors at the end of a deep and ancient ritual. From her cerebellum
to her loins, her nervous system purrs like an ocelot. She couldn't
quite put it into words; all she knows is that she has a visceral feeling
that all is right with the world. And she would do almost anything
to have that feeling again.

THE TREE OF TROPICAL KNOWLEDGE

There's a little of the blood sacrifice in every piece of chocolate.
Those chocolate hearts on Valentine's Day tiptoe close to the
truth, which was flaunted by the Maya and Aztec, who were to
chocolate what America was to the hamburger—they inherited the basic concept, perfected it, and ritualized it. The basics
haven't changed. Just like the Maya, we gather the seeds of

cacao* pods, ferment them, dry them, roast them to a nutty brown, and then grind them into a thick paste.

We do this because chocolate is our most complex food. More than six hundred different aromatic molecules have been identified in it. Chocolate is not one specific flavor so much as everything you can think of; it's the brown taste you get when you mix together all the colors in the flavor box. The raw bean contributes astringency and bitterness. The pulp supplies a tart alcoholic nose of sake and sherry as it ferments, eventually turning to vinegar. The vinegar burns through the cells in the beans, triggering enzymatic reactions that create brothy umami compounds and buttery blue-cheese flavors. The drying process adds a raisiny must. Then the whole mass gets roasted to bring out flavors of nuts, grilled meat, coffee, and flowery caramel. Practically the only missing flavor categories are sweetness and saltiness. A little crunch is nice. Almond Joy, anyone?

If you were ask to an ancient Aztec princess or a contemporary New Yorker what it is about chocolate that's so captivating, she probably wouldn't say, "because it has six hundred different flavor chemicals in it," but that gets to the heart of the matter. From a single pod in the rainforest comes the vast library of edible experience. The tree of knowledge is alive and well.

We process our chocolate into a smooth, solid form. The Maya and Aztec usually drank their chocolate as a thick, dark liquid. With its caffeine and theobromine (a related, milder stimulant), it was as restorative as a transfusion. Chocolate had a singular vitality to it, and the ancients became even more addicted to it than we are. Maya children were baptized in chocolate. It flowed at weddings.

---

* Per slightly screwy tradition, "cacao" refers to the tree and its pods, "cocoa" refers to the seeds/beans inside the pods, as well as the dried product made from them, and "chocolate" refers to the final product once it's been smoothed out with additional cocoa butter and, usually, sugar.

Husbands and wives even swapped cacao beans as part of their vows. If maize built the body of the Maya and Aztec empires, cacao was their lifeblood.

The Mesoamericans had a fluid, cyclical view of time and nature that showed a precocious inkling of ecology. Life flowed from other life, and human beings were no exception. There was a sense of recycling. Even a Maya creation myth tells how the sun and moon were formed from the beheading of twin gods. Blood was among the most valuable currencies. Mesoamericans were fond of pricking themselves with maguey thorns and offering up the blood as needed. Sometimes chocolate filled in for blood, and sometimes the cosmic composting went the other way. One Maya hieroglyph shows four gods pricking their ears with obsidian knives and dripping their blood onto cacao pods. There was a powerful essence in those beans, awaiting human ingenuity to unlock it.

Chocolate's extreme symbolic, culinary, and pharmacological value (it was Mesoamerica's only source of caffeine) brought tremendous wealth to the regions that could produce it. Foremost was Soconusco, the Napa Valley of its day, which stretched along the Pacific coastal plain of what is now the Mexican province of Chiapas. Cacao will grow only in truly tropical and moist areas. The Maya, whose civilization was based in the tropical lowlands of the Yucatán, had numerous regions that lent themselves to cacao production. But the Aztec empire was based in the volcanic highlands of the Valley of Mexico (modern-day Mexico City), an area much too cool for cacao. The Aztec had to import all their cacao, most of it from Soconusco, which they annexed around 1500 A.D. for that very purpose.

The Aztec were to the Maya as the Romans were to the Greeks. They borrowed heavily from the earlier culture's art and science, then added a militaristic discipline that enabled the efficiency of empire to replace the city-state squabbling of their predecessors. Through trade and conquest, the fingers of the Aztec reached far, and kept a stranglehold on Soconusco.

The Aztec nickname for chocolate was "heart blood." This was possibly due to its color and viscosity, or possibly because cacao beans come in a reddish, oval pod that might look like a heart if you squint hard. For Aztec priests, this was enough to link the two in certain rituals.

Chicken Little had nothing on the Aztec. They believed that the world was going to end in cataclysm and that they would go with it. I can sympathize with the notion; it's in what to do about it that we part ways. For the Aztec, the only way to put off Armageddon was through endless sacrifice. Since everything came from the gods' own sacrifices, something had to be returned to replenish their reserves. Beans, maize, flowers, dogs, rabbits, hummingbirds, and cacao, of course—it all had to go to keep the gods upright another few days.

Being responsible for the continuation of the entire universe, the Aztec had a lot on their plates. The tears of children were effective in stimulating the rain god, and a few captives burned alive went a long way toward appeasing the fire god. But their primary concern was in keeping the sun god rising every day, and that meant feeding him a steady supply of hearts. Each human heart was believed to be a tiny shard of the sun; since there were new people and new hearts coming into existence every day, it only made sense to repay the loan. Cutting the body open with a knife and ripping out the still-beating heart helped it return to the sun a little faster. Scholars debate the number of human sacrifices in Tenochtitlán. Was it ten a day? Twenty? Suffice it to say that the stairs of the ziggurat temples were thickly stained.

Most sacrificial victims went willingly to their doom. We tend to frown on human sacrifice, but try to see it from the Aztec point of view. Sacrificial victims were generally prisoners of war. Faced with a quick death or spending a tortuous life as Aztec slave, you, too, might opt for the altar. For the religious-minded, the Mesoamerican hell was a place you wouldn't want to be caught dead in, but it was exactly where you'd wind up if you died the ignominious death of a captive slave. To qualify for heaven, death in combat was tops, bettered only by ritual death on the altar. It's not so different from the ever-popular bargain offered to suicide bombers: In exchange for your sacrifice, you further the cause, nail down everlasting respect on Earth, and score admission to an eternity of earthly and unearthly delights—which may explain why the victims freed in the nick of time by the Spanish conquerors objected strenuously and demanded that the show go on.

Some sacrificial victims got the added benefit of being treated as gods on Earth prior to their departure. Once a year, for example, a particularly virile captive was chosen to represent Quetzalcoatl, the creator god. But more than a representative, he became something of an avatar of the god. Bedecked in feathers and jewels, he got to promenade around Tenochtitlán being worshipped by the people and treated like a king. After forty days of this, he was told that the jig was up; he'd have his heart torn out that night, but only after completing a dance of joy.

The success of the ceremony hinged on the dance, but sometimes, surprise, surprise, despite everything that had been done for him, despite the promise of babes and beverages in heaven, the victim would react to the news of his fate with something other than joy. A morose victim would ruin everything, would ensure future doom, and this is where the chocolate came in. At the first sign of gloominess, the priests would whip out their obsidian knives, wash off the blood of the previous victims, and then brew up a batch of chocolate with the bloody washing water. Fed to the victim, this apparently restored his spirits, and the dancing, sacrifice, and world went on.

The sun god was appeased for about five hundred years. Then, apparently, he got very, very pissed at the Aztec. Whether they were skimping on the chocolate or human hearts is unclear. What we know is that a guy named Columbus cruised up to the coast of what is now Honduras in 1502 and captured a large Maya dugout canoe on a trading mission. In addition to some clothing, maize beer, and obsidian-edged Aztec war clubs, Columbus scored a collection of what turned out to be dried cacao beans. The sailor got a clue as to the surprising value of these nuggets when a few spilled and the locals went scrambling for them "as if an eye had fallen."

The die had been cast, though it wouldn't come up snake eyes for the Aztec for another seventeen years, when Hernán Cortés and his conquistadores tromped into Tenochtitlán. Abetted by neighboring tribes only too happy to see the Aztec fall—as well as by smallpox, which wiped out a third of the population in six months—the Spaniards demolished the empire in three short years and established New Spain, gaining control over the millions of cacao beans in Montezuma's coffers, as well as the prized plantations of Soconusco. "The whole province was a garden of cacao trees," wrote one conquistador. And it was all Spain's.

The ultimate example of fusion cuisine was under way. The Spanish introduced wheat, beef, cheese, and limes to the Mexican repertoire. Meanwhile, in Europe, a related fusion cuisine was stirring. Where would the Italians be without Mexico's corn, tomatoes, peppers, and chocolate? This last, in particular, took Europe by storm.

The cacao tree's plan for world domination was going swimmingly. But it was about to take a Faustian turn.

THE WRONG CHOCOLATE

A raw cacao bean is profoundly inedible. Generations of primates have tried, with a mouthful of yuck to show for it. That's the plan. The cacao tree enlists the services of monkeys to spread its seeds far and wide, wrapping the seeds in a sweet and goopy pulp, and then encasing the whole thing in a portable, durable oval pod the size and colors of a Nerf football. The pods hang pendulously from the tree's trunk and main stems, making it look for all the world like one of those many-breasted Hindu goddesses. Monkeys grab the pods, carry them on their arboreal wanderings, and devour the pulp. They would eat the seeds, too, if the tree didn't pump its seeds full of polyphenols, the same compounds that make tea, red wine, and coffee bitter and astringent. Monkeys quickly learn to discard the seeds. This is the basic strategy for fruit all over the planet— tasty flesh, nasty seeds—but cacao takes it to an extreme.

Using monkeys, birds, rats, and other couriers, cacao spread throughout the Amazonian rainforest, its ancestral home. It stuck to the river valleys, which contained the rich alluvial soil it required, and it stuck to the forest understory, thriving as a twenty- or thirty-foot tree beneath the canopy of Amazon giants. Its tiny flowers sprout straight from the trunk and point downward— perfect for getting the pollinating attention of the midges that fill the leaf litter of the rainforest floor.*

Then, perhaps twelve thousand years ago, a new sort of monkey arrived on the scene, a partner beyond cacao's wildest dreams. This monkey carried cacao's seeds farther than ever before. It even helped cacao escape its Amazon cradle, carrying seeds up the headwaters of the Amazon and over the Andes to the Pacific side. And then, unthinkably, it did something that cacao never, ever could have anticipated. *It began to eat the seeds.* A disaster? Actually, the beginning of a beautiful friendship.

No one knows when people hit upon the process for turning cacao into chocolate, but it must have been eons ago, and it must have happened in Mesoamerica. The oldest evidence we have of chocolate making was found on a four-thousand-year-old clay potsherd from Soconusco. In addition to being the birthplace of

---

* Today, cacao plantations must still ensure enough leaf mulch and understory growth at the base of their trees to support a midge population; otherwise the trees won't set fruit.

chocolate culture, this region may well have been the birthplace of all Mesoamerican civilization. In short order, the citizens of Izapa, the region's leading ancient city, seem to have invented the calendar, writing, and chocolate, which some would argue are the three pillars of civilization.

But the cacao beans and chocolate found throughout Mesoamerica are all of a particular cultivar known as *criollo*, which is just one of numerous cultivars found in South America. Criollo seeds are much less bitter than those of most cacao trees—something that would be a serious disadvantage in the wild. And the criollo genes show signs of inbreeding. Somebody selected a particularly delicious strain of cacao and brought it north.

Criollo chocolate was incredibly aromatic and only slightly bitter. Criollo was the cacao that stimulated the Maya, the Aztec, and eventually the Europeans (once they had learned to dump sugar in it to suit their palates). Indeed, rumors of its powers of stimulation caught Europeans' fancy. The early-sixteenth-century historian Gonzalo Fernández de Oviedo y Valdés, in his *General y natural historia de las Indias*, noted that ten cocoa beans could get you a rabbit or a prostitute, and better still, that "it is the habit among Central American Indians to rub each other all over with pulpy cocoa mass and then nibble at each other."

Unfortunately, because of the inbreeding that had eliminated so much bitterness, criollo was also highly susceptible to a host of diseases that were soon playing havoc with cacao plantations throughout Mesoamerica. With disease decimating their trees and their labor force, New Spain's lucrative new industry soon couldn't keep up with demand. Prices soared, ensuring that chocolate remained the drink of the elite.

Competition came in the 1600s from Brazil, where another variety of cacao tree had been established. More disease-resistant, less finicky in its growing conditions, and higher yielding, this variety seemed to be the answer to growers' prayers. They called it *forastero*, which meant "foreign" (in other words, not the criollo they were used to). By then the slave trade was filling South America with free African labor, the final factor that allowed growers to provide forastero chocolate at a fraction of the price of criollo.

Only one catch. It tasted terrible. The plentiful polyphenols that helped protect its seeds from disease and pest were obvious in the purple color and intense bitterness.

A deal breaker? Perhaps not. With cane plantations up and running throughout the Caribbean, Europe had already developed a nice little sugar habit. A few extra scoops of white crystal in the cocoa covered the sins of even the nastiest beans, and the toothless aristocrats of Europe never knew the difference.

The colonists in New Spain, however, weren't fooled, just as Californians aren't tricked by the cheap Australian wines that wow 'em in Wichita. They still sought out their Soconusco chocolate, and if they couldn't get it, opted for criollo chocolate from Venezuela as a second choice and accepted Brazilian and Ecuadoran forastero only as a last resort. But with the price of chocolate having fallen within anyone's reach, they were becoming an insignificant part of chocolate's increasingly global market. Most of that market had never tasted good beans, and never would. When companies like Hershey and Mars thrive on products that are mostly milk and sugar, cocoa quality is little more than an afterthought.

The abolition of slavery put a dent in Brazil's cacao industry, but only until the industry realized it could bring its operation to the labor force. The first cacao trees in Africa were planted on the islands of Príncipe in 1822 and São Tomé in 1824. Today West Africa, led by Ivory Coast,* produces about 70 percent of the world's

---

* The industry there is still dogged by accusations of slave labor, though most investigations have turned up little evidence. Still, if not slave labor, the industry is at least floated on the backs of very cheap labor (about one dollar per day for the average worker), with all the ethical questions that entails.

cacao, followed by Indonesia at 13 percent and Brazil at 5 percent. Most of this is low-quality "bulk beans," which make up 95 percent of the world supply. "Flavor beans," the surprisingly frank industry name for the good stuff, make up the rest. Most come from Venezuelan, Caribbean, and Mexican plantations too small or remote to have been touched by big industry, or too poor to have replaced their old trees with the high-yield kind.[*]

And there you have the key to understanding chocolate terroir. The groves of aromatic flavor beans are still out there, hiding in the fertile backwaters of the Americas, the old indigenous strongholds. To find them, you have to put on your fedora and get in touch with your inner anthropologist.

THE COCOA WARS

Criollo's resurrection began in 1985, when the French chocolate legend Valrhona began offering its line of Grand Cru bars (appropriating the designation given to Burgundy's top vineyards), starting with the now-canonized Guanaja bar, named for the island where Columbus had his run-in with the Maya in 1502. Guanaja doesn't exhibit any one terroir—it's a blend from many different sources—but is a perfect mix of the highest-quality beans, a dazzling kaleidoscope of berries and coffee and creamy dates, and when introduced, it alerted the world to what chocolate could be. You mean there isn't one standard chocolate flavor? You mean chocolate can be challenging, surprising, and playful? In 1985, who knew?

Valrhona's other Grand Cru offerings have specific, if broad, provenance. The Manjari is from Madagascar, the Caraïbe from the Caribbean. Each has a distinct profile. Demand for chocolate with unique terroir went from nonexistent to thunderous, and in 1999

---

[*] This all sounds remarkably similar to coffee's story, and indeed the two beans lead parallel lives, one in the tropical highlands, the other in the lowlands.

Valrhona complied with its first single-domain chocolates: Gran Couva, made with beans from an estate in Trinidad, and Chuao, from a Venezuelan coastal town that is the single most famous appellation in chocolate.

No roads lead to Chuao. To reach it, you have to journey to the beachside party town of Choroní, then requisition a fishing boat to transport you a few miles east to a loading dock. Walk a couple of miles up into the steamy mountains that press tight against the shore, and you reach the fifteen-hundred-person village. Cacao has always been Chuao's reason for being. It was founded as a Spanish cacao plantation using slave labor in 1660. Today the descendants of those slaves control their own destiny, which lately looks pretty bright. Rumored to possess the finest cacao beans on the planet, the Chuao farmers' cooperative has been the focus of an intense bidding war between Valrhona, which for years bought every single one of the twenty tons of beans produced annually in Chuao, and the Italian upstart Amedei, which in 2002 stole Valrhona's monopoly in a much-publicized coup. Amedei scored the goods the old-fashioned way—they paid through the nose. The Chuao cooperative had been getting $1.30 a kilo from Valrhona; Amedei paid $9 per kilo and went on to produce a chocolate bar that has been hailed as the greatest of all time.

Chuao's greatness rests on its inaccessibility. When the industrial chocolate giants were modernizing the chocolate industry, inconvenient plantations like Chuao received little attention. The old cacao varieties survived there and in its neighboring valleys, where scientists in the 1940s discovered unusually vigorous stands of cacao with pale, pinkish seeds—the sign of few polyphenols.

Perhaps more important, the old traditions survived in Chuao, too. The villagers have tended their criollo-heavy groves with incredible care for centuries. Unlike most cocoa beans in the world, Chuao beans are slowly and carefully sun-dried on the village square in front of the white and blue stucco church. That's essential.

For, as much as you need good beans to produce great chocolate, you also need to get the fermentation and sun-drying right. This is what few modern companies are willing or able to bother with. And it shows.

Years ago I wrote a small book about the health benefits of dark chocolate. I spent months tasting every dark chocolate bar on the market, pushing the envelope of cacao percentage higher and higher in the quest for the ultimate antioxidant bomb: 60 percent, 65, 70, 72! Then 85! And I came to the demoralizing conclusion that chocolate wasn't very good. Most dark chocolate has the tarry, burnt-rubber flavor of something that was scraped off the street in the wake of a drag race. Gone in sixty seconds? If only. My blood may have been surging with health, but my mouth was twitching with bitterness, and my tongue felt coated in paraffin. People show an astonishing ability to choke down pure awfulness in the name of health. Chocolate maker Colin Gasko often gets asked about the health benefits of the bars from Rogue Chocolatier, his boutique brand, a question he laughs off. "The most god-awful, astringent, bitter, wretched-tasting chocolate is always going to be the best for you. If that's what you're looking for, you might as well take a pill."

Was this really the experience that had bewitched four thousand years of Mesoamericans, who took no sweetener in their chocolate? No, it turns out. They were having a very different experience than most of us are. To understand why, we need to go back to that raw, inedible cocoa bean.

MAKING THE INEDIBLE EDIBLE

A lot of things have to go right to make good chocolate. A single misstep at any stage—poor fermentation, drying, roasting, or grinding—can ruin everything, which is why almost all chocolatiers, even the most famous, buy their bulk chocolate from companies like Valrhona. Only a handful of artisans in America have the talent and daring to work with the beans themselves. Amano, De Vries, Patric, Rogue, Scharffen Berger, Taza, and Theo are the only companies I know doing high-quality bean-to-bar chocolate. All are tiny operations. And all share a quixotic desire to make edible art despite devilishly difficult details.

The only good way of getting rid of the bitterness and astringency in a raw cocoa bean is through fermentation—something that, if given the chance, the pods will do on their own, thanks to their sticky, sweet pulp. After harvesting the cacao pods, splitting them open, and scooping out the beans and pulp, workers heap up the mass and cover it with plantain leaves to encourage fermentation. Tropical yeasts answer the dinner bell, digesting the sugary pulp and converting it to alcohol. Some minor flavors are contributed by this process, including the fruity and flowery notes I associate with sake, but the main goal of this fermentation is to provide the "wine" for the important fermentation, this one conducted by acetic acid bacteria, the microbes responsible for turning wine into vinegar. All that corrosive vinegar burns its way into the beans, breaking cells apart and mixing their contents together. Thus begins the extraordinary chemical reactions that lead to chocolate.

This process "cooks off" some of the harsh flavors in the beans and breaks down the protein and sugars into a dazzling array of flavor precursors that will blossom into full-fledged cocoa flavors during the roasting stage, but it also leaves very sour, vinegar-soaked beans. To arrest the fermentation process, the beans are dried. When the moisture level drops to around 8 percent, fermentation stops. The ancients dried their beans in the sun, turning the piles periodically to keep the heat and moisture consistent, covering the beans at night and during rain. The best beans are still slowly sun-dried over six or seven days, turned every twenty minutes or so and shielded from the intense heat of the midday sun. Only slow drying allows the vinegar to exit the beans without causing unwanted changes. Overly intense sun-drying can cause the outer shell of the beans to harden and encapsulate before enough moisture has left the beans, leading to internal mold growth.

But proper sun-drying is a great challenge in the soggy tropics. Most cacao is mechanically dried over heat, leading to all sorts of problems. Cacao's high fat content makes it quite fragile. If your chocolate tastes burnt, the beans may have been scorched in hot drums. If it tastes cooked and acrid, it was probably dried too hot, too fast, and the vinegar never had time to exit. If it tastes smoky, you may be experiencing the infamous "hammy beans" of Indonesia, dried over open fires.

Most of us think of these off-flavors as part of the profile of dark chocolate, because that's all we've ever had. High-end markets are full of righteous dark chocolate bars sporting cute, endangered animals on the labels and horrendously caustic chocolate inside. Sadly, organic chocolate is one of the worst offenders here, because growers can earn a top rate for organic cacao regardless of flavor. So long as they keep pesticides out of the equation, they have no incentive for quality control.

The standard way to get the vinegar out of chocolate is to beat the crap out of it. This is done in slow motion, in a machine called a conch (the original was shaped like a shell), which acts like an industrial dough mixture, kneading the crushed, semi-liquid chocolate for an astonishingly long time—around seventy-two hours in the case of premium chocolates. The heat produced by the process helps develop roasty caramel flavors in the finished chocolate, and the constant kneading coats particles with cocoa butter to achieve that perfectly smooth meltability most connoisseur's look for in their chocolate. But the conch's most important task is to mellow the chocolate by letting the volatile acetic acid escape into the air. "It will really make your eyes water," said Colin Gasko. "A ton of vinegar comes off. You'd think that, working in a chocolate factory, I'd go home smelling good. I go home smelling like rotting fruit. It's awful. People don't want to sit next to me."

Conching long and hard eliminates much of the sourness, but many interesting aromatic molecules escape along with the acetic acid. The resulting chocolate is "mellowed," the flavor flattened. That had been my experience of most "gourmet" dark chocolate—acrid, waxy cardboard. Then I tasted a chocolate bar that opened my eyes. With a 70 percent cocoa content, it was intensely fruity and aromatic, yet it had only the slightest hint of bitterness. It had a strange, rough texture. And it made me realize that many things I'd been taught to value in chocolate were all wrong.

The beans had been ground into chocolate using stone mills the Aztec would certainly have recognized. I had a strong suspicion that this was as close as I could get in the United States to the chocolate of a thousand years ago. Which made the address on the chocolate bar all the more perplexing: Somerville, Massachusetts. If I wanted to get to the heart of dark chocolate, I'd have to head to the suburbs.

AGAINST THE GRAIN

An unassuming brick office building in an industrial oxbow of Somerville, surrounded by acres of crushed automobiles, is an unlikely place to find an authentic Oaxacan stone chocolate mill, but there it was, churning out a thick, pungent brown paste. Standing amid heavy aromas straight out of the dried-fruit and nut section of a natural foods store, Alex Whitmore, cofounder of Taza Chocolate, explained to me the epiphany that had brought it here. "I was an anthropology major in college," he said. "My entire entry into this line of business was inspired by a trip I took to Oaxaca City. Oaxaca is *the* culinary destination in Mexico. You can literally eat your way through Oaxaca for a week and not have the same thing twice. There's a hundred different types of chili peppers in the market. There's *so* much. The pre-European food traditions are still vibrant. There's stuff that's been going on for hundreds of years exactly as it's going on today. The way they mill chocolate there is very simple. They grind everything from chocolate to corn to chilies on stone mills. You see these old ladies bringing big trash bags full of chilies and little bags of herbs and garlic and spices to a miller, and the miller grinds them all together and gives the ladies a bag of the family sauce. Every family has its own recipe. It's this amazing culture."

Alex was particularly taken with the chocolate in Oaxaca. The best of it had a vibrancy he'd never encountered before. The quality of the beans was one factor, but the milling process, he learned, was another. The imperfect surface of the millstones left a texture rougher than that achieved with modern steel milling equipment, and the Oaxacans didn't bother to conch at all—anathema to a European chocolate maker. Texture wasn't all that important to the Oaxacans, who, like their Maya ancestors, drink most of their chocolate, but Alex found that he preferred the grainy texture for eating chocolate, too. And he wondered whether other Americans would fall for the rustic style.

From the start, Alex wanted the terroir of Taza's chocolate to be true to its roots. "Cocoa is indigenous to the Americas," he said. "As a company, we've been very focused on sourcing all of our ingredients from the Americas."

Taza sold its first chocolate bars in 2007. At the beginning, though, Alex knew he had an uphill battle on his hands. "Chocolate's a very crowded category," he said. "One of the ways we've distinguished ourselves is with this texture. It was difficult at first. There were a lot of doubts in my mind. I knew people in Mexico were used to it, but I didn't know if I could convince people here that this was a really enjoyable way to eat chocolate. It's one of the biggest challenges. The people that don't like it tend to hate it. They're like, 'Oh my god, that's not chocolate. That sucks.' They want waxy, smooth, sugary. They want Lindt. They think that finer chocolate is literally finer. Well, we're not making European-style chocolate; we're making American-style chocolate. It usually takes two tries. At first people are skeptical. You have to get them over that hump. But the people who are converted become die-hard fans. They love it. It's not candy; it's real food. It's got a texture to it. And I think that's hitting home."

It worked on me. Like most people, my first bite of a grainy Taza chocolate bar caught me off guard. My initial thought was that something had gone wrong. But once I knew what to expect, I quickly came to anticipate it. It's great fun to crunch down on a square of chocolate and roll it around in your mouth as the particles break apart and release their surprises. You can chew on Taza. When I went back to traditional European-style chocolate, I missed that substantialness. I found the ultrasmooth texture cloying. That fine particle size coated my tongue like clay and I couldn't get rid of it. I was unlearning a lifetime of indoctrination. While textured chocolate seems weird to those who have grown up on the smooth stuff, the opposite is true, too. It's like the difference between a crumbly, clothbound cheddar and American cheese. Those who believe that cheese comes squirting out of a can find a wheel of the real stuff impossibly strange, even sinister, while the rest of us find "cheese food" dreadfully overprocessed, so removed from nature that it can't even refer back to its origins on a farm.

When I told Alex this, he nodded and said, "People want food that's real, that's simple, that's not superprocessed. And they want to know where their food's coming from. We're answering to that, too."

Making chocolate with such a transparent connection to its terroir is like performing unplugged; there are no tricks to hide behind. Alex likes it that way: "Because we minimally process our chocolate—we roast very lightly, we grind very simply on stone mills, we don't conch—all of our ingredients have to taste good naturally. When you eat our chocolate, especially when it's fresh, you can taste all the disparate ingredients. As it ages, they become more unified. But it's pretty important that we have those finished flavors in the ingredients before we start."

That's in contrast to most European-style chocolate makers, who logically emphasize qualities—such as superfine texture, creaminess, and toasty, nutty chocolate flavors—that can be created in the factory with less-than-perfect beans. It's much easier to control factory conditions than to control cultivation and fermentation in remote cacao plantations across the third world.

To get the beans it needs, Taza instigated what it has coined "direct trade," which takes fair trade to the next level. Fair trade guarantees third world farmers a fair price for their crop, but it includes no incentive for quality. Taza pays a premium well above the fair-trade standard to ensure a rare level of hands-on care. Beans are fermented for a full week, to maximize aromatics and minimize bitterness, then dried in the shade for another week. The slow drying cycle allows more vinegar to evaporate from the beans before the outer shell encapsulates. And that's what allows Taza to process its beans so lightly.

The beans themselves are trinitario stock, a hybrid that combines the old, aromatic criollo traits with the robust forastero traits. Trinitario was created in Trinidad in the 1720s in response to a blight that wiped out most of the original criollo stock. New trees were brought up from the Orinoco Basin of the Amazon and crossed with the old trees to produce a fine-tasting and commercially viable cultivar. Many of the world's finer chocolates are made with trinitario beans. The terroir of Taza's beans is a particularly Dominican take on trinitario, with the juicy-fruit vibrancy enhanced by the volcanic soils of the island and the slow-drying and balanced by the deep chocolatey base of the forastero genes.

Taza is so confident in the quality of its raw beans that it even sells them by the bagful. They remind me of sour walnuts: perfumed, crunchy, rich, just a tad bitter. The astringency is already gone. The base notes that we think of as chocolate—the sweet, toasted, buttery cocoa qualities—aren't there, and no one would think "chocolate" after biting down on a raw bean, yet all the flavors present are clearly part of the complex effect of good dark chocolate.

Other than ensuring the impeccable quality of its beans, Taza's biggest contribution to the flavor of its chocolate is the roasting. Taza uses a German-built Barth Sirocco 200 that Alex found used in Italy. It cost $35,000, versus $225,000 for a new machine, and that was important for Taza, which was started on a shoestring budget. It's a convection roaster that resembles the roasting machines seen in coffee shops, and it could roast coffee or just about anything else, but it was made for cocoa and hazelnuts. Cocoa beans, which are fragile and more than 50 percent fat (cocoa butter), require a much gentler roast than coffee, and Taza roasts gentler still. The goal is to eliminate any remaining moisture, which can play havoc in the milling stage, and to contribute the caramel and roasted meat flavors that are the backbone of chocolate, without driving off the bright floral and fruity notes or burning the beans.

This is far different from the intense roasting of the big industrial players, which is intended to destroy some of the "offest" of off flavors. "Most of the cacao that's grown in Africa is not fermented," Alex told me. "It's shipped out and used to make cocoa powder and bulk chocolate. They just roast the bejeezus out of it to get rid of the astringency and to give it that toasty, chocolaty flavor. Then they mix it with a ton of sugar. Most of the stuff that goes on the outside of a Snickers bar is not fermented."

"It's given me new respect for the big guys," Colin Gasko added. "I don't know how they're able to make a palatable product out of such awful raw material. It's some impressive chemistry."

If you get used to premium chocolate, and then you go back and eat one of the mass-market chocolate products of your youth and really pay attention, you'll be shocked. None of the complex flavors created by the fermentation process are present. The flavors that are present are truly bizarre, a testament to the fact that almost anything can be made palatable if sufficiently sweetened. Hershey's, in particular, is famous for an odd sour quality that, I'm told, derives from the soured milk originally used. "Vomit" is how one expert describes it, though I more charitably think of it as chocolate yogurt.

After roasting, Taza's beans are broken up in a winnowing machine that was liberated from a defunct candy company in the Dominican Republic. Again, the price was right. (New machines go for half a million dollars.) The winnower breaks the beans and separates the light and cardboardy shells from the rest using air. (Some of the shells are traded for vegetables with a local farmer, who uses them for organic mulch.) Then the beans are put through the stone mill. The two stones, each a twenty-pound disk with an identical pattern incised into one face, turn against each other, sucking the beans through and crushing them. The pattern is essential to getting proper texture in the chocolate, and the stones must be redressed every three months with a disk grinder and a hammer and chisel—something Alex had to learn from masters in Mexico. "No one wants to tell you how to do it," he said. "It's one of these things that gets passed down from generation to generation. Two guys in Oaxaca City taught me how to dress in exchange for money and fame. But they didn't teach me much. I was never allowed to look at one of their stones."

The industry term for ground cacao is "cocoa liquor," but it is neither liquid nor alcoholic. It's like gritty mud. This mud then gets combined with sugar and run back through the grinder so it's well combined. A tiny bit of vanilla bean brings out the natural flavors of the chocolate. ("Like a steak likes salt, chocolate likes vanilla," Alex said.) A touch of extra cocoa butter softens the mouthfeel. Then it gets worked in a stone roller mill for about a day, which reduces the size of the sugar crystals and emulsifies the chocolate a bit without losing the volatile components that evaporate during a true conch.

Straight off the assembly line, Taza's chocolate is a revelation. It has a much softer crumb than you expect from chocolate, like a buttery graham cracker crust. It's bright beyond belief, sparkling with citrus and balsamic vinegar notes and especially the green zing of *guarapo*, fresh-squeezed cane juice. Whether this flavor is from the sugar or the cocoa is unclear. In any case, it departs after about ten days, yielding to an intense nose of dried fruit, especially blueberries, overlaying a foundation of port, nuts, and coffee. It's surprisingly reminiscent of Amarone, the great Italian wine made from shriveled grapes. The texture becomes snappier, though it never quite resembles the hard plastic of most dark chocolate.

That's Taza's standard chocolate, made with beans from a handful of family farms in the Dominican Republic. Its Chiapan chocolate, available as an extremely limited edition (just seventeen sacks of cacao were available in 2009, its inaugural year), expresses an entirely different terroir. Being the former home of the finest cacao groves of the Maya and Aztec, Chiapas has a sacred name in the world of chocolate. But just try finding some. Mexico drinks chocolate like we drink coffee. It's a net importer of cacao beans, with a fine appreciation for the finer ones. What grows in Chiapas stays in Chiapas.

And boy, does it grow there. "In Chiapas there's some really old, really unique tree stocks that are thought to be the classical, pre-Columbian cocoa," Alex told me. "A lot is just growing in the jungle. We've found some amazing beans where there's actually no way to get them out. No roads, no organization. We could go up into those hills with the Zapatistas, but it's a very challenging environment. We could do limited-edition bars with really small quantities that travel down the river in canoes and go across the mountain range on donkeys, but we've been focusing on becoming a viable business. We've still gotta make chocolate every day. Maybe we can get into that fun stuff later."

The arrival in October 2009 of Taza's first Chiapan bars marked the beginning of the "fun stuff." Their predominantly pre-Columbian gene pool highlights the old qualities prized by the Maya and Aztec, cut with enough feral survivor genes to allow them to endure five hundred years of rainforest neglect. They have something new to tell us, and something very old. The chocolate has an exotic, worldly smell, like well-oiled teak. Notes of pipe tobacco and Keemun tea make you think of being in a captain's stateroom on an eighteenth-century trading ship, or maybe an ancient library. There is knowledge in it, some sweet, some bitter. It's a bar you wouldn't want to hand to someone until they were ready. But once they are, they'll be glad you let them taste of it, glad to know that the trees are still out there, nurturing their pods in some overgrown garden, their roots patiently coiling around the base of an old, blackened ziggurat.

RECIPES

CHOCO-CHILI SAUCE

As he was making a mole verde when we were in Mexico, Rick Bayless said, "One thing that's strange to read in people's descriptions of mole is how they could taste all the different parts. They say, 'Oh, I can taste the ancho and the mulatto and the pasilla and the chocolate.' Well, in Mexico, that would be considered the worst mole that's ever been made. In bringing all those flavors together, you're supposed to be creating a brand-new flavor in an almost alchemical way." Rick's right, no question, but a true mole calls for hours or even days of prep time, as each of the laundry list of ingredients is griddled and charred and added to the mix. Rarely can I commit to such a project, but there is a lesser alchemy that takes place in a mere fifteen minutes when you combine pasilla chilies and chocolate. It's a richly earthy flavor outside of time that makes me think of Maya traders and thick rivers slipping through the jungle. It's a showstopper. Versatile, too. I serve it as a dip for chips, as a salsa for tacos or enchiladas, as a sauce for grilled meat or vegetables, or as the base of Poor Man's Mole (next page).

Makes about 1 cup (enough to sauce four entrées)

2 ounces dried pasilla or ancho chilies
1 clove garlic, peeled and minced
1 to 2 ounces baking or dark chocolate (at least 70 percent cocoa), finely chopped
1 teaspoon honey
zest and juice of ½ lime
½ teaspoon salt

1. Stem and seed the chilies. (This is easiest when they're in a dried state. The seeds rattle around inside the skins like beans in a maraca and simply fall out when you cut open the chilies.)

Put them in a bowl and cover them with boiling water. Let them sit for at least 15 minutes.

2. Drain the chilies, reserving the soaking liquid, and puree them in a food processor with the other ingredients, adding small amounts of soaking liquid as needed to make it blend smoothly. (You may also want to use the soaking liquid in Poor Man's Mole, below.) Taste and add more lime or salt if desired. The sauce will keep for at least a week (possibly forever; I've never tested its longevity) and its flavor will actually improve after a day or so.

POOR MAN'S MOLE

Not as complex as an authentic mole, but a hell of a lot faster to make, and still damn good. *Mole* simply means "sauce" in Nahuatl, and there are practically as many versions of mole in Mexico as there are grandmothers, so ignore everyone who tries to burden you with mole rules; anything goes. This one sticks to New World ingredients just for kicks. The pepitas are key; when blended, they give sauces a creamy texture and an inimitable flavor. Serve with homemade corn tortillas (easier to make than you might think) or over a bed of polenta (less traditional, but also less messy). Like many dishes, this is actually better the next day, when the flavors have really bonded.

Serves 4

1 tablespoon corn oil or lard
1 onion, peeled and chopped
1 cup toasted pepitas (pumpkin seeds)
1 14.5-ounce can diced or whole tomatoes (preferably fire-roasted) and their juice
1 cup Choco-Chili Sauce (page 264)

4 cups shredded or chunked cooked meat (chicken, turkey, pork,
   guinea pig, or capybara) or vegetables
salt to taste
1 cup fresh cilantro, chopped

1. Heat the oil or lard in a skillet large enough to hold all the
    ingredients. When it's shimmering, add the onion and sauté,
    stirring occasionally, until soft, about 4 minutes.
2. Combine the pepitas, tomatoes, Choco-Chili Sauce, and sau-
    téed onions in a blender or food processor and blend until
    fairly smooth. A little texture is fine.
3. Return the sauce to the skillet and cook over low heat until it
    begins to bubble, about 5 minutes. Keep scraping the bottom
    of the skillet with a flat spatula, as the thick sauce likes to
    stick.
4. Add the meat or vegetables and simmer until everything is hot
    and the flavors have melded, about 15 minutes. The sauce thick-
    ens as it cooks, so you may need to add liquid as you go. Water
    or stock is fine, but if you've really planned ahead, you'll have
    the leftover soaking water from the Choco-Chili Sauce. Taste
    and add salt if needed.
5. Garnish with the cilantro and serve.

RESOURCES

Let me say right now that I'm put off by most chocolate. Milk chocolate is a sugary joke, and even a lot of high-quality dark stuff, to me, goes in a category with habanero peppers, bungee jumping, and Thomas Pynchon novels: extreme pastimes that will develop their cult followers but are devoid of inherent pleasure or value. It's exceedingly difficult to deprogram a member of any cult, and I'm not going to try here; if you are part of the dark-chocolate cult, and think that most of it tastes just fine, then I don't want to spoil your party. But if you've started to wonder, secretly, whether it really makes sense to treat cacao percentages like school grades, then you may enjoy the following recommendations.

AMANO

www.amanochocolate.com
801-655-1996
If more traditional, highly refined chocolate with ultrasmooth mouthfeel is to your liking, Amano is an excellent source, making a number of high-quality single-origin bars. Look for its Cuyagua bar, from the third of Venezuela's prized cacao valleys, along with Chuao and Ocumare. Cuyagua may be the best of the bunch, combining an initial blast of intense cocoa aromatics with the earthy and bitter-sweet flavor of walnuts—a *rancio* note found in good Amontillado. The overall effect has more intrigue and richness than Chuao or Ocumare, making it my favorite of the Venezuelan appellations. Amano also makes an Ocumare that is remarkable for its lack of bitterness; even at 70 percent cocoa content, it is creamy and mild. The overall flavor is not unlike cola (which is better than it sounds), with just enough licorice and goji berry notes to keep things from getting boring.

THE CHOCOLATE LIFE

www.thechocolatelife.com

Want to dive even deeper into the heart of dark chocolate? Two words for you: Clay Gordon. His book, *Discover Chocolate*, is the best on the subject, and the Chocolate Life, the online forum he administers, is the best place to mix it up with passionate amateurs and even the occasional pro.

CHOCOSPHERE

www.chocosphere.com

The best one-stop-shopping for unusual and unusually delicious chocolate, including most of the appellations discussed here.

FELCHLIN

www.new.felchlin.com

In the Beni region of the Bolivian Amazon, wild cacao still grows along riverbanks and in the forest understory. It isn't rare; thousands of acres of "chocolatales," as the cacao forests are called, are utilized by the indigenous peoples of the area. Each rainy season, they gather the pods, ferment and dry the beans, and sell them to traders who ply the rivers in canoes. In March 2010, I visited these chocolatales. Seeing the beans piled in dugout canoes, hearing the screeching macaws in the cacao trees, watching monkeys swipe pods from the higher branches, was like stepping into the pre-Columbian past. The wild cacao pods were small and yellow, and their beans were only about half the size of typical beans. The flavor was extraordinary, deeply chocolatey, without a trace of sourness or bitterness. Sugar was unnecessary. This was as close as one could get to the origins of chocolate. Historically, all this cacao has been used by the domestic Bolivian chocolate industry. Most of the world didn't even know of its existence, and it was too isolated to be brought out. Now one man, Volker Lehmann, is buying the wild beans and exporting them. They travel by boat to the jungle town of Trinidad, by truck a thousand miles to La Paz, then over a 15,000-foot pass in the Andes to the Chilean port of Arica. From there, a feeder ship takes the beans to Panama, where they are loaded onto a container ship for the journey through the canal and across the Atlantic to Rotterdam, where another feeder ship picks up the beans and runs them up the Rhine to Basel, where the Swiss chocolate company Felchlin makes them into an unforgettable bar named Cru Sauvage. Seek it out.

ROGUE CHOCOLATIER

www.roguechocolatier.com

Handmade in tiny batches by Colin Gasko ("My office is a five-gallon bucket"), Rogue has three different bars: Rio Caribe (Venezuela), Hispaniola (Dominican Republic), and Sambirano. Look for the Sambirano Valley bar, from Madagascar.* The Sambirano Valley is full of quality cacao beans that produce a ton of fruitiness but also intense acidity. The unusual strains of microbes in Madagascar create extra acetic acid during fermentation. When carefully dried and generously conched, the tart and fruit can be beautifully balanced. To me, it's the chocolate equivalent of New Zealand Sauvignon Blanc wines. Madagascar chocolates are invariably described as having citrus notes, but to me it's more wild blueberries and tamarind.

TAZA CHOCOLATE

www.tazachocolate.com

617-623-0804

---

* Okay, Madagascar is so *not* the Americas, but the Sambirano Valley is the source for such excellent and unusual chocolate that it needs a quick mention here. It's encountered a lot, and it provides a nice contrast with American beans.

The only authentic Mesoamerican chocolate available in the United States. Rustic, gritty, intensely flavored. Look for its limited-edition Chiapas bar, as well as forthcoming bars from Belize, Bolivia, and elsewhere.

Acknowledgments

*T*OOLING DOWN THE aisles of the produce or seafood or wine section of your local market, it's impossible to sense the amount of work that went into getting that product to you in the art-worthy condition it tends to be in. You certainly don't see all the imperfect versions that were culled to make sure you get the best of the best. But, since I started working on this book two years ago, I've had the opportunity to visit many food producers at the source and see the incredible care they take in their work. Even something as common as an apple or a potato goes through such an elaborate process of nurturing, harvesting, washing, packing, and shipping—all without being bruised—that it's a miracle you can buy one in your market for pocket change. I no longer take it for granted. The nature of farming is that disaster is always shadowing you in the form of floods, droughts, diseases, and market fluctuations. The producers profiled in this book keep their standards so high purely because they believe growing good food is an important thing to do; if it weren't for them, as well as their generosity in sharing precious time and information with me, I wouldn't have had anything to write about.

And if it weren't for Kathy Belden, my editor at Bloomsbury, it wouldn't have been nearly so much fun. Sometimes I think every writer thinks communicating with his editor is like chatting with an old friend, and then I hear the horror stories. If it weren't for that 10010 zip code, I'd swear she was hanging out in the country somewhere.

A few other magazine editors I count as friends contributed to this book by publishing pieces that helped me research and write certain chapters. Some of that material shows up here in different form. Thank you Ed Behr at *The Art of Eating*, Luke Mitchell at *Harper's*, Carolyn Malcoun and Lisa Gosselin at *Eating Well*, Justin Paul at *Virtuoso Life*, and Jeremy Spencer at *Outside*. I'm also grateful to Amy Trubek, who helped me contextualize my thoughts on terroir through conversation, maple tastings, and her book *The Taste of Place*, and to Dr. Montserrat Almena-Alista—a goddess of sensory evaluation.   *

A special thanks to Jon Rowley, who lurks behind the scenes in several chapters of this book. Jon's nose for remarkable foods and places, and generosity in making introductions, helped immensely, and his fine photographs are a great plus. Ditto for Brian Kingzett; Brian and I traveled around PEI together and took pictures of the same damn things, but his were always superior.

Then there are the friends and family members who have been forced—forced!—to taste their way through multiple varieties of some food product at my table. It may sound like it would be fun to come over, taste these six wines with these six oysters, and tell me what you think, but when I slide pen and paper into your hand and make you start writing things down (*"Fruity? What's 'fruity?' Try again!"*), sometimes the fun goes away. Anyway, thanks. You know who you are, you did good work, and I'm sorry about the calipers.

A NOTE ON THE AUTHOR

ROWAN JACOBSEN writes about food, the environment, and the connections between the two. His work has appeared in the *New York Times*, *Harper's*, *Newsweek*, *Eating Well*, and elsewhere. He is the author of the James Beard Award–winning *A Geography of Oysters*, *Fruitless Fall*, and *The Living Shore*. He lives in rural Vermont with his wife and son and speaks frequently on the subjects of food, wine, and sustainability.